M000213753

The Church
of the Fundamentalists

*An Examination of Ecclesiastical Separation
in the Twentieth Century*

Larry R. Oats

Library of Congress Cataloging-in-Publication Data

Author
    The Church of the Fundamentalists/Larry R. Oats
        205 p.   cm.
    Includes bibliographical references.
    ISBN-13:   978-0-9821426-2-2 (paper)
    ISBN-10:   0-9821426-2-5
    1.   Ecclesiology. 2. Fundamentalism, History of. 3. Evangelicalism, History of. 4. Oats, Larry.
BT82.2
277.3

CONTENTS

PREFACE

The issue and, especially, the application of ecclesiastical separation were at the heart of the division which occurred between evangelicalism and fundamentalism in the middle of the twentieth century. While much has been written on the histories of the fundamentalist and evangelical movement, the theological basis of that division has frequently been overlooked. The purpose of this book is to examine how the ecclesiologies of mid-twentieth century fundamentalists and evangelicals affected their views of ecclesiastical separation and how those views led individuals to establish, abandon, or modify their views of ecclesiastical separation. While the causes of this separation are multitudinous and nuanced, leaders in both movements claimed that a misunderstanding of the doctrine of the church was instrumental in the division between the two movements.

It would be impossible to cover the positions of every significant individual in the movements, so the following key leaders and publications have been chosen in the historical examination of the division: Bob Jones, Sr., Bob Jones, Jr., John R. Rice, Robert T. Ketchum, and Carl McIntire among the fundamentalists and Carl F. H. Henry, Billy Graham, Harold J. Ockenga, and Edward J. Carnell among the evangelicals. Fundamentalist institutions such as the American Council of Christian Churches, Bob Jones University, the *Christian Beacon*, and the *Sword of the Lord* will be contrasted with evangelical institutions such as the National Association of Evangelicals, Fuller Seminary, and *Christianity Today*. Numerous readers will undoubtedly wonder why someone or some institution was not included. This writer would encourage each such reader to personally evaluate that person or institution in light of the context of the movements. Should someone undertake such a study, this author would appreciate hearing from him or her.

A brief survey of the doctrine of the church seeks to exhibit where the evangelicals and fundamentalists fit in the historic scheme of ecclesiologies. The fundamentalists placed emphasis on the local church and its purity; most used a dispensational hermeneutic. The early evangelicals tended toward a more universal and covenant church position. A short history of the fundamentalist/evangelical ecclesiological debate follows. The purpose is to demonstrate the role that ecclesiology played in the fundamentalist movement and the reaction of the evangelical movement in the mid-twentieth century.

Particular attention will be paid to the meaning of the word "church;" when the church began (which affects the relationship between the Old and New Testaments); the relationship of the church to Scripture (which determines whether the church can modify the teaching of the Bible); the connection between the concepts of the local church, visible church, universal church, and invisible church (which has significant relevance to the concepts of fellowship and separation); who is qualified for membership in the church (which affects the purity of the individual church); and the relative importance of purity and unity within the church, denomination, and association.

INTRODUCTION

Conservative Christianity in North America was a fairly homogenous movement during the later nineteenth and early twentieth centuries. The rise of liberalism in the latter half of the 1800s brought about the discrete and defined movement eventually called "Fundamentalism," an amalgamation of various churches and denominational leaders who stood for the truth of Scripture against the rise of unbelief in many of the mainstream denominations and their schools. During the first half of the twentieth century, "'fundamentalist' and 'evangelical' meant roughly the same things. People might use either name to describe those who preserved and practiced the revivalist heritage of soul winning and maintained a traditional insistence on orthodoxy."[1]

> In the 1930s we were all fundamentalists.... The term "evangelical" became a significant option when the NAE [National Association of Evangelicals] was organized.... In the context of the debate with modernism, fundamentalism was an appropriate alternative; in other contexts (of the debate within the fundamentalist movement), the term evangelical was preferable.[2]

Battles over the control of various denominations, primarily those of the Baptists, Presbyterians, and Methodists, took place until the middle of the twentieth century; by then most fundamentalists had voluntarily left or been evicted from their denominations. After the Fundamentalist-Modernist controversies, fundamental groups and individuals became increasingly prone to fracture, resulting in the emergence of two major divisions: new evangelicalism and fundamentalism.

In 1976 Harold J. Ockenga made the following declaration:

---

[1] Nancy Ammerman, "North American Protestant Fundamentalism" in *Fundamentalisms Observed*, ed. Martin E. Marty and R. Scott Appleby (Chicago: University of Chicago Press, 1991), 8.

[2] George Marsden, *Reforming Fundamentalism: Fuller Seminary and the New Evangelicalism* (Grand Rapids: Eerdmans, 1987), 10. There were "evangelical" groups in England and Europe, but the triumph of modernism in those groups had been so great in the early twentieth century, that no one in the United States desired to be called "evangelical."

New-evangelicalism was born in 1948 in connection with a convocation address which I gave in the Civic Auditorium in Pasadena. While reaffirming the theological view of fundamentalism, this address *repudiated its ecclesiology and its social theory*. The ringing call for a *repudiation of separatism and the summons to social involvement* received a hearty response from many evangelicals. The name caught on and spokesmen such as Drs. Harold Lindsell, Carl F. H. Henry, Edward Carnell, and Gleason Archer supported this viewpoint. We had no intention of launching a movement, but found that the emphasis attracted widespread support and exercised great influence. Neo-evangelicalism differed from modernism in its acceptance of the supernatural and its emphasis on the fundamental doctrines of Scripture. It differed from neo-orthodoxy in its emphasis upon the written Word as inerrant, over against the Word of God which was above and different from the Scripture, but was manifested in Scripture. It differed from fundamentalism in its *repudiation of separatism and its determination to engage itself in the theological dialogue of the day. It had a new emphasis upon the application of the gospel to the sociological, political, and economic areas of life.*[3]

While reaffirming traditional fundamentalist theology, three times in this short statement Ockenga identified two elements that distinguished the emerging "new evangelicalism" from the old fundamentalism: a rejection of fundamentalist ecclesiology with its attendant separatism and the fundamentalist social theory.

Fundamentalists responded with a call for separation from new evangelicalism. For instance, George Dollar, fundamentalist historian, declared, "[A] new and powerful movement began in the 1940's. It was carefully defined in the 1950's and then became a national menace in the 1960's, even spilling over onto the mission field. . . . The movement has a

---

[3] Harold J. Ockenga, "Foreword," in Harold Lindsell, *The Battle for the Bible* (Grand Rapids: Zondervan, 1976), 11. Emphasis mine. Lindsell's book is about bibliology, not ecclesiology. The move away from belief in an inerrant Scripture was a later development and not part of the original new evangelicalism. Ockenga had previously declared: "The evangelical and the fundamentalist could sign the same creed," but "an evangelical must be distinguished from a fundamentalist in areas of intellectual and ecclesiastical attitude." Harold J. Ockenga, "Resurgent Evangelical Leadership," *Christianity Today* 4 (10 October 1960): 12–13.

permissive attitude on personal and ecclesiastical separation . . . and a new toleration of the ecumenical movement."[4]

The result was a rift in the movement. The concept of "ecclesiastical separation," particularly as used in the debates of the time frame under consideration, is not restricted to the organic separation of churches from apostate churches or denominations. The new evangelical movement was in one sense a separatistic group—the NAE separated from the Federal Council of Churches. The debate centered on the extent of separation and from whom one should separate. The new evangelicals generally insisted that separation should take place only from full-fledged, documented apostasy; fundamentalists insisted that they must separate from those holding almost any form of biblical denial, even when that church or denomination could be viewed as essentially free from full-fledged apostasy. Ecclesiastical separation referred as much to separation from what the fundamentalists considered to be "disobedient brothers" as to separation from theological liberalism or heresy.

A number of explanations for the varying positions on separation have been explored: sociological distinctions, disagreements over the doctrine of salvation, diversities of interpretive methodologies, or even disagreements among the personalities and some attendant kingdom-building. This study, however, will limit itself primarily to a single theological difference—ecclesiology.

While much has been written concerning new evangelicalism and its separation from fundamentalism, there has been minimal study of fundamentalism as a movement or of the fundamentalists who remained in the movement. There has also been little *theological* discussion of the differences between the two movements. The issue of ecclesiology was frequently raised as a point of division, but there has been little serious study of just how these ecclesiologies differed.

It is appropriate to begin a study of ecclesiastical separation with an examination of the historical views of the nature of the church. These views of the church will be analyzed to determine the distinguishing characteristics of each view and will become a basis for comparison of the evangelical and fundamentalist views of the church.

---

[4] George Dollar, *A History of Fundamentalism in America* (Greenville, SC: Bob Jones University Press, 1973), 192.

Then the ecclesiologies of representative evangelicals and fundamentalists will be examined to determine each one's view of the church. The time frame will begin in the early decades of the emergence of "new evangelicalism" when it and fundamentalism divided into two fairly distinct movements (the 1940s, 1950s, and 1960s). The two movements during this time were very similar in doctrinal belief. Since then, both evangelicalism and fundamentalism have changed and enlarged their borders. By limiting the study primarily to this time frame, most doctrinal differences that developed later are minimized.[5] Since Christian fundamentalism is originally a North American phenomenon, the study will be restricted to individuals and organizations in North America.

No single person or institution is fully representative of either movement, nor may the combination of the representatives be viewed as completely typical of either movement. There were, however, significant players on each side whose arguments and declarations carried weight within the respective movements.

Among the leading fundamentalists of that time were Bob Jones, Sr., and Bob Jones, Jr., ("Junior," as he was often called). They were successive presidents of Bob Jones College (founded in 1927), later to become Bob Jones University. This school was one of the leading fundamentalist institutions of higher education and developed into a pattern for later fundamentalist schools. Both men were Methodists, and both were proponents of fundamentalism and vocal antagonists of the new evangelicals. Jones, Sr., had been involved in the starting of the NAE, but eventually withdrew. Billy Graham attended Bob Jones College briefly and developed a friendship with Bob Jones, Jr., but eventually Junior, rejecting Graham's inclusive evangelism, became one of his most vocal critics.

Another fundamentalist leader was Baptist John R. Rice. The most widely-circulated and influential fundamentalist periodical in the middle of the twentieth century was the *Sword of the Lord,* which Rice began in 1934 and of which he was the editor until his death. George Marsden declares that Rice was "the most influential fundamentalist publicist of

---

[5] Later developments included bibliology, creationism, cessationism and more.

the era."[6] He was a mentor of Billy Graham and helped form the NAE, but along with the Bob Joneses separated from the NAE in the 1950s. Rice was less militant than the Joneses, however, and at one point broke fellowship with Bob Jones University over the separation issue. Rice's greatest sphere of influence was among the independent Baptists, especially those who had ties to the Southern Baptist Convention but had either withdrawn from the convention or were considering withdrawing.

Another leading fundamentalist was Carl McIntire, who began to publish the *Christian Beacon* in 1936. He founded Faith Theological Seminary in 1937. He was influential in the starting of the American Council of Christian Churches (ACCC) in 1941 and the International Council of Christian Churches (ICCC) in 1948. Associated with him were Allan MacRae and J. Oliver Buswell. McIntire was frequently identified in the secular and popular press as the quintessential fundamentalist. This was undoubtedly due to his protest marches and open hostility toward the National and World Councils of Churches, just the type of activity that would attract the popular press.

A fourth element among the fundamentalists consisted of the General Association of Regular Baptist Churches and the Conservative Baptist Association. These two organizations consisted of fundamentalist Baptists who left the Northern Baptist Convention because of its liberalism. They developed in different ways, but both were involved in the fundamentalist-evangelical debates of the mid-twentieth century and later.

In a December 8, 1957, press release entitled "The New Evangelicalism," Ockenga named what he considered to be the new evangelical forces of the day: the National Association of Evangelicals, Fuller Seminary, Billy Graham, and *Christianity Today*. David Wells agrees, describing the new evangelical movement as a united front, rallying behind Billy Graham, working under the aegis of the NAE, and finding intellectual coherence in *Christianity Today* and its first editor, Carl F. H. Henry.[7] In 1968 Millard Erickson viewed the leading theologians of the new evangelicalism movement to be Harold Ockenga, Carl Henry, Billy

---

[6] Marsden, *Reforming Fundamentalism*, 159.

[7] David Wells, "No Offense: I Am an Evangelical: A Search for Self-Definition," in *A Time to Speak Out: The Evangelical-Jewish Encounter*, ed. A. James Rudin and Marvin R. Wilson (Grand Rapids: Eerdmans, 1987), 37.

Graham, Bernard Ramm, Vernon Grounds, and Edward John Carnell,[8] men who, for the most part, had been connected to Fuller Seminary or *Christianity Today*.

The NAE was founded in 1942 and formed the basis for organizational unity for the emerging evangelical movement. Harold J. Ockenga, future president of Fuller Seminary, along with a leading New England layman, J. Elwin Wright, was instrumental in its founding and was its first president.

Fuller Theological Seminary began classes in 1947 and became the early premier institution of higher learning among the evangelicals. On its first faculty were Wilbur Smith, Carl F. H. Henry, Everett F. Harrison, and Harold Lindsell. Fuller's first president was Harold John Ockenga, who served *in absentia*, and its second was Edward J. Carnell.[9]

Christianity Today was first published in 1956. It became the voice of the new evangelicalism. Ockenga and Graham were instrumental in the founding of the magazine. Its first two editors were Henry and Lindsell.[10] Henry had a significant influence on the direction evangelicalism, particularly in its more cognitive form, would take in its formative years.

No study of the debate over ecclesiastical separation between fundamentalists and new evangelicals would be complete without including the "Billy Graham issue." It was Graham's 1957 New York crusade that became the foil for fundamentalist attacks against inclusive evangelism particularly and new evangelicalism in general.[11] Ockenga viewed Billy Graham as the spokesman of the convictions and ideals of the new evangelicalism.[12] Fundamentalists viewed Graham as a

---

[8] Millard Erickson, *New Evangelical Theology* (Westwood: Revell, 1968), 8.

[9] Timothy George, Southern Baptist historian, says of Henry and Carnell, "If Carl Henry is the Calvin of evangelicalism—masterminding, publicizing, systematic—Carnell was its Kierkegaard—brilliant, brooding, single-minded." Timothy George, "Partly Fearing, Partly Hoping: Evangelicals, Southern Baptists, and the Quest for a New Consensus," *Perspectives in Religious Studies* 17 (Summer 1990), 169.

[10] *Christianity Today* "was to become the official periodical voice of the new Evangelicals." Richard Quebedeaux, *The Young Evangelicals: Revolution in Orthodoxy* (New York: Harper and Row, 1974), 13.

[11] Dollar, *A History of Fundamentalism*, 204.

[12] Marsden, *Reforming Fundamentalism*, 167.

compromiser and friend of the modernists.[13] The attacks of fundamentalism on new evangelicalism often centered on Graham and his inclusive evangelism.

When Fuller Seminary began, Ockenga argued for a theological similarity between the old fundamentalism and the new evangelicalism. He argued that the start of the seminary was not the starting of a new movement. In less than a decade, however, Ockenga was in the forefront of the new evangelicalism. In the March 1956 issue of *Christian Life* the new evangelicals identified eight areas of change in their theology. While not intending to start a new movement in 1948, by 1957 a new movement was formed and being promoted.

It was this constellation of forces, along with untold others, that debated the issue of ecclesiastical separation with fundamentalists. This work shall focus primarily on these early institutions and individuals as the most significant representatives of the movement, at least in its early period.

Fundamentalist and Evangelical Historiography

Historian Ernest R. Sandeen observed in 1967, "The fate of Fundamentalism in historiography has been worse than its lot in history."[14] The following pages explain the various approaches individuals have taken in the study of the fundamentalist and evangelical movements.

The first discussion of the history of fundamentalism as a movement was undertaken by Stewart Cole in *The History of Fundamentalism*. He argued that the initial stages of the movement were to be found in the late nineteenth century Bible conferences, the Bible school movement, and revivals. Cole declared, "In 1895 the Niagara group put forth the famous Five-points statement of doctrine, in which they insisted upon the universal Church, acceptance of the Inerrancy of the Scripture, the Deity of Christ, His Virgin Birth, the substitutionary Atonement of Christ, and

---

[13] See Farley Potter Butler, "Billy Graham and the End of Evangelical Unity" (PhD diss., University of Florida, 1976).

[14] Ernest R. Sandeen, "Toward a Historical Interpretation of the Origins of Fundamentalism," *Church History* 36 (March 1967): 66.

His physical Resurrection and coming bodily Return to earth."[15] Cole made two mistakes. First, he seems to have ignored the historic context of the 1878 Niagara Creed, from which the five points came. The five points were a condensation of the earlier fourteen-point creed, which identified the core beliefs of the Niagara Conference: The verbal, plenary inspiration of the Scriptures in the original manuscripts; the Trinity; the creation of man, the fall into sin, and total depravity; the universal transmission of spiritual death from Adam; the necessity of the new birth; redemption by the blood of Christ; salvation by faith alone in Christ; the assurance of salvation; the centrality of Jesus Christ in the Scriptures; the constitution of the true church by genuine believers; the personality of the Holy Spirit; the believer's call to a holy life; the immediate passing of the souls of believers to be with Christ at death; and the premillennial Second Coming of Christ.

Second, he attributed these five characteristics to fundamentalism as a whole, rather than simply to the Niagara group. The Niagara Conference leaders, however, had created a broader theological position in the 1878 Niagara Creed. "Through uncritical acceptance of Cole's mistake, generations of students have been taught to identify the Fundamentalist beast by its five points. That Fundamentalists defended many traditional doctrines is obvious. They did not define themselves in relation to any five particular points, however."[16] Doctrine was of only minimal concern to Cole, who saw the rising tide of secularism as the major problem disturbing fundamentalists.

Norman Furniss saw fundamentalists as people "who had failed to keep pace with the intellectual progress of the nation after 1870."[17] Most of his work was dedicated to a discussion of the anti-evolution crusade of the 1920s. For Furniss fundamentalists were people engaged in an "aggressive attempt to force orthodoxy upon all."[18]

Another writer who equated fundamentalism with reactionism was Richard Hofstadter. Hofstadter developed the "status anxiety" hypothesis

---

[15] Stewart Cole, *The History of Fundamentalism* (Westport, Conn.: Greenwood, 1931), 34.

[16] Sandeen, "Toward a Historical Interpretation," 80.

[17] Norman Furniss, *The Fundamentalist Controversy 1918-1931* (New Haven: Yale University Press, 1954), 29.

[18] Ibid., 32.

to describe fundamentalism. Orthodoxy had lost respectability in the face of the social gospel, evolution, and higher criticism. The result was a mindset among fundamentalism that could "tolerate no ambiguities, no equivocations, no reservations and no criticism."[19] For him fundamentalism was a passing reaction to the tide of secularization and an obstacle to enlightened and rational public discourse.

Several historians who wrote more general histories of religion or Protestantism also saw fundamentalism as a reactionary movement. H. Richard Niebuhr, in 1931, viewed the rise of fundamentalism as parallel to the depression of agricultural values after the World War.[20] A similar position was taken by Winthrop S. Hudson. He argued that urban, middle-class America adjusted to new ideas easily, while rural and mainly fundamentalist America adopted an obscurantist stance.[21] In 1965 George Mowry summarized the fundamentalist/modernist controversy as "countryside versus the big city, the West and the South against the East, Anglo-Saxonism against the polyglots."[22]

The first significant sociological study of fundamentalism and evangelicalism was Robert Webber's attempt to analyze the distinct subcultures constituting the two movements.[23] His first category was that of "Fundamentalist Evangelicalism," a subgroup characterized by "personal and ecclesiastical separation" and "biblicism" and represented by Bob Jones University, the ACCC, and John R. Rice's periodical, the *Sword of the Lord*. He identified "Cooperative Evangelicalism" as an inclusive group with a broad theological base, represented by the NAE, Billy Graham, and *Christianity Today*.

---

[19] Richard Hofstadter, *Anti-Intellectualism in American Life* (New York: Alfred A. Knopf, 1964), 119. Especially see pages 117–136. William McLoughlin took a similar position. William G. McLoughlin, *Revivals, Awakenings, and Reforms* (Chicago: Chicago University Press, 1978).

[20] H. Richard Niebuhr, "Fundamentalism," in *Encyclopedia of Social Sciences* (New York: 1937), 527. Interestingly enough, he referred to the movement in the past tense.

[21] Winthrop S. Hudson, *American Protestantism* (Chicago: University of Chicago Press, 1961), 145.

[22] George Mowry, *The Urban Nation* (New York: Hill and Wang, 1965), 30.

[23] Robert Webber, *Common Roots: A Call to Evangelical Maturity* (Grand Rapids: Zondervan, 1978), 32.

Nancy Ammerman argued that what separated fundamentalism and evangelicalism was an uncompromising attitude of separation. Fundamentalists were willing to separate from theological liberals and accommodating evangelicals, as well as from worldly attitudes and practices that might compromise personal holiness.[24] Sociologist James Davison Hunter held that evangelicalism had won the battle, absorbing almost all of fundamentalism, and, thus dismissing fundamentalism, focused the majority of his writing on evangelicalism.[25]

These studies viewed fundamentalism as an aberration, as a reaction to cultural change, or merely as a temporary phenomenon. Other than Cole's five points, they gave scant attention to theology or the debate over ecclesiastical separation.

Theological discussions of the movements began to appear in the latter 1960s. Paul Carter recognized that fundamentalism was far more complex than had been earlier realized. He was surprised that forty years after the fundamentalist/modernist controversy, fundamentalism was still alive while the word modernism had all but dropped out of the nation's vocabulary.[26] He questioned the old stereotype that fundamentalism was anti-scientific and anti-intellectual. He instead postulated that there was simply a difference between the fundamentalists' nineteenth century Baconian view of science and the twentieth century's analytical view.

A new phase in the interpretation of fundamentalism began with Ernest Sandeen.[27] Having acknowledged that scholars before him had

---

[24] Nancy Ammerman, *Bible Believers: Fundamentalists in the Modern World* (New Brunswick: Rutgers University Press, 1987), 193.

[25] James Davison Hunter, *American Evangelicalism: Conservative Religion and the Quandary of Modernity* (New Brunswick: Rutgers University Press, 1983) and *Evangelicalism: The Coming Generation* (Chicago: University of Chicago Press, 1987).

[26] Paul Carter, "The Fundamentalist Defense of the Faith," in *Change and Continuity in Twentieth Century America*, ed. John Braeman (Columbus: Ohio State University Press, 1968), 180.

[27] Ernest Sandeen, "Toward a Historical Interpretation"; "Fundamentalism and American Identity," *Annals of the American Academy of Social and Political Sciences* 387 (January 1970): 64–66; and *The Roots of Fundamentalism: British*

confused the fundamentalist movement with the fundamentalist/modernist controversy, he was among the first to evaluate fundamentalism as a theological movement. He understood fundamentalism to be the alliance between the adherents of the Princeton doctrine of biblical inerrancy and whose who espoused dispensational premillennialism.[28] He stressed that the movement was more than merely anti-modern or anti-liberal and that it was not simply conservative Protestantism. He argued that the strength of fundamentalism was in the large cities such as Philadelphia and New York, while the south was virtually unrepresented.[29] He attacked Cole's five-point basis of fundamentalism as obscuring its real roots.[30] He argued that the roots of fundamentalism were to be found in the dispensational premillennialism that John Darby had brought to America and the doctrine of verbal inspiration and biblical inerrancy that had developed at Princeton.[31] In reference to the dispensational view of the church, he stated, "It is impossible to overestimate the importance of this ecclesiology for the history of Fundamentalism."[32]

One of the first to respond to Sandeen was Leroy Moore, Jr. He accused Sandeen of committing the same anachronisms as Cole and Furniss: they had ignored the nineteenth century, and Sandeen had ignored the twentieth by ending his study with 1919. Moore asked how fundamentalism could be understood without examining its most important conflict.[33] Moore also argued that Sandeen had reduced the fundamentals to just two: dispensationalism and inerrancy.

---

and American Millenarianism, 1800–1930 (Chicago: University of Chicago Press, 1970).

[28] This thesis was challenged by Randall Balmer and John D. Woodbridge, "The Princetonians' Viewpoint of Biblical Authority: An Evaluation of the Ernest Sandeen Proposal," in *Scripture and Truth*, ed. D. A. Carson and John D. Woodbridge (Grand Rapids: Zondervan, 1983), 251–286.

[29] Sandeen, "Toward a Historical Interpretation," 77.

[30] Sandeen, *The Roots of Fundamentalism*, xii.

[31] Ibid., 190–91.

[32] Sandeen, "Toward a Historical Interpretation," 69.

[33] Leroy Moore, "Another Look at Fundamentalism: A Response to Ernest R. Sandeen," *Church History* 37 (June 1968): 196.

The most significant response to Sandeen's proposals, however, came from George Marsden.[34] Marsden contended that Sandeen had ignored vital ingredients within nineteenth century evangelicalism. In a theological study of Presbyterianism, Marsden identified the importance of the ecclesiastical practice of New Presbyterianism in Presbyterian fundamentalism.[35] His research appeared in 1980 in the seminal work *Fundamentalism and American Culture: The Shaping of Twentieth Century Evangelicalism 1870–1925*. This was the most thorough treatment of fundamentalism to its time and is still a critical work in the understanding of the movement. He contended that fundamentalism was the direct descendant of nineteenth-century evangelicalism and included revivalism, pietism, holiness teaching, millenarianism, and Common Sense philosophy. He argued that the movement was broader than the Sandeen thesis of a coalition of Darbyite millenarians and Princetonians. He saw evangelicalism as the dominant worldview of Americans in the mid-nineteenth century. Integral to this worldview were Scottish Common Sense realism and Baconianism. Religious views during the nineteenth century had expanded to include the moral, political, and economic realms.[36]

Marsden argued that evangelicalism turned into fundamentalism after World War I. Fundamentalists saw modernism and evolution subverting the Christian roots of America. It was not merely that their theological beliefs were under attack; they believed that the very existence of Christian civilization was at stake. Fundamentalism thus became militant in its opposition, a nineteenth-century evangelicalism

---

[34] George Marsden, "Defining Fundamentalism," *Christian Scholar's Review* 1 (Winter 1971): 141–151. Sandeen's responded in "Defining Fundamentalism: A Reply to Professor Marsden," *Christian Scholar's Review* 1 (Spring 1971): 227–233.

[35] George Marsden, "The New School Heritage and Presbyterian Fundamentalism," *Westminster Theological Journal* 32 (1970): 129–147. This is an analysis of Presbyterian fundamentalism, based on the aspects of New School Presbyterianism: dispensational eschatology, revivalism, independent agencies, and strict moral codes.

[36] George Marsden, *Fundamentalism and American Culture: The Shaping of Twentieth Century Evangelicalism, 1870–1925* (New York: Oxford University Press, 1980), 3–11.

reshaped in the crucible of the upheavals of the 1920s.[37] Fundamentalists championed traditional conservative theology, but exercised a religious and cultural separation unknown to their forbearers.

After the battles with modernism subsided, a portion of fundamentalism became dissatisfied with its separatism. Calling themselves "new evangelicals," they precipitated a major split in the ranks of fundamentalism. In Marsden's view, fundamentalism became a coalition of dispensationalists and separatists, while evangelicalism sought to retain its essential commitment to evangelical orthodoxy and anti-modernism while getting rid of "these more recent aspects of fundamentalism."[38] He viewed the primary manifestations of evangelicalism to be the establishment of Fuller Seminary, the ministry of Billy Graham, and the formation of the NAE. Marsden argued that the clashes between fundamentalism and evangelicalism were over the biblical parameters of ecclesiastical and personal separation.

Joel Carpenter examined fundamentalism in the years following the Scopes' Monkey trial, from the 1920s to the middle of the century. During these decades fundamentalism as a movement seemed to have disappeared.[39] Carpenter clearly demonstrates that fundamentalism was alive and well during that time. He argues that during those years, however, fundamentalism suffered from "cultural alienation, sectarian behavior, and intellectual stagnation."[40]

Another major writer on American religion was Martin Marty, who attempted to link American fundamentalism with other worldwide conservative religious movements.[41] He argued that fundamentalism was characterized by two key doctrines—biblical inerrancy and

---

[37] Ibid., 4. See A. C. Dixon, Louis Meyer, and R. A. Torrey, eds., *The Fundamentals: A Testimony to the Truth* (Chicago: Testimony Publishing Company, [1910–1915]).

[38] George Marsden, *Fundamentalism and American Culture: The Shaping of Twentieth Century Evangelicalism, 1870–1925* (New York: Oxford University Press, 1980), 10.

[39] Joel A. Carpenter, *Revive Us Again: The Reawakening of American Fundamentalism* (New York: Oxford University Press, 1997).

[40] Ibid., 3.

[41] See Martin Marty, "Fundamentalism Reborn," *Saturday Review* 7 (May 1980): 37–38.

premillennialism.[42] He spoke of the fracture in the 1950s and 1960s between separatists and non-separatists and pointed to the inclusive ministry of Billy Graham as the litmus test of this division.[43]

Fundamentalism was not very productive in defense of itself. *A History of Fundamentalism in America* by George W. Dollar was the first historical defense of fundamentalism by one of its own.[44] The work was purely historical, with little attention to theology. After Dollar's departure from Bob Jones University, his replacement, David O. Beale, wrote another history of fundamentalism.[45] This, too, was primarily historical and not theological. A third work, by Jerry Falwell, combined history with an apologetic for the fundamentalist political agenda.[46] This work was also non-theological. The most recent history of fundamentalism focuses on the Baptists in the movement. Written by two fundamentalist educators, Kevin Bauder and Robert Delnay, this work is a detailed history mainly of the internal struggle that the fundamental Baptists in the Northern Baptist Convention had in attempting to reform and finally separate from the convention.[47]

More theological in his discussion of fundamentalism was Ernest Pickering. He wrote an apologetic for separatism in two books, *Biblical Separation: The Struggle for a Pure Church*, a historical view of the issue of separation, beginning with the Donatists and Novatianists and continuing to the mid-twentieth century, and *The Tragedy of Compromise*, a look at new evangelicalism from the viewpoint of a

---

[42] Martin Marty, "Modern Fundamentalism," *America* 155 (27 Sept 1986): 134.

[43] Martin Marty, "Fundamentalism as a Social Phenomenon," *Review and Expositor* 76 (Winter 1982): 27.

[44] Dollar, *A History of Fundamentalism*. He followed this with *The Fight for Fundamentalism: American Fundamentalism, 1973–1983* (Sarasota, Fla.: George Dollar, 1983).

[45] David O. Beale, *In Pursuit of Purity: American Fundamentalism since 1850* (Greenville, SC: Unusual Publications, 1986).

[46] Jerry Falwell, ed., *The Fundamentalist Phenomenon: The Resurgence of Conservative Christianity* (Garden City: Doubleday, 1981).

[47] Kevin Bauder and Robert Delnay, *One in Hope and Doctrine: Origins of Baptist Fundamentalism 1870-1950* (Schaumburg, IL: Regular Baptist Books, 2014).

fundamentalist.[48] Fred Moritz developed a biblical and philosophical base for separatism in *"Be Ye Holy" The Call to Christian Separation*.[49] A similar work was written by Mark Sidwell who includes a short discussion of how the doctrine of separation was fleshed out by the fundamentalists.[50]

One of the first historical works specifically on new evangelicalism as a distinct movement was James D. Murch's history of the NAE published in 1956.[51] Two years later Louis Gasper examined the contrast between the ACCC and the NAE in *The Fundamentalist Movement*.[52] Ronald Nash wrote an apology for new evangelicalism. He was hard on the separatists and ignored any problem areas in evangelicalism.[53] He dealt particularly with bibliology, ecclesiology (and the problems of separation and unity), and, to a limited extent, apologetics. In 1967, on the twenty-fifth anniversary of the beginning of the NAE, Bruce Shelley produced an update of Murch's work.[54] Several years later, Joel Carpenter wrote a shorter history of the NAE, "The Fundamentalist Leaven and the Rise of an Evangelical United Front," in *The Evangelical Tradition in America*.[55]

---

[48] Ernest D. Pickering, *Biblical Separation: The Struggle for a Pure Church* (Schaumburg, Ill.: Regular Baptist, 1979) and *The Tragedy of Compromise* (Greenville, SC: Bob Jones University Press, 1994). A similar work is Rolland McCune, *Promise Unfulfilled: The Failed Strategy of Modern Evangelicalism* (Greenville, SC: Ambassador Emerald, 2004).

[49] Fred Moritz, *"Be Ye Holy" The Call to Christian Separation* (Greenville, SC: Bob Jones University Press, 1994).

[50] Mark Sidwell, *The Dividing Line: Understanding and Applying Biblical Separation* (Greenville, SC: Bob Jones University Press, 1998).

[51] James D. Murch, *Cooperation without Compromise: A History of the National Association of Evangelicals* (Grand Rapids: Eerdmans, 1956).

[52] Louis Gasper, *The Fundamentalist Movement* (The Hague, Netherlands: Mouton, 1963). This came from his dissertation, "Fundamentalist Movement in American Protestant Christianity since 1930," (PhD dissertation, Case Western Reserve University, 1958).

[53] Ronald H. Nash, *The New Evangelicalism* (Grand Rapids: Zondervan, 1963).

[54] Bruce Shelley, *Evangelicalism in America* (Grand Rapids: Eerdmans, 1967).

[55] Joel Carpenter, "The Fundamentalist Leaven and the Rise of an Evangelical United Front," in *The Evangelical Tradition in America*, Leonard I. Sweet, ed. (Macon: Mercer University, 1984), 257–88.

These works were, for the most part, historical studies and did little to contribute to a theological understanding of the movement.

Millard Erickson wrote a theological work in 1968, emphasizing the theology of the new evangelicals.[56] He sketched out the historical background to the new evangelical movement, surveyed its doctrinal contents, and analyzed the "subdivisions" into which evangelicalism had fractured by the time of his writing. Five years later Donald Bloesch and Bernard L. Ramm both produced works attempting to define evangelicalism and identify its roots.[57] Bloesch attempted to systematize what had happened in evangelicalism since World War II. Ramm was more comprehensive than Bloesch. He took a historical theology approach and identified evangelicalism as the legacy of the Reformation and Protestant Orthodoxy. He noted the conflicts it had faced since the Enlightenment and then suggested a possible future. Richard Quebedeaux wrote from the perspective of a young evangelical who had moved further away from evangelicalism's fundamentalist origins.[58] He described his own intellectual pilgrimage away from conservative evangelicalism, with an emphasis on the emergence of a group within evangelicalism "motivated on the one hand by the concerns of the new evangelicalism, and on the other hand by the conscious-rending social and political unrest of the 1960's."[59]

One of the most useful theological works appeared in 1975: *The Evangelicals: What They Believe, Who They Are, and Where They Are Changing* by David Wells and John Woodbridge.[60] This work consists of

---

[56] Erickson, *New Evangelical Theology*.

[57] Donald G. Bloesch, *The Evangelical Renaissance* (Grand Rapids: Eerdmans, 1973) and Bernard L. Ramm, *The Evangelical Heritage* (Waco: Word, 1973). Ten years later, Ramm updated his work in *After Fundamentalism* (San Francisco: Harper and Row, 1983).

[58] Quebedeaux, *The Young Evangelicals*. This was followed up with a sequel in which he described a wide spectrum of evangelicals, from left to right, although he acknowledged that "the boundaries of these designations are very hard to delineate with accuracy." Richard Quebedeaux, *The Worldly Evangelicals* (New York: Harper and Row, 1978), 28.

[59] Ibid., 40.

[60] David F. Wells and John D. Woodbridge, *The Evangelicals: What They Believe, Who They Are, and Where They Are Changing* (Nashville: Abingdon, 1975).

twelve essays, and the second edition contains a "Guide to Further Reading." It is important because it was written by leading evangelicals when evangelicalism was gaining national attention and when others were beginning to seriously assess its stance. It went beyond the typical historical study and introduced a theological basis for the movement. It particularly identified the changes new evangelicalism was making to the older fundamentalism. The book also revealed the continuing lack of consensus on just what an evangelical was.[61]

Kenneth Kantzer edited a *Festschrift* to Wilbur Smith. The sixteen chapters include important works on the history or position of new evangelicalism.[62] Included are a short history of evangelicalism by Ockenga, several articles on the importance of the inerrancy and authority of Scripture, and a missiological emphasis. In 1978 Robert Webber and Donald Bloesch edited *The Orthodox Evangelicals*, which centered its discussion on the May 1977 "Chicago Call," which, among other things, issued a call for church unity in strongly ecumenical tones.[63]

Since the 1970s the direction of much of the writing has moved to a debate over historiography. The debate is between those who use a reformed-doctrinal-creedal base for the interpretation of the current evangelical/fundamentalist scene (represented by George Marsden, Joel Carpenter, Mark Noll, Donald Bloesch, and Bernard Ramm) and those who understand evangelicalism as the child of the holiness-revivalistic-experiential factions of the nineteenth century (represented by Donald Dayton, Timothy Smith, and Leonard Sweet). Some (such as Douglas Sweeney) argue that both interpretations must be used.[64]

Two major works critical of the new evangelical movement were written by leading fundamentalists. Ernest Pickering wrote briefly of the

---

[61] This lack of consensus was still present in 1989 when more than 350 evangelicals gathered for four days at Trinity Evangelical Divinity School to produce a concise definition of evangelical belief and practice. See "What Does It Mean to Be Evangelical?" *Christianity Today* 33 (16 June 1989): 60, 63.

[62] Kenneth Kantzer, ed., *Evangelical Roots* (Nashville: Thomas Nelson, 1978).

[63] Robert Webber and Donald Bloesch, eds., *The Orthodox Evangelicals* (New York: Nelson, 1978). See especially page 7.

[64] Douglas A. Sweeney, "The Essential Evangelicalism Dialectic: The Historiography of the Early New-Evangelical Movement and the Observer-Participant Dilemma," *Church History* 60 (March 1991): 71.

fundamentalist-modernist battles of the early twentieth century and the beginnings of the new evangelicalism. While the criticisms have a broad range, Billy Graham was particularly singled out for his role in the ecumenical evangelism that troubled so many of the fundamentalists.[65] A more extensive work was written by seminary professor, Rolland McCune.[66] This work includes four chapters on the historical background of the rise of the fundamentalist-evangelical debates but focuses much of its attention on theological issues, such as ecumenism, separation, apologetics, social involvement, and the doctrinal deviations of some segments of evangelicalism.

A number of biographical and institutional histories have been written. By far the most common subject has been Billy Graham, although much of the material has been in popular format. For example, in the two decades after the 1954 London crusade, *Newsweek* alone featured Graham and his work in more than fifty articles. More than three hundred books in part or in whole treat Graham's life and ministry.[67] His origins in southern fundamentalism are well documented in numerous official and unofficial biographies. The more useful early studies were done by Stanley High and William McLoughlin, Jr.[68] McLoughlin was critical of Graham, arguing that he mirrored the simplistic piety of the postwar revival of religion. He viewed Graham as a typical revival figure, born into the milieu of modern communications technology, but with nothing new in his techniques or message except that "it emphasized more heavily than any previous revivalists the note of world-wide catastrophe associated with the Second Coming of Christ."[69] John Pollock wrote two "insider" works. He

---

[65] Ernest Pickering, *The Tragedy of Compromise: The Origin and Impact of the New Evangelicalism* (Greenville, SC: Bob Jones University Press, 1994).

[66] McCune, *Promise Unfulfilled*.

[67] An ongoing bibliography of Graham is kept at the Billy Graham Center Library, Wheaton, Illinois.

[68] Stanley High, *Billy Graham: The Personal Story of the Man, His Message and His Mission* (New York: McGraw-Hill, 1956) and William McLoughlin, Jr., *Billy Graham: Revivalist in a Secular Age* (New York: Ronald, 1960).

[69] William McLoughlin, *Modern Revivalism: Charles Grandison Finney to Billy Graham* (New York: Ronald, 1959), 519.

clearly admired Graham and attributed his success to God.[70] Early supporters of Graham's cooperative evangelism included Robert O. Ferm and John R. W. Stott.[71] Lowell Streiker and Gerald Strober identified Graham as an essential agent of new evangelicalism. "At the moment Graham ascended to national stature he assumed leadership of the burgeoning new evangelical movement which developed in the forties around a circle of sophisticated theological conservatives led by the seminary professors, Carl F. H. Henry and Edward John Carnell."[72] The

---

[70] John Pollock, *Billy Graham: The Authorized Biography* (New York: McGraw-Hill, 1966) and *Billy Graham, Evangelist to the World: An Authorized Biography of the Decisive Years* (New York: Harper and Row, 1979). Other useful works are David Poling, *Why Billy Graham?* (Grand Rapids: Zondervan, 1977) and Marshall Frady, *Billy Graham: A Parable of American Righteousness* (Boston: Little, Brown, 1979). Frady, however, left out of his story men like Carl Henry, Wilbur Smith, and V. R. Erdman, a significant omission indicative of Frady's missing the whole issue of Graham's relationship to his own primary community of support. Frady tried to make Graham an enigma. For instance, Frady concentrates on Graham's relationship with Ruth Bell at Wheaton, rather than on his educational experiences. Frady does, however, attempt to show how Graham fused religious and national values to create a guide for how one should think and act. A useful outsider's view of Graham's life was given by William Martin, *A Prophet With Honor: The Billy Graham Story* (New York: William Morrow, 1991). Another useful study of Graham, if used with caution, is W. David Lockard, *The Unheard Billy Graham* (Waco: Word, 1971), a collection of his declarations on social issues and other themes.

[71] Robert O. Ferm, *Cooperative Evangelism: Is Billy Graham Right or Wrong?* (Grand Rapids: Zondervan, 1958) and John R. W. Stott, *Fundamentalism and Evangelism* (Grand Rapids: Eerdmans, 1959). Many were in agreement with Graham's message and methodology, as evidenced in the glowing reports and evaluations of men like Curtis Mitchell, *God in the Garden: The Story of the Billy Graham New York Crusade* (Garden City, NJ: Doubleday, 1957); Frank Colquhoun, *Harringay Story: The Official Record of the Billy Graham Greater London Crusade, 1954* (London: Hodder and Stoughton, 1955); and Sherwood Eliot Wirt, *Crusade at the Golden Gate* (New York: Harper and Brothers, 1959).

[72] Lowell D. Streiker and Gerald S. Strober, *Religion and the New Majority: Billy Graham, Middle America, and the Politics of the 70s* (New York: Association, 1972), 32. The treatment is too simplistic, however; Graham could not have "assumed leadership" of a movement too fluid to be contained.

most "authentic" work on Graham is undoubtedly his own autobiography, *Just As I Am: The Autobiography of Billy Graham.*[73]

Fundamentalists opposed his ministry. Gary Cohen and Errol Hulse were two men from the Reformed viewpoint who were critical of Graham's ministry.[74] George W. Dollar made numerous references to the problems that fundamentalism had with Graham, particularly his "ecumenical evangelism."[75] Robert P. Lightner, William E. Ashbrook, and Charles Woodbridge wrote works critical of new evangelicalism in general and of Graham's cooperative evangelism in particular.[76] These attacks from the fundamentalist circles actually may have broadened Graham's appeal to the audiences he was seeking, since it distanced him from his roots.

The first biography of Carl F. H. Henry was in the Makers of the Modern Theological Mind Series.[77] Henry's autobiography provides helpful information on events at Fuller Seminary and *Christianity Today.*[78]

Rudolph Nelson wrote a critical biography of E. J. Carnell.[79] The larger portion was a moderately sympathetic, yet honest account of Carnell's troubled life; the remainder was an examination of Carnell's works, including an analysis of the strengths and weaknesses of Carnell's

---

[73] Billy Graham, *Just As I Am: The Autobiography of Billy Graham* (San Francisco: HarperCollins, 1997).

[74] Gary G. Cohen, *Biblical Separation Defended: A Biblical Critique of Ten New Evangelical Arguments* (Philadelphia: Presbyterian and Reformed, 1966); and Errol Hulse, *Billy Graham—the Pastor's Dilemma* (Hounslow, Middlesex, England: Maurice Allan Ltd., 1966).

[75] Dollar, *A History of Fundamentalism*, 325.

[76] Robert P. Lightner, *Neo-Evangelicalism* (Des Plaines, Ill.: Regular Baptist, 1969); William E. Ashbrook, *Evangelicalism: The New Neutralism* (Columbus, Ohio: William E. Ashbrook, n.d.); and Charles Woodbridge, *The New Evangelicalism* (Greenville, SC: Bob Jones University Press, 1969).

[77] Bob E. Patterson, *Carl F. H. Henry*, Makers of the Modern Theological Mind (Waco: Word, 1983).

[78] Carl F. H. Henry, *Confessions of a Theologian: An Autobiography* (Waco: Word, 1986).

[79] Rudolph Nelson, *The Making and Unmaking of an Evangelical Mind* (New York: Cambridge University Press, 1977).

apologetics. Joseph L. Rosas, III, included a short biography of Carnell in *Baptist Theologians*.[80]

Harold Lindsell wrote the first substantive biography on Harold John Ockenga.[81] Years later a Baylor University PhD student, John Adams, wrote his dissertation on Ockenga.[82] A third major work was written by Garth Rosell, who produced a history of evangelicalism with an emphasis on Ockenga and his relationship with Billy Graham.[83] For as important a role as he played in the emergence of the new evangelical movement and his part in the beginning of institutions such as the NAE, Fuller Seminary, and *Christianity Today*, however, Ockenga has not received much attention.

On the fundamentalist side, many scholars who have explored Carl McIntire's career have been content to see him as an example of religious extremism, fanaticism, militant anti-communism, or a combination of these.[84] John Fea believed that McIntire's ideological and religious makeup caused this. He was "an outspoken critic of theological

---

[80] Joseph L. Rosas, III, "Edward John Carnell," in *Baptist Theologians*, ed. Timothy George and David Dockery (Nashville: Broadman, 1990): 606–626.

[81] Harold Lindsell, *Park Street Prophet: A Life of Harold John Ockenga* (Wheaton: Van Kampen, 1951).

[82] John M. Adams, "The Making of a Neo-Evangelical Statesman: The Case of Harold John Ockenga," (PhD diss., Baylor University, 1994).

[83] Garth M. Rosell, *The Surprising Work of God: Harold John Ockenga, Billy Graham, and the Rebirth of Evangelicalism* (Grand Rapids: Baker, 2008).

[84] See, for example, Ralph Lord Roy, *Apostles of Discord: A Study of Organized Bigotry and Disruption on the Fringes of Protestantism* (Boston: Beacon, 1953), who placed McIntire on the outside of mainstream American politics; Benjamin Epstein and Arnold Forster, *Danger on the Right* (New York: Random House, 1964), written from the perspective of the Anti-Defamation League; and Gary Clabaugh, *Thunder on the Right: The Protestant Fundamentalists* (Chicago: Nelson-Hall, 1974), which continued the anti-McIntire view. Most interpretations of fundamentalism in the Presbyterian Church tend to stop with Machen's death after 1936, when he was ousted from the denomination for violating his ordination vows. This, however, neglects the fact that a fundamentalist current continued to exist into the 1940s and beyond. McIntire provides a good study of this post-1940s fundamentalism. Marsden makes reference to him on several occasions, but only to contrast his brand of separatism with that of the more open-minded new evangelicals.

modernism, a dogged champion of ecclesiastical separation, a militant opponent of ecumenism, and a devout anticommunist."[85] Others took him more seriously. R. Laurence Moore reminded the historical community not to neglect religious "outsiders." He argued that such people are important for understanding American history no matter how "politically useless or even pernicious their dissent often was."[86] Another writer in this vein was Leo Ribuffo, who warned historians to avoid the simplicity of reducing men like McIntire to the realm of mere religious fanatic.[87] He argued that the extremists on the right often converged with the cultural and political mainstream. Erling Jorstad may provide the best means of understanding McIntire's career. He saw McIntire as high-lighting not so much the tension between separatism and politicism as the amalgamation of these two elements into a variant civil religion. Jorstad notes that McIntire's most serious problem was that of equating American values and citizenship with Christianity itself.[88] Not all the biographers took a negative and critical position. Two with a positive view of McIntire were Clarence Laman and James Morris.[89]

---

[85] John Fea, "Carl McIntire: From Fundamentalist Presbyterian to Presbyterian Fundamentalist," *American Presbyterians* 72 (Winter 1994): 254.

[86] R. Laurence Moore, *Religious Outsiders and the Making of Americans* (New York: Oxford, 1986), xii.

[87] Leo Ribuffo, *The Old Christian Right: The Protestant Far Right from the Great Depression to the Cold War* (Philadelphia: Temple University Press, 1983), xi–xix, 247.

[88] Erling Jorstad, *The Politics of Doomsday: Fundamentalists of the Far Right* (Nashville: Abingdon Press, 1970). Other works helpful to understanding McIntire and his impression on American Fundamentalism include: William R. Hutchison, *The Modernist Impulse in American Protestantism* (Cambridge, Mass.: Harvard University Press, 1976); and Robert C. Leibman and Robert Wuthrow, *The New Christian Right: Mobilization and Legitimation* (New York: Aldine, 1983).

[89] Clarence Laman, *God Calls a Man* (Collingswood, NJ: Christian Beacon, 1959) and James Morris, *The Preachers* (New York: St. Martin, 1973). A close associate of Carl McIntire was Robert T. Ketcham, early leader of the General Association of Regular Baptist Churches and of the American Council of Christian Churches. J. Murray Murdoch wrote a sympathetic biography of Ketcham. J. Murray Murdoch, *Portrait of Obedience: The Biography of Robert T. Ketcham* (Regular Baptist, 1979).

There have been few works on the Joneses. The standard source of biographical information is *Builder of Bridges* by R. K. Johnson.[90] While fiercely partisan, this work provides valuable biographical information on the first three generations of the Joneses. The autobiography of Bob Jones, Jr., also contains helpful background information to the Jones family.[91] Another important source of information is from George Dollar, former professor of Church History at Bob Jones University.[92] Wider in scope than just the Joneses, Dollar's work provides a good background and locates them within the context of American Fundamentalism. There are two histories of the University written by insiders, yet they provide good basic information on the school.[93] An outsider, Mark Taylor Dalhouse, wrote a more objective history of Bob Jones University and especially its position on separatism.[94] A very helpful book on the theology of the Joneses is Robert Campbell's *Spectrum of Protestant Beliefs*.[95] The Joneses' own writings are not theologically oriented. Most of them are collections of sermons, although Bob Jones, Jr., did write a series of Old Testament commentaries.

---

[90] R. K. Johnson, *Builder of Bridges: The Biography of Dr. Bob Jones, Sr.* (Murfreesboro, Tenn.: Sword of the Lord, 1969).

[91] Bob Jones, Jr., *Cornbread and Caviar: Reminiscence and Reflections* (Greenville, SC: Bob Jones University Press, 1985).

[92] Dollar, *A History of Fundamentalism.* Dollar's work was replaced as the standard history of fundamentalism by David O. Beale, *In Pursuit of Purity: American Fundamentalism since 1850* (Greenville, SC: Bob Jones University Press, 1986).

[93] Margaret Beall Tice, *Bob Jones University* (Greenville, SC: Bob Jones University Press, 1976) and Melton Wright, *Fortress of Faith* (Grand Rapids: Eerdmans, 1960).

[94] Mark Taylor Dalhouse, *An Island in the Lake of Fire: Bob Jones University, Fundamentalism, and The Separatist Movement* (Athens: University of Georgia Press, 1996).

[95] Five writers contributed answers to questions from Campbell. These were divided into five bands "which seem most closely to represent the reality of the situation: radical, liberal, confessional, new evangelical, and fundamentalist." Robert Campbell, *Spectrum of Protestant Beliefs* (Milwaukee: Bruce, 1968), v. While the answers are short and thus not very thorough, the book provides one of the few places where any of the Joneses explicated their theology.

Three key biographies have been written on John R. Rice. The first was by his friend and fellow evangelist Robert L. Sumner.[96] This highlights his early career. A later work by a staff member of the *Sword of the Lord*, Viola Walden, while partisan to an extreme, provides helpful information on his life and ministry.[97] A more recent work was done by Andrew Himes, the first grandson of Rice. Himes was seventeen when he left fundamentalism for the communistic ideals of Karl Marx and Mao Zedong. Himes felt disillusioned with God because to Himes God was "an elderly white male who lived in a golden city beyond the sky, who apparently liked white people better than black people, who ordered women to be subservient to men, who supported the war aims of the United States in Vietnam," and who sent most people to a literal lake of fire. Forty-four years after this decision, Himes recognized the emptiness of communism and came to appreciate, but not agree with, his fundamentalist heritage.[98] These work are not theological, however. To determine the theology of Rice, one must read through his articles in the *Sword of the Lord* and his various books.

Conclusion

Much has been written on these two movements and on the leaders within them. Much more needs to be done to fully comprehend the complexity of these men and institutions and the extent to which they have affected their spiritual descendants. It is the purpose of this work to explore one theological segment—the doctrine of the church, including how the various men and movements came to understand this doctrine and how that understanding affected their affiliations and actions.

---

[96] Robert L. Sumner, *Man Sent From God: A Biography of John R. Rice* (Grand Rapids: Eerdmans, 1959).

[97] Viola Walden, *John R. Rice, "Captain of our Team"* (Murfreesboro, Tenn.: Sword of the Lord, 1990).

[98] Andrew Himes, *The Roots of Fundamentalism in an American Family* (Seattle: Chiara, 2010).

Chapter 1

VARIETIES OF ECCLESIOLOGIES

"Church history has great value as an explanation of the present."[1] In order to better understand the theological climate in which the debates over ecclesiastical separation took place, it will be helpful to examine how the doctrine of the church developed. The ecclesiologies of fundamentalism and evangelicalism did not develop in a vacuum. This chapter will undertake a brief examination of the primary historical views of the nature of the church to set the background for the positions taken by the representatives of fundamentalism and new evangelicalism.

Pre-Reformation Ecclesiologies

As early as the second century, two contradictory trends had developed which would affect the doctrine of the church in later periods. One trend was toward external unity; the other was toward internal purity.

External Unity

The early church fathers, in refuting heresies in the second century, established external characteristics by which they argued the true church could be known: the church was ruled by a bishop as the direct successor of the apostles, the church possessed the true tradition, the universal church was the historical basis of all local churches, and a local church was a true church only as long as it remained faithful to the catholic church.[2] The most significant early writer on the doctrine of the church was Augustine. His ecclesiology held sway until the Reformation and continued to affect ecclesiologies long after that. Augustine did not

---

[1] Earl D. Radmacher, *What the Church is All About* (Chicago: Moody, 1978), 27.

[2] Louis Berkhof, *The History of Christian Doctrines* (Grand Rapids: Eerdmans, 1937; reprint, Grand Rapids: Eerdmans, 1994), 233.

create a new ecclesiology; he was influenced by those who had gone before him and those against whom he stood. Three of the more significant writers prior to Augustine were Ignatius, Irenaeus, and Cyprian.

Ignatius (who died about AD 107) spoke of "one Church which the holy apostles established from one end of the earth to the other by the blood of Christ."[3] He was one of the first to use the phrase "catholic church," although he used it in a local sense. Submission to the bishop was the way to avoid heresy and maintain the unity of the church: "Wherever the bishop shall appear, there let the multitude also be."[4] Ignatius, however, saw no hierarchy outside the church.

Irenaeus (about AD 130–202) emphasized a universal, visible church. "The Church, though dispensed throughout the whole world, even to the ends of the earth, has received from the apostles and their disciples this faith."[5] For Irenaeus, those who met in other "churches" (he viewed them as unauthorized meetings) were not part of the universal church: "The very great, the very ancient, and universally known Church founded and organized at Rome, by the two most glorious apostles, Peter and Paul. . . . For it is a matter of necessity that every Church should agree with this Church, on account of its preeminent authority, that is, the faithful everywhere, inasmuch as the apostolic tradition has been preserved continuously by those who exist everywhere."[6]

Irenaeus viewed the church as the divine custodian and dispenser of truth and limited salvation to those within this catholic church. Although he had a strong interest in maintaining the purity of the church, his desire to stem the rising tide of heresy resulted in a strong emphasis on external unity.[7]

---

[3] Ignatius, *To Philadelphia* 4. English translations are from Alexander Roberts and James Donaldson, eds., *The Ante-Nicene Fathers*, American Reprint of the Edinburgh Edition (Grand Rapids: Eerdmans, 1971) or Philip Schaff and Henry Wace, eds., *A Select Library of Nicene and Post-Nicene Fathers of the Christian Church*, Second Series (Grand Rapids: Eerdmans, 1969).

[4] Ignatius, *To the Smyrnaeans* 8.

[5] Irenaeus, *Against Heresies* 1.10.1.

[6] Ibid., 3.3.2.

[7] Radmacher, *What the Church is All About*, 41.

Cyprian (AD 200–258), the great North African bishop, was among the first to develop the doctrine of the episcopal church.[8] With the church threatened from without by persecution and from within by schism, Cyprian emphasized the unity of the catholic church under the authority of the bishop.[9] He argued that schism is totally and absolutely unjustified. Unity cannot be broken, for to step outside the church was to forfeit any possibility of salvation.[10] The crux of Cyprian's conception of the unity of the church is found in his defense of the unbroken chain of succession beginning with Peter.[11] According to Cyprian's view of Matthew 16:18, the church was founded on the bishops. The bishop was the absolute lord of the church, while the clergy were priests by virtue of their sacrificial ministry. The unity of the church was based on the unity of the bishops, and rebellion against the bishop was rebellion against God.

> Whence you ought to know that the bishop is in the Church, and the Church is in the bishop; and if any one be not with the bishop, that he is not in the Church . . . the Church, which is Catholic and one, is not cut nor divided, but is indeed connected and bound together by the cement of priests who cohere with one another.[12]

For Cyprian, schism was a satanic trick whereby he "might subvert the faith, might corrupt the truth, and might divide the unity."[13] Unity was the clear teaching of Scripture.[14] The view of the church as the bride of

---

[8] The English "bishop" comes from *episcopos* in the Greek and thus the reference to the *episcopal* form of the church.

[9] Cyprian wrote *On the Unity of the Church* in AD 251 as a result of the division which developed between the lenient party (represented by Cyprian) and strict party (represented by Novatian) regarding readmission of those Christians who had forsaken their faith during the Decian persecution.

[10] Alister McGrath, *Christian Theology, An Introduction* (Oxford: Blackwell, 1994), 408.

[11] "While the other apostles were endowed with an equal share of office and power, Christ arranged that the church should take its beginning from one man, Peter." Cyprian, *On the Unity of the Church* 4.

[12] Cyprian, *Epistles* 68.8.

[13] Cyprian, *On the Unity of the Church* 3.

[14] Ibid., 4. Cant 6:9, "My dove, my spotless one, is one" and Eph 4:4–6, where Paul declares the mystery of unity of the "unum corpus" ("one body").

Christ meant that the schismatics were adulteresses. The idea of bride moved easily into the picture of mother; one bride obviously means one mother. Hence his decisive conclusion:

> He can no longer have God for his Father, who has not the Church for his mother. . . . Whoever is separated from the Church and is joined to an adulteress, is separated from the promises of the Church; nor can he who forsakes the Church of Christ attain to the rewards of Christ. He is a stranger; he is profane; he is an enemy.[15]

Although Rome was an important city and church, Cyprian did not recognize any special authority of the Roman bishop, for the Roman Catholic Church, with its papal authority, did not yet exist.[16]

Augustine. Of Augustine (AD 354–430), Dana states:

> If Cyprian laid the foundation for Romanism, Augustine erected the papal throne, and blazed the way for the colossal tyranny of the Roman Church hierarchy, which cast its blighting shadow upon the succeeding centuries, and was a potent factor in determining medieval history as the "Dark Ages." But these consequences were, of course, never

---

[15] Ibid., 6.

[16] Although there were numerous bishops in Rome who held great influence in the Empire, it is thought by some non-Catholics that Leo I (Bishop of Rome from 440–461) may be considered the first real pope, for several reasons. Leo I was the first to assert scriptural authority for the earlier claim by Innocent I (Bishop of Rome from 402–417) that the bishop of Rome had universal jurisdiction on the basis of the tradition surrounding Peter. Leo secured the emperor's recognition of his claims of primacy. He oversaw the doctrinal conclusions of the Council of Chalcedon; when Leo's statement was read at Chalcedon, the bishops proclaimed, "Peter has spoken." Robert A. Baker, *A Summary of Christian History,* rev. John M. Landers (Nashville: Broadman and Holman, 1994), 75–76. Others would argue that the first true pope was Gregory the Great, who reigned as bishop of Rome from 590 to 604. He was the first to centralize and amass the power and trappings of the papacy. He led the Roman church into the medieval world and institutionalized much of the culture under the umbrella of the bishop of Rome. In 602 the Eastern (Orthodox) church recognized the bishop of Rome as the "head of all the churches." Earle E. Cairns, *Christianity Through the Centuries* (Grand Rapids: Zondervan, 1981), 167–68.

anticipated by Augustine, even though they were the logical outgrowth of his theory of the church.[17]

Augustine developed his doctrine of the church in the heat of the Donatist controversy. During the Diocletian persecution (which lasted from AD 303 to 305 in Africa and longer in the East), Christians were ordered to surrender their Christian writings and register their church property with the government. The handing over or surrender (*traditio* in the Latin) of the writings was considered by many to be a kind of apostasy, and those who gave up their Christian writings were known as *traditores* ("surrenderers" of the Scriptures). In 311, the bishop of Carthage died. Cecilian was chosen as his successor and ordained by three men, one of whom had been a *traditore*. Secundus of Tigisis rejected the ordination of Cecilian and called a local synod. Cyprian had taught that sacraments given by wicked people were not valid. Secundus argued that included ordination. This synod then elected their own bishop for Carthage, Donatus of Casae Nigrae. The result was division.[18]

There had been previous divisions in the African church during the Severan and Decian persecutions. These divisions had been quickly healed, however, when reconciliation was obtained between the various parties. This time was different. The Donatists were unwilling to accept the offers of reconciliation, and the division lasted for three centuries. Augustine spent two decades attempting to win the Donatists back to the catholic church. When argument failed, he turned to force. Out of this debate came Augustine's view of the nature of the church.[19]

Augustine believed the church was a "mixed body" (*corpus permixtum*) of saints and sinners. The holiness of the church is not that of its members, but that of Christ.[20] Augustine also believed that schism was a worse sin than *traditio*. Sin is an inevitable aspect of the church. The wicked cannot be outwardly excluded from the church, but they are

---

[17] H. E. Dana, *A Manual of Ecclesiology* (Kansas City: Central Seminary, 1945), 116.

[18] There appears also to have been numerous personal reasons for the division. See W. H. C. Frend, *The Donatist Church* (Oxford: Clarendon, 1952), 3–24.

[19] Radmacher, *What the Church is All About*, 44–45.

[20] McGrath, *Christian Theology*, 409.

nevertheless inwardly separated from the pious. They are in the house, but do not belong to the house.[21]

Augustine placed an emphasis on the universal church: the one, holy, catholic church. The Donatist controversy drove Augustine to declare explicitly that there was no possibility of salvation outside of the church and without being baptized into the visible organization. Augustine declared:

> And so there is one Church which alone is called Catholic; and whenever it has anything of its own in these communions of different bodies which are separate from itself, it is most certainly in virtue of this which is its own in each of them that it, not they, has the power of generation. For neither is it their separation that generates, but what they have retained of the essence of the Church; and if they were to go on to abandon this, they would lose the power of generation. The generation then in each case proceeds from the Church.[22]

Elsewhere he stated that the "remission of sins, seeing it is not given but by the Holy Spirit, can only be given in that Church which hath the Holy Spirit."[23]

In their argument against baptismal regeneration, the Donatists asked Augustine how he could account for those who were baptized but were obviously not Christians. He responded by distinguishing between the visible church and the invisible church. The invisible church was found within the catholic church. His main illustration and proof was found in Matthew 13 in the parable of the wheat and the tares.[24] He was willing to acknowledge that the devil had some of his own children in the church, but he argued that God had no children outside the church.[25] "I tell you of a truth, my Beloved, even in these high seats there is both wheat and

---

[21] Berkhof, *History of Christian Doctrines*, 236.

[22] Augustine, *On Baptism, Against the Donatists* 1.9.14.

[23] Augustine, *Sermons on Selected Lessons of the New Testament* 21.33.

[24] Ibid., 23.1. That he made the church identical to the kingdom of heaven and identical to the world in the same parable apparently did not trouble him.

[25] Augustine, *On Baptism, Against the Donatists* 4.10.16. Here he refers to Donatists as the "party of the devil."

tares, and among the laity there is wheat, and tares. Let the good tolerate the bad; let the bad change themselves and imitate the good."[26]

Augustine's use of the parable of the wheat and tares was based on the identification of the kingdom of God with the church.[27] He identified the kingdom as the pious and holy individuals of the church, but he also identified the kingdom as the episcopally-organized church (which included the lost).[28] Augustine never synthesized these divergent views. In fact, his position on the church is so fraught with difficulties that Berkhof declares, "It is doubtful that a consistent theory of the church can be forged from the mass of materials Augustine has given."[29] In spite of his lack of theological clarity and consistency, Augustine laid the foundation for papal supremacy and developed the idea that the church was a *corpus mixtum*, a "mixed body" of good and bad men. He became the first "to distinguish an invisible church within the one, holy, visible, catholic church, outside of which is neither possibility of salvation nor knowledge of the truth."[30]

This laid the foundation for the gradual development toward external unity. Ancient Christianity faced internal problems and external pressures. There needed to be a common faith, which would produce a catholic consciousness, a unity of all Christian forces. As many began to move away from the "spiritual values of their religion and toward tangible

---

[26] Augustine, *Sermons* 23.4.

[27] Early church fathers had usually identified the kingdom as the eschatological millennium.

[28] Berkhof, *History of Christian Doctrines*, 236.

[29] Ibid., 237–38.

[30] Radmacher, *What the Church is All About*, 51. In a meeting between Augustine and Emeritus, the Donatist bishop of Caesarea in Mauretania, Augustine asked the people to pray for Emeritus' salvation and declared, "No one can be saved except in the Catholic Church. He can have everything but salvation outside the Catholic Church. He can have honors, he can have the sacraments, he can sing 'Alleluia,' he can answer 'Amen,' he can hold the Gospels, he can have faith and preach in the name of the Father and of the Son and of the Holy Spirit. But nowhere except in the Catholic Church will he find salvation." Augustine, *Sermo ad Caesariensis Ecclesiae plebem, MPL* 43, 695.

expression and externalism, they came more to gravitate around an earthly center of control."[31]

There were three stages in this development.[32] The first was the appearance of the monarchical bishop, to whom fellow elders were subservient. The Catholic Church developed the three-fold office of the ministerial priesthood (bishop, presbyter or priest, and deacon), in which the bishop ruled as the "monarch." The bishop became the custodian of the faith, and unity in the church was maintained by loyalty to the bishop.

The second stage was the gaining of preeminence by bishops of large cities. Bishops of smaller cities looked up to the bishops of the larger cities, who were usually older and more experienced. Thus developed both the metropolitan bishop[33] and the pattern for an episcopacy. The conception of the church under a bishop grew until the concept of the local church practically disappeared.

Then came the third stage, the development of the Roman supremacy. The concept of a visible, universal church demanded a centralized authority. Rome was the obvious choice. It was the center of the empire, the chief city in early theological debates, and the church which Peter was supposed to have started. It was easy for Cyprian and Augustine to convince the church at large of the primacy of the Roman see.

Internal Purity

A separatist movement developed in opposition to the growing centralized authority in the institutional church. These separatist churches considered the holiness of their members to be the real mark of the true church. They grew as a reaction against the gradual secularization and increasing worldliness of the larger church. Information on these churches is scarce and its reliability questionable, since it often comes from their opposition. The movements cannot be

---

[31] Ibid., 49–50.

[32] Ibid., 50–51.

[33] The metropolitan bishop is the bishop (or archbishop) over a large city or area. He maintains ecclesiastical control over the priests and churches in that area.

whitewashed of their errors, but they should be credited with whatever contributions they did make.

Tertullian rejected the emphasis on unity of the churches. He viewed the church as a community of saints awaiting the end of the world and as a brotherhood overseen by elders.[34] There were no bishops or episcopal power of any kind in Tertullian's ecclesiology. He suggested that any Christian could dispense the sacraments.[35] The church existed anywhere there were two or three gathered in the unity of the Spirit. Tertullian also argued that the Holy Spirit was present in the water of baptism. Since a heretic could not possess the Spirit, baptism by a heretic was invalid.[36] Therefore, anyone baptized by a heretic had to be rebaptized to be admitted to the true church. This theology demonstrates that separatism based on an ecclesiastical practice was present as early as the second and third centuries.

The Donatist controversy of the fourth century is important for two reasons. One positive result was the development of a church free from the influences of the institutional church. The second is the impetus the Donatists gave to Augustine to develop his ecclesiology. The Donatist controversy began in 303 when Diocletian, emperor of the Roman Empire, sought to return the empire to its former glory. Placing the blame for the empire's decline on Christianity, Diocletian instituted three edicts. First, all Christian books were to be given to the Roman authorities and burned. Second, the Christian bishops were imprisoned. Finally, torture was used to turn Christians back to Roman paganism. In 311, Diocletian's successor, Galerius, dying from a horrible disease, ordered all persecution of Christians to cease. This was continued by Constantine, who granted toleration to all who professed Christianity. The controversy centered on the validity (or invalidity) of Christians who had surrendered their Christian books during the persecution resuming places of leadership in the church. The end result of this controversy was the division of the church into the Catholics, who were content with the authority of someone who had been willing to yield to the persecution, and the Donatists, who sought to remain a pure church.

---

[34] Tertullian, *Apologetics* 39.4.

[35] Tertullian, *Of Baptism* 17.

[36] Ibid., 5–15.

The overall theology of the Donatists and the Catholics differed very little. Their differences centered in their views of the church. The Donatists insisted that the true church was a fellowship of real saints; therefore, they endeavored to purge the church of unholy elements. The Catholics had allowed their church to become corrupted. For the Donatists, the church consisted of righteous people under the guidance of the Holy Spirit and the Word of God. Discipline was to be a church practice. Monasticism was rejected. Church leaders were highly exalted and the standards for their conduct were appropriately high as well. The Catholics argued that the sacraments remained valid, even though the administrator may be unworthy to administer them; the Donatists argued that the worthiness of the administrator was critical. The Donatists also eventually refused to allow the state to interfere in the affairs of the church, although they came to this position only after repeated losses in their appeals to various emperors.

Until the Reformation, the churches that desired and worked for purity over unity were small, few and persecuted. Nevertheless, there were those who were unwilling to sacrifice purity for the sake of unity.

Middle Ages

There was essentially no development of the doctrine of the church among the Catholics during the Middle Ages (about 500 to 1500 AD). "This system [of Catholic theology] was taken over by the Scholastics of the Middle Ages, and then was handed down by them, practically in the same condition in which they received it, to their successors who came after the Council of Trent."[37] The important major change was the practical disregard for the church as the *communio sanctorum* ("the communion of saints").[38]

The leading theologian of this time was Thomas Aquinas. While giving theology a modern reworking, he "added nothing of new content to the doctrine of the church."[39] MacGregor notes, "It is noteworthy that St.

---

[37] Bernard John Otten, *Manual of the History of Dogmas* (St. Louis: Herder, 1918), 2:214. Otten was a Roman Catholic.

[38] Berkhof, *History of Christian Doctrines*, 238.

[39] Radmacher, *What the Church is All About*, 56.

Thomas, who neglected little that pertained to 'sacred doctrine,' devotes less space to the doctrine of the Church, in the course of all his vast theological writings, than almost any modern theologian would give this subject within the compass of a single book covering major theological issues of the day."[40] His predominant thought was that the church was a mystical body made up of the faithful on earth and the beatified in heaven. He strengthened the position of the pope, setting forth the doctrine of the infallibility of the pope and his unrestricted sovereignty over the church and state.[41] The Roman Catholic Church was viewed as the Kingdom of God on earth. Therefore, any Christian duty done for the Kingdom had to be done for and through the Catholic Church. This led to the practical secularization of the church. More attention was paid to politics than to the salvation of souls; worldliness took the place of other-worldliness.[42] The result in Roman Catholicism was a fivefold view of the nature of the church.[43]

First, the visible nature of the church was strongly emphasized. The church is visible since Jesus was visible. The ultimate basis of the visibility of the church was the incarnation of the Word. Jesus passed his authority on to Peter who, according to Catholicism, was the head of the apostles. Since the popes are the successors of Peter, the pope then is the visible head of the visible church.

Second, a distinction was made between the teaching church (*ecclesia docens*) and the believing church (*ecclesia audiens, discens,* or *credens*). The former is comprised of the clergy with the pope at its head; the latter consists of the faithful who honor the authority of their pastors. It was only to the teaching church that Roman Catholicism ascribes the attributes of the church.

Third, the one true (Roman Catholic) church was composed of body and soul, like a human person. The soul of the church consisted of those who were called to faith and united to Christ. Not all the elect were in the

---

[40] Geddes MacGregor, *Corpus Christi: The Nature of the Church According to the Reformed Tradition* (Philadelphia: Westminster, 1958), 28.

[41] Thomas Aquinas, *The Summa Theologica of Saint Thomas Aquinas* 2.2.1.10.

[42] Berkhof, *History of Christian Doctrines*, 240.

[43] Ibid., 241.

church (such as the catechumens); neither were all those in the church the elect, for they may have fallen away.

Fourth, Christ distributed the fullness of the graces through the agency of the clergy. The *teaching church* preceded the *believing church* and was superior to it. The church was a faithful mother (*mater fidelium*) before she was a faithful child (*coetus fidelium*).

Finally, the church was exclusively an institute of salvation, a saving ark. Her three functions were to propagate the true faith through the ministry of the Word, to effect sanctification by means of the sacraments, and to govern believers through ecclesiastical law. However, it was only the *teaching church* which was able to do this. Therefore, this alone was the true church. God, by means of his Word, did not lead men to the church; rather, the church led men to Christ and his Word.

The prelude to Reformation ecclesiology was centered in the distinction between the Roman Catholics, who promoted the unity of the universal church, and non-Catholics, who argued for the purity of the local church. This difference would continue into and past the Reformation.

Reformation Views of the Church

A number of theological issues were raised during the Reformation, but a central issue was the church. "There is, to say the least, a *prima facie* case for saying that they were all rooted in ecclesiological questions. . . . [T]he Reformation was about the nature of the Church more than it was about justification or grace."[44]

Lutheran Church

There was no desire on Luther's part to form a new church; his intention was "to serve the Church that was there, and which was, he believed, *una sancta ecclesia* [one holy church]."[45] He translated the classic Latin *una sancta ecclesia catholica* (one holy catholic church) by the German *eine vorsamlung aller Christgläubigen auf erden* (an assembly

---

[44] MacGregor, *Corpus Christi*, 5.

[45] Ibid., 8.

of all believers on earth).[46] He did not like the common German term
Kirche (church), but preferred to use *Christenheit* (Christian fellowship) in
the sense of a society of believers.

Luther viewed the priesthood and ministry as God's gift to the church
and as receiving authority from Christ. The church knows it consists of
sinners, always dependent on God's justification. The church contains
both the saint and the hypocrite.[47] He rejected the Catholic concept of an
infallible church, a special priesthood, and magical sacraments.[48] He
believed that the one true church is a spiritual community composed of
all living believers in Christ and sustained by Christ its Head. He rejected
the Roman universal, visible church:

> Scripture speaks about Christendom very simply and in only one
> way. . . . Christendom means an assembly of all the people upon earth
> who believe in Christ. . . . This community or assembly means all those
> who live in true faith, hope and love. Thus the essence, life and nature
> of Christendom is not a physical assembly, but an assembly of hearts in
> one faith. . . . Accordingly, regardless of whether a thousand miles
> separates them physically, they are still called one assembly in spirit, as
> long as each one preaches, believes, hopes, loves, and lives like the
> other. . . . This unity alone is sufficient to create Christendom, and
> without it, no unity—be it that of city, time, persons, work, or whatever
> else it may be—can create Christendom.[49]

---

[46] Martin Luther, "On the Papacy in Rome Against the Most Celebrated
Romanist in Leipzig" (1520), in *D. Martin Luthers Werke*, Weimar edition (1888),
6:292 and "Of the Councils and the Churches" (1539), in *D. Martin Luthers
Werke*, Weimar edition (1914), 50:624.

[47] "Augsburg Confession" in *Triglot Concordia: The Symbolic Books of the Ev.
Lutheran Church* (St. Louis: Concordia, 1921), 46. This edition contains the official
German version, the Latin version, and an English translation. The Confession
was initially written in both Latin and German. "The theological language was
Latin; the language of diplomacy at the diet was German. . . . The official text is
the German one." Wilhelm Maurer, *Historical Commentary on the Augsburg
Confession*, translated by H. George Anderson (Philadelphia: Fortress, 1968), 35.

[48] Berkhof, *History of Christian Doctrines*, 243.

[49] Martin Luther, "On the Papacy in Rome," in *Luther's Works*, ed. Eric W.
Gritsch (Philadelphia: Fortress, 1966), 39:65.

Using John 18:36 and Luke 17:20–21 as proof passages, however, he maintained the Augustinian tradition of equating the church and the kingdom.

Luther acknowledged both the local, visible congregation as well as the greater universal church. He realized that this position was similar to Catholicism, although he argued that while the medieval church may have looked like the real thing, it was really something different.[50]

He believed that the invisible and visible churches were not two churches, but two aspects of the same church.

> Therefore, for the sake of better understanding and brevity, we shall call the two churches by two distinct names. The first, which is natural, basic, essential, and true, we shall call "spiritual, internal Christendom." The second, which is man-made and external, we shall call "physical, external Christendom." Not that we want to separate them from each other; rather, it is just as if I were talking about a man and called him "spiritual" according to his soul, and "physical" according to his body, or as the Apostle is accustomed to speak of an "internal" and "external" man [Rom. 7:22–23]. So, too, the Christian assembly is a community united in one faith according to the soul, although, according to the body, it cannot be assembled at one place since every group of people is assembled in its own place.[51]

Berkhof demonstrates Luther's rejection of the church as an external organization:

> His insistence on the invisibility of the Church served the purpose of *denying* that the Church is *essentially* an *external society with a visible head*, and of affirming that the essence of the Church is to be found in the sphere of the invisible: in faith, communion with Christ, and in participation in the blessings of salvation through the Holy Spirit.[52]

The church becomes visible and known when the pure administration of the Word and the sacraments takes place. The important thing is for a person to belong to the spiritual or invisible church, but membership with the visible church is closely associated with this.

---

[50] McGrath, *Christian Theology,* 411.

[51] Luther, "On the Papacy in Rome," 39:70.

[52] Berkhof, *History of Christian Doctrines*, 243.

For Luther, the church consisted of whoever was true to the Word. An episcopally-ordained ministry was not necessary to safeguard the existence of the church, but the preaching of the gospel was essential to the identity of the church. For Luther it was more important to preach the same gospel as the Apostles than to be a member of an institution which was historically derived from them.[53]

Luther identified two external marks of the true church: baptism and the gospel. The characteristics of a true church had nothing to do with locality: "Not Rome or this place or that place. Wherever there is baptism and the gospel no one should doubt the presence of saints—even if they were only children in the cradle."[54] Questions of ecclesiastical order were only external and incidental, the "clothes" of the church, but not its fundamental nature. Thus the constitutions of various Lutheran bodies may vary, while they view themselves all to be truly Lutheran.[55]

Having saints and sinners in the same church was not a problem for Luther. He quickly fell back on the concept of the invisible church. Luther preferred the word *abscondita* (hidden) over the usual *invisibilisi* (invisible).[56] Only God can know precisely who the members of the church are, although the true believers (the *fideles*) can recognize what is the true church by the presence of its marks.

The Augsburg Confession of 1530, Articles 7, "Of the Church," and 8, "What the Church Is," allowed the Lutheran church to move beyond the New Testament pattern. These articles state:

> Article VII: Of the Church.
> Also they teach that *one holy church* is to continue forever. The Church is the congregation of saints, in which the Gospel is rightly taught and the Sacraments are rightly administered.
> And to the true unity of the church it is enough to agree concerning the doctrine of the Gospel and the administration of the Sacraments. Nor is it necessary that human traditions, that is, rites or ceremonies,

---

[53] McGrath, *Christian Theology,* 410–11.

[54] Luther, "On the Papacy in Rome," 70.

[55] MacGregor, *Corpus Christi*, 8.

[56] Martin Luther, "Ad librum eximii Magistri Nostri Magistri Ambrosii Catharini, defensoris Silvestri Prieratis acerrimi, responsio," in *D. Martin Luthers Werke*, Weimar edition (1521), 7:722.

instituted by men, should be everywhere alike. As Paul says: *One faith, one Baptism, one God and Father of all,* etc. Eph. 4, 5. 6.

Article VIII: What the Church Is.

Although *the Church* properly is the congregation of saints and true believers, nevertheless, since in this life many hypocrites and evil persons are mingled therewith, it is lawful to use Sacraments administered by evil men, according to the saying of Christ: *The Scribes and the Pharisees sit in Moses' seat,* etc. Matt. 23, 2. Both the Sacraments and the Word are effectual by reason of the institution and commandment of Christ, notwithstanding they be administered by evil men.

They condemn the Donatists, and such like, who denied it to be lawful to use the ministry of evil men in the Church, and who thought the ministry of evil men to be unprofitable and of none effect.[57]

Their doctrine of the universal church allowed the Lutherans to pay scant attention to the New Testament pattern of the church. John Yoder, an Anabaptist, indicts them for this:

The Reformers formed a persecuting church, but at the same time they were protected themselves against any criticism which might have objected that their church was not what a church should be by the fact that their church, being visible, could never be the true church anyway. Since our church is not the true church, they said in effect, the state is free to organize and administer it as it seems best. This concession to Hellenism, the admission that the invisible and timeless is more real than the visible and historical, has avenged itself a hundred fold in accidental piety, ethics, and social responsibility.[58]

---

[57] "Augsburg Confession," 46. McGrath suggests that there was no development of the doctrine of the church in early Lutheranism because they believed that separation from Catholicism was only temporary. Why develop extensive theories of the church when reunion with a church that would soon correct its faults was only a matter of time? McGrath, *Christian Theology*, 411.

[58] John H. Yoder, "The Prophetic Dissent of the Anabaptists," in *The Recovery of the Anabaptist Vision*, ed. Guy Franklin Hershberger (Scottdale, Penn.: Herald, 1957), 98–99.

Reformed Churches

In contrast to Luther's vagueness concerning the doctrine of the church, John Calvin developed a specific theory on the relationship of the invisible church to the external ecclesiastical institution.[59] In so doing he used the term "church" in three ways.

First, Calvin spoke of the invisible church as consisting of all the elect (in agreement with Augustine and Luther).

> Sometimes, when they mention the Church, they intend that which is really such in the sight of God, into which none are received but those who by adoption and grace are the children of God, and by the sanctification of the Spirit are true members of Christ. And then it comprehends not only the saints at any one time resident on earth, but all the elect who have lived from the beginning of the world.[60]

The church, for Calvin, was invisible, in the sense that it is spiritual, but also in the sense that it is able at times to survive only in a hidden state. "But because a small and contemptible number is concealed among a vast multitude, and a few grains of wheat are covered with a heap of chaff, we must leave to God alone the knowledge of his Church whose foundation is his secret election."[61]

Calvin's second concept of church was the universal church. In Calvin's mind, the universal church is an aggregation of all the local churches on earth.

> But the word *Church* is frequently used in the Scriptures to designate the whole multitude, dispersed all over the world, who profess to worship one God and Jesus Christ. . . . In this Church are included many hypocrites, who have nothing of Christ but the name and

---

[59] With the collapse of the Colloquy of Regensburg, all hope of reunification with Catholicism was lost. Therefore, the second-generation reformers, such as Calvin, needed a more extensive ecclesiology. McGrath, *Christian Theology*, 412.

[60] John Calvin, *Institutes of the Christian Religion*, translated by John Allen (Philadelphia: Presbyterian Board of Christian Education, n.d.), 4.l.7. All English translations of Calvin are from this work. The *Institutes* were first published in Latin in 1536; the definitive version was finished in 1559. French translations were made in 1541 and finally in 1560.

[61] Ibid., 4.1.2.

appearance; many persons ambitious, avaricious, envious, slanderous, and dissolute in their lives, who are tolerated for a time, either because they cannot be convicted by a legitimate process, or because discipline is not always maintained with sufficient vigour. As it is necessary, therefore, to believe that Church, which is invisible to us, and known to God alone, so this Church, which is visible to men, we are commanded to honour and maintain communion with it. . . .

[T]he universal Church is the whole multitude, collected from all nations, who, though dispersed in countries widely distant from each other, nevertheless consent to the same truth of Divine doctrine . . . that in this universal Church are comprehended particular churches, distributed according to human necessity in various towns and villages; and that each of these respectively is justly distinguished by the name and authority of a church.[62]

He argued for a single universal church, because if there were more than one church, Christ would have to be divided.[63] Calvin hoped that by means of the reform taking place around him the unity of the visible church, long obscured, would be clearly seen again in the light of purified doctrine and practice.

From this insistence on the unity of the church as visible, together with his recognition elsewhere that even under the tyranny of Rome the visibility of the True Church had not been entirely destroyed, it is plain that from the time of his earliest formulation of an ecclesiology, Calvin never thought of the organization of the Reformed Church as involving a separation from the medieval institution; it was, rather, a vivification of the Body of Christ that had become oppressed and encumbered by a diabolical cancer that sought to destroy it.[64]

Calvin thus made a theological distinction between the invisible and visible churches. The community of Christian believers is the visible church; the fellowship of saints (the company of all the elect) is the invisible church (in keeping with Augustinian ecclesiology). The invisible church is known only to God; it lies beyond human competence to discern the difference between the two. The invisible church is made up of only the elect; the visible church is composed of both good and evil, the elect

---

[62] Ibid., 4.1.7–9.

[63] Ibid., 4.1.2.

[64] MacGregor, *Corpus Christi*, 47.

and the reprobate. The invisible church is the object of hope and faith; the visible church is the object of present experience. The invisible church comes into being at the end of time; the visible church now exists. The invisible church is the basis for the visible church and is the true body of Christ; the believer is required to honor and remain committed to the visible church despite its weaknesses.[65]

The problem with Calvin's ecclesiology was determining which visible church corresponded to the invisible church. Calvin recognized this problem and sought to articulate objective criteria to judge the authenticity of the church: the pure Word of God purely preached and listened to and the sacraments administered according to the institution of Christ. "For wherever we find the word of God purely preached and heard, and the sacraments [sic] administered according to the institution of Christ, there, it is not to be doubted, is a Church of God."[66]

It was not the quality of the members that was important, but the presence of the authorized means of grace. Discipline, therefore, was not essential to a church.

Calvin followed and restated Cyprian's doctrine that outside the church there is no salvation. The church was the divinely-founded body within which God effects the salvation of the elect. Therefore, he taught, like Cyprian, that he cannot have God for his Father who has not the church for his mother.

> But as our present design is to treat of the *visible* Church, we may learn even from the title of *mother*, how useful and even necessary it is for us to know her; since there is no other way of entrance into life, unless we are conceived by her, born of her, nourished at her breast, and continually preserved under her care and government till we are divested of this mortal flesh, and "become like the angels." . . . It is also to be remarked, that out of her bosom there can be no hope of remission of sins, or any salvation.[67]

Unlike the Roman Catholic Church, however, Calvin did not insist that salvation could be found in only one specific church, thus the importance of the marks of a true church.

---

[65] McGrath, *Christian Theology*, 413.

[66] Calvin, *Institutes*, 4.1.9.

[67] Ibid., 4.1.4.

Since the Roman Catholic Church did not agree with either of these two distinguishing marks, the evangelicals were perfectly justified in leaving it; but since all evangelicals conformed to this definition, they should be unified.[68] Calvin never severed soteriology from ecclesiology, but in his concept of the universal church, he took a small step, moving away from organizational unity to sacramental unity.

Calvin perpetuated the church-state amalgamation that characterized the Roman Church. He made the specific form of ecclesiastical order an item of doctrine by including government as part of "the gospel purely preached."[69] He gave explicit instructions concerning the duties of civil government.

> [T]his civil government is designed, so long as we live in this world, to cherish and support the external worship of God, to preserve the pure doctrine of religion, to defend the constitution of the Church, to regulate our lives in a manner requisite for the society of men, to form our manners to civil justice, to promote our concord with each another, and to establish general peace and tranquility. . . . [I]ts objects also are, that idolatry, sacrileges against the name of God, blasphemies against his truth, and other offenses against religion, may not openly appear and be disseminated among the people.[70]

Perry Miller states concerning Calvin's association of church and state:

> The Deity Himself had commanded that all men's thoughts be turned toward redemption, and had prescribed certain ways and means. The Church could not accomplish this unaided by civil authority. The reformers envisaged a simple and plausible arrangement, wherein they, the professional experts in Biblical knowledge, should teach the state its duties, and the state should silence contradiction. The highest function of the State, therefore, was the loving care of the Church, the maintenance of its eternal being in uniformity throughout the kingdom, and the physical support of its censures.[71]

---

[68] McGrath, *Christian Theology*, 412.

[69] Ibid., 413.

[70] Calvin, *Institutes*, 4.20.2–3.

[71] Perry Miller, *Orthodoxy in Massachusetts, 1630–1650* (Cambridge: University Press, 1933), 7.

This Genevan development of the doctrine of the Church became the characteristic Protestant theory. These teachings were incorporated, for the most part, into the Westminster Confession of Faith (1647) and accepted by the majority of Reformed Churches.[72] Since the seventeenth century, most Puritans and Reformed theologians have added discipline as a third mark of a true church.

Radical Reformers

The "Radical Reformers" consisted of numerous groups, some political and some religious. Only one of these groups will be examined in this work—the Anabaptists. These were the more conservative of the Radical Reformers and argued that baptism was a requirement for church membership and only believers could be baptized.

The most obvious difference between the Anabaptists and the Reformers was baptism. The Reformers maintained the Catholic practice of infant baptism, while the Anabaptists argued that only true believers, ones able to express their faith, could be baptized. When a person came to trust Christ as Savior, he would be truly baptized; thus the name "Anabaptist" came to be the pejorative used against these people.

> "Anabaptist" was a popular term with the authorities because it afforded them an excuse for forcefully suppressing the radicals. The enemies of the movement were insistent on the use of the term "Wiedertäufer" or "Anabaptistici" because the radical groups thereby became subject to the death penalty. Under the ancient Roman law against the rebaptizers (Donatists), those called "Anabaptist" could be suppressed by the sword.[73]

Baptism, however, was really only an external demonstration of their distinctive ecclesiology, not a root of it. While the magisterial reformers had seen the church as *corrupted* by Catholicism, the Anabaptists saw it as *fallen*. Reformers such as Luther and Calvin had a tremendous regard for the living tradition of the historic church. They hesitated to abandon

---

[72] Philip Schaff, *The Creeds of Christendom* (New York: Harper, 1931; reprint, Grand Rapids: Baker, 1985), 3:657–59.

[73] Franklin Hamlin Littell, *The Origins of Sectarian Protestantism: A Study of the Anabaptist View of the Church* (New York: Macmillan, 1964), xv.

the principle of the territorial church and the linkage of church and state. As they saw it, the Roman Catholic Church was the true church, but it had fallen on evil days and into unworthy hands. Therefore, they sought to bring about a spiritual renewal, initially from within, but eventually from without. In contrast, the Anabaptists set out to discard the territorial and state-church pattern and replace it with the pattern they saw in the New Testament. They did not seek to introduce something new, but to restore something old. "Restitution" was their slogan.

For Menno Simons, founder of the Mennonites, the church was "an assembly of the righteous" and not a "mixed body."[74]

> The priestly hierarchy claimed to have apostolic tradition, sacramental grace, and the jurisdiction of the Church. The free churches, on the other hand, stressed voluntary fellowship patterned after the practice of the early church, the demand for holy living, and the absolute authority of the Bible.
>
> The sects maintained that these ideas and principles of primitive Christianity were not simply starting points for the historical development of Christ's church but that they were ideals and patterns for all generations.[75]

Theron Price expands on this idea: "As the Anabaptists saw it, the task for the sixteenth century Christians was nothing else than the reconstitution of the true church itself, restoring that which had lapsed rather than reforming that which had erred."[76]

A key difference between the Reformers and the Restorers was the mutually exclusive concepts of the church. Rome and the Reformers had based their views of the church largely on the Old Testament; the Anabaptists denied the identity of an Old Testament church with that of the New Testament and insisted on a church of believers only.[77]

> The difference in the interpretation of the *subject* of baptism only served to highlight the irreconcilability of the two views of the church.

---

[74] McGrath, *Christian Theology*, 415.

[75] Gunnar Westin, *The Free Church Through the Ages*, Virgil A. Olson, tr. (Nashville: Broadman, 1958), 40.

[76] Theron D. Price, "The Anabaptist View of the Church" in *What is the Church?*, ed. Duke McCall (Nashville: Broadman, 1958), 101.

[77] Berkhof, *History of Christian Doctrines*, 244.

Basic to an understanding of the Anabaptist viewpoint is the understanding of the terms *fall* and *restitution* as applied to the church. The whole idea of the recovery of the New Testament Christianity was tied up with the thought that at some point in Christian history the pattern was lost. The church experienced a fall from the golden age when martyr-heroes followed Christ to death.[78]

Most Anabaptists dated this fall to Constantine and included the Reformers in the period of the fall. The criticisms of the Reformers against Rome were the same criticisms the Anabaptists raised against the Reformers: amalgamation of church and state, empty formalism, and spiritual slackness, to which the Anabaptists added infant baptism.[79] The basic factor in the fall was the union of church and state. The "fall" flooded the church with nominal Christians, and infant baptism continued this flood.

For the Anabaptists the restitution was a result of a regenerate church membership:

> [Restitution was] accomplished wherever churches were gathered on the principle of responsible faith and regenerate life (of which believer's baptism is the sign but not the cause); whenever congregations were spiritually governed and cohered on the principle of mutual nurture and mutual rebuke; whenever the terms of communion were essentially moral and ethical rather than sacramental (with the sacraments being primarily symbols of a communion between the church and God, and between believer and believers).[80]

There were strong parallels between the Anabaptists and the Donatists. Both groups believed in a pure and holy body of believers, isolated from the corrupting influences of the world, and prepared to maintain their purity and distinctiveness. This harmonized with their persecution by the magistrates. Discipline was maintained by heavy use of the "ban," and they separated from other churches that failed to maintain proper discipline within their ranks.[81]

---

[78] Radmacher, *What the Church is All About*, 69–70.

[79] Littell, *Sectarian Protestantism*, 64–65.

[80] Price, "The Anabaptist View of the Church," 106.

[81] McGrath, *Christian Theology*, 416.

Anglicanism

The Reformation movement with the greatest impact on American Christianity (and thus for the fundamentalist and evangelical movements in America) was Anglicanism. It was formed under the impetus of a political, not a religious, leader. The Act of Supremacy in 1534 declared that the king of England was "the only supreme head in earth of the Church of England."[82] Theologically, however, the Church of England remained true to Roman Catholic doctrine under Henry's rule. It was not until Elizabeth's reign that the reform moved forward and the *Thirty-Nine Articles* were accepted by Parliament as the official creed of the Anglican Church. Article 19 states concerning the church:

> The visible Church of Christ is a congregation of faithful men, in the which the pure Word of God is preached, and the Sacraments be duly ministered according to Christ's ordinance in all those things that of necessity are requisite to the same.[83]

There is no mention of an invisible church in this statement. "The opening words, when taken in conjunction with the title, imply that there is only one Church, the visible. Moreover, Article XXVI (7) shows that 'faithful' must mean professed believers, not those whose faith is known to God alone."[84]

> Among Anglicans the term Invisible Church seems quite meaningless. They do not see how the New Testament attitude of "telling it" to the Church could be rational if the Church were invisible and, equally, would they find it difficult to "hear" an invisible Church. It cannot be too strongly emphasized that for Anglicans the Church is the society of people, primarily here on earth. When Anglicans use the term

---

[82] Henry Bettenson, *Documents of the Christian Church* (New York: Oxford University Press, 1947), 321–23.

[83] B. J. Kidd, *The Thirty-Nine Articles: Their History and Explanation* (New York: Edwin S. Gorham, 1906), 2:161.

[84] Leonard Hodgson, "The Doctrine of the Church as Held and Taught in the Church of England," in *The Nature of the Church*, ed. R. Newton Flew (New York: Harper, 1952), 133.

Invisible Church they mean by it that larger part of the visible Church which has passed from this life to the life beyond.[85]

Not all Anglicans were content with Anglicanism as it had developed. A movement arose that was committed to purifying the morality and theology of the church and changing the church's governmental structure. The "Puritans," for the most part, preferred the Presbyterian structure, although some preferred a Congregational system. A few were content to live under the Anglican (Episcopalian) system. Initially the Puritan party was unclear in its ecclesiology, but when the Presbyterians and Separatists came into conflict, their views of the nature of the church were clarified.

The Congregationalists among the Puritans identified two essential features of the church: the restriction of church membership to the proven elect and the autonomy of particular congregations. Henry Jacob declared in 1605 that a true church is "a particular Congregation being a spirituall perfect Corporation of Believers, & having power in it selfe immediately from Christ to administer all Religious meanes of faith to members thereof."[86] All Puritans, however, were still part of the Anglican Church; their debate centered on what form of church system should be used in Anglicanism. The Congregationalists desired a congregational church, but not separation from the Anglican Church. Associated with the Congregationalists were the Separatists, who also desired a Congregational church system, but one outside of Anglican or governmental control.

> Thanks to their deft stratagems they [the Separatists] were always prepared to protest that they were not Separatists, even at the very moment when they were erecting independent churches in England or gathering them on foreign shores. They were trying to show that men who wished simply to realize potentialities already inherent in the Church were far different from men who wish to destroy it and begin anew. Those who never questioned that they should be coerced into conformity, even when a temporarily misguided monarch was coercing

---

[85] Leicester C. Lewis, "The Anglican Church," in *The Nature of the Church*, ed. R. Newton Flew (New York: Harper, 1952), 309.

[86] Champlin Burrage, *Early English Dissenters in the Light of Recent Research* (New York: Putnam, 1912), 2:157.

them in the wrong direction, might reasonably be considered loyal Englishmen. . . . They denied that any *ecclesiastical* authority had a right to expel ministers from particular churches; but just so soon as the King himself authorized the expulsion, though it remained intrinsically an unjust act, still, as it was the act of a *magistrate*, they did not rebel. . . . The peculiar twist of their philosophy enabled them to look upon these depravations with equanimity, even while they continued to declare that the act had not affected the essential character of the true churches.[87]

The Separatists, however, would have nothing to do with the state church. The first Congregationalist to set forth the principle of separation of church and state was Robert Browne (1550–1633), although he was later reconciled to the English church. There were two basic principles that distinguished the Separatists from the Presbyterians. First, they demanded a regenerate membership (although they continued to baptize infants). Only those who could demonstrate that they were "redeemed by Christ unto holiness and happiness for ever" could be members of the church.[88] Admission of the wicked and ungodly would infect and corrupt the rest. Officials could not force a church to be gathered, constrain an individual to join, or compel the church to receive or retain members. When a church was formed, the visible saints were to join freely, profess their faith, and take a covenant of allegiance to Christ their King.[89] The real marks of this church were faith and order; for the Separatists, Calvin, the Church of England, and the Puritans were wrong when they declared the marks of a true church to be the preaching of the Word and the administration of the sacraments. These marks could be administered to assemblies of unbelievers. Only where God had called his people together could faith be found, and only where faith exists can there be proper order. They were still Reformed enough, however, to maintain infant baptism.

---

[87] Miller, *Orthodoxy in Massachusetts,* 92–93.

[88] Williston Walker, *Creeds and Platforms of Congregationalism* (Boston: Pilgrim, 1960), 19.

[89] John Robinson, *The Works of John Robinson, Pastor of the Pilgrim Fathers, with a Memoir and Annotations by Robert Ashton,* ed. Robert Ashton (Boston: Doctrinal Tract and Book Society, 1851), 2:316.

A second distinctive of the Separatists was that the individual churches were directly related to Christ. According to Browne, every believer was "a Kinge, a Priest, and a Prophet vnder Christ, to vpholde and further the kingdom of God."[90] Each such church was self-sufficient, independent of all external controls, and competent to manage its own affairs.

> To [Browne's] thinking a Christian church is a body of professed believers in Christ, united to one another and to their Lord by a voluntary covenant. This covenant is the constitutive element which transforms an assembly of Christians into a church. Its members are not all the baptized inhabitants of a kingdom, but only those possessed of Christian character. Such a church is under the immediate headship of Christ, and is to be ruled only by laws and officers of his appointment. To each church Christ has entrusted its own government, discipline, and choice of officers.[91]

The similarities between the English Separatists and the Anabaptists are striking. While there may not be clear evidence of direct influence upon the Separatists by the Anabaptists, there were a significant number of Dutch Anabaptists in England during this time. "[T]he similarity of the system which [Browne] now worked out to that of the Anabaptists is so great in many respects that the conclusion is hard to avoid that the resemblance is more than accidental."[92]

An important Separatist was John Smyth who went from Puritan to Separatist to Baptist to Mennonite.[93] Smyth graduated from Christ's

---

[90] Robert Browne, "Extracts from Browne's 'Booke which Sheweth the life and manners of all true Christians, etc.,' Middelburg, 1582" in Walker, *Creeds and Platforms*, 22–23.

[91] Williston Walker, *A History of the Congregational Churches in the United States*, The American Church History Series (New York: Christian Literature, 1894), 3:38.

[92] Ibid., 36.

[93] Smyth's writings are available in John Smyth, *The Works of John Smyth*, W. T. Whitley, ed. (Cambridge: University Press, 1915). Works on the life and theology of John Smyth include: Jason K. Lee, *The Theology of John Smyth: Puritan, Separatist, Baptist, Mennonite* (Macon, Ga.: Mercer University Press, 2003); Walter Herbert Burgess, *John Smyth, the Se-Baptist, Thomas Helwys and the First Baptist Church in England with Fresh Light upon the Pilgrim Fathers'*

College, Cambridge, with his Bachelor of Arts in 1590, Master of Arts in 1593, and served as a fellow at the college from 1594 to 1598.[94] Christ's College was a hotbed of Puritan beliefs at that time, although Reformed views such as predestination were rebuffed. One of Smyth's tutors was Francis Johnson, who would later serve in the "Ancient Church" in Amsterdam.[95] In 1600 he was elected "city lecturer" of Lincoln, although he became the victim of a political struggle and two years later lost his position.[96] While Smyth was not at that time a Separatist, he preached like one. In 1603 his license to preach was revoked, but he continued to preach. By 1607, Smyth, along with William Bradford, William Brewster, Thomas Helwys, John Robinson and others had formed a Separatist church in Gainsborough.[97] In July 1607, Joan Helwys (wife of Thomas Helwys) was imprisoned in York Castle; this prompted the removal of the church from England to the Netherlands.

In 1608 or perhaps early 1609, Smyth rejected the Separatist practice of infant baptism and re-established his church on the principle of believers' baptism. Three arguments have been suggested for Smyth's change to believer's baptism.[98] One was that the Separatists were uneasy about accepting Anglican baptism; Smyth carried that uneasiness to a logical conclusion. A second was that Smyth became convinced that the apostolic example was believer's baptism. A third suggestion was that Smyth became aware of and influenced by the Mennonite practice of believer's baptism. For instance, his church had moved into the former

---

Church (London: James Clarke, 1911). The reader is directed to Lee, *The Theology of John Smyth*, for further information on Smyth's broad theological positions.

[94] John Venn and J. A. Venn, *Alumni Cantabrigiensis* (Cambridge: University Press, 1913), 4: 101.

[95] British Puritans who fled England founded a church of their own in Amsterdam and called it the "Ancient Church." Although they were calvinistic, their church was not officially recognized by the Dutch Reformed Church. They were not allowed to use any of the official church buildings in the city, and their ministers were not paid for by the city.

[96] Lee, *Theology of John Smyth*, 43.

[97] William Bradford, *Of Plymouth Plantation*, ed. Samuel Eliot Morison (New York: Alfred A. Knopf, 1952), 9.

[98] B. R. White, *The English Baptists of the Seventeenth Century* (Didcot: Baptist Historical Society, 1996), 19.

East India Company Bakehouse, which belonged to Mennonite Jan Hunter, probably in 1609.

Smyth argued for only two ordinances and rejected any notion that baptism or the Lord's Table "convey grace and regeneration." Instead, the ordinances served "to support and stire up the repentance and faith of the communicants." Baptism was only for repentant adults and specifically not for "innocent infants, or wicked persons." Water baptism was linked to the spiritual baptism of Christ and the Holy Spirit and the baptism of fire (which he did not explain). It was baptism into the death and resurrection of Christ.[99] The Lord's Supper was only for the baptized. It represents the spiritual supper in which Christ gives his flesh and blood, a picture of Calvary.[100]

When Smyth adopted the Mennonite positions on oaths, war, and the magistracy and thus became too Mennonite for some of his church members, the church split. Smyth eventually requested membership in the Mennonite community, but Thomas Helwys (ca. 1550–1616) and John Murton (1585 – ca. 1626), along with several others in the church, refused to do this. Why did these early Baptists not simply become Mennonites? The answer concerns an issue of great concern to the first Baptists and later to the fundamentalist movement in America, namely, how churches ought to relate to society at large. Like all separatist Puritan groups, the Baptists withdrew from the Church of England. Because this was an illegal act, they tended not to be engaged as a group with society at large. However, in principle they had no reason not to be so engaged. The Mennonites did have a reason. For reasons of principle they excluded civil magistrates from membership in their churches. This was one of the reasons that Helwys and other members of the church did not want to align themselves with the Mennonites. The decision of the early Baptists to be engaged with larger society has had important consequences in Baptist life ever since, for Baptists were the first to engage society over the issue of religious freedom.

---

[99] John Smyth, "Propositions and Conclusions concerning True Christian Religion, containing a Confession of Faith of certain English people living at Amsterdam," in W. J. McGlothlin, *Baptist Confessions of Faith* (Philadelphia: American Baptist Publication Society, 1911), 66ff.

[100] Ibid., 79.

Helwys and Murton took less than a dozen members of the church back to England and established the first modern Baptist church on English soil. In 1610, before leaving for England, Helwys and Murton wrote *A Declaration of Faith of English People.* They argued for congregational church government and discipline (but not Mennonite shunning) and rejected infant baptism.[101] Leonard Busher, a member of Helwys' church, wrote *Religious Peace: or, a Plea for Liberty of Conscience* in 1614 and presented the work to King James and the Parliament. The focus of the work was on religious liberty, but he also expressed the Baptist emphasis on adult baptism: "And therefore Christ commanded his disciples to teach all nations, and baptize them; that is, to preach the word of salvation to every creature of all sorts of nations that are worthy and willing to receive it. And such as shall willingly and gladly receive, He has commanded to be baptized in the water; that is, dipped for dead in the water."[102]

> While more moderate Puritans were concentrating upon the doctrine of salvation and, in particular, the morphology of the soul's conversation, it was the writings of men ... such as the Baptist followers of Thomas Helwys and the older Separatists who kept the question of the nature of the true Church alive and in print in England.[103]

Three of the principal concerns of these Baptists were believer's baptism, sectarian withdrawal from society, and religious liberty. When Smyth and Helwys, with their church, adopted the practice of believer's baptism, they were responding to two impulses at once. One was the restorationist impulse, the desire to order contemporary church life as closely as possible to the life of New Testament churches. Once Smyth and his church became convinced that only believers were baptized in

---

[101] James Leo Garrett, Jr., *Baptist Theology: A Four-Century Study* (Macon: Mercer University Press, 2009), 32.

[102] Leonard Busher, *Religious Peace: or, a Plea for Liberty of Conscience*, 1614 in John T. Christian, *Did They Dip? or, An examination into the act of baptism as practiced by the English and American Baptists before the year 1641* (Louisville: Baptist Book Concern, 1896), 95.

[103] B. R. White, *The English Separatist Tradition* (London: Oxford University Press, 1971), 168.

New Testament churches, they were determined to imitate that practice. The other impulse was to achieve a believers' church. The Separatist churches in England had left the Church of England to achieve a more pure church, but their practice of baptizing infants meant that their congregations continued to have members who had not made a public profession of their faith. The act of believer's baptism by Smyth and Helwys represented a dramatic departure from what was being done by other English churches.

Perhaps the most memorable words concerning the separation of church and state are found in the inscription which Helwys wrote in the copy of his book *The Mystery of Iniquity* which he sent to King James. Inside the cover, Helwys wrote:

> Hear, O king, and despise not the counsel of the poor, and let their complaints come before thee.
>
> The king is a mortal man and not God, therefore has no power over the immortal souls of his subjects, to make laws and ordinances for them, and to set spiritual lords over them.
>
> If the king has authority to make spiritual lords and laws, then he is an immortal God and not a mortal man.
>
> O king, be not seduced by deceivers to sin against God whom you ought to obey, nor against your poor subjects who ought and will obey you in all things with body, life, and goods, or else let their lives be taken from the earth.
>
> God save the king.[104]

The Reformers argued that the medieval church was corrupted and a new form of the church had to begin, one more in keeping with New Testament principles. This, however, created a contradiction between their theoretical belief in "one church" and the reality of a plurality of churches and denominations. The Anabaptists extended Reformation thought and sought to bring experience in line with theory. They laid emphasis on the empirical holiness of the church, leading to the exclusion of lapsed members from the church. The Baptists continued the return to the New Testament by adopting believer's baptism, the purity of church membership, and a plea for religious liberty for all. These views of the

---

[104] Thomas Helwys, *A Short Declaration of the Mystery of Iniquity*, Classics of Religious Liberty 1, ed. Richard Groves (Macon, GA: Mercer University Press, 1998), xxiv.

church set the stage for the modern approaches to the church, including the fundamentalist and evangelical views.

Modern Views of the Church

After the Reformation, the denominations sharpened and delineated their ecclesiologies. The modifications to the views of the church that most affected evangelicalism and fundamentalism took place in America and Germany. In Germany, liberalism and later neo-orthodoxy developed. In America the old ecclesiologies were placed into the new light of political and religious liberty. In addition, America was the scene of the greatest growth of dispensationalism, a theological approach that would carry great influence within fundamentalists.

Early American Views

The doctrine of the church that developed in the early American denominations was an outgrowth of the preceding views. An important American contribution to the discussion was the freedom to put doctrinal developments into practice in a way never allowed before.

Many English Puritans who were opposed to the English hierarchy—but who also refused to separate from it—came to the New World, putting between themselves and the Church of England a ditch so wide "they could not leap over it with a lope-staff."[105] The Puritans had no desire to break with the Church of England, as did the Pilgrims, although they did seek to break from the corruptions of the Church. They still viewed the Church as "our dear mother."[106] In Walker's history of the Congregational Church in America, he states concerning the adoption of the principles of the Separatists (the "Congregationalizing" of English Puritanism) that "no step . . . is more obscure or more important than

---

[105] Edward Johnson, *The Wonder Working Providences of Zion's Saviour in New England*, Original Narratives of Early American History, ed. J. Franklin Jameson (New York: Barnes and Noble, 1959), 15:20.

[106] Alexander Young, ed., *Chronicles of the First Planters of the Colony of Massachusetts Bay, 1623–1636* (New York: Da Capo, n.d.), 296.

this."[107] America provided the opportunity for the Puritans to stop protesting and start constructing. Cotton Mather stated, "It is one thing for the church, or members of the church, loyally to submit unto any form of government, when it is above their calling to reform it, another thing to chuse a form of government and governore discrepant from the rule."[108]

Their aim was not religious liberty or democracy, but a theocracy, a "Government of the Society of God's subjects by a sovereign subordinate to God, for the common good, and the Glory and Pleasing of God."[109] Church and state were still united, and church membership was still a prerequisite for election to civil office. It remained for Roger Williams and others like him to bring to bear the true principles of religious liberty and the separation of church and state.

Having left England for the colonies in 1631, Williams was surprised to discover that the churches of Massachusetts were still strongly attached to the Church of England. After a ministry in Plymouth and then Salem, Williams was called before the General Court in 1635 to answer questions of disloyalty to the King and the Church. Before he could be arrested, however, he fled south and eventually established the colony of Rhode Island, based upon what was then termed the "Anabaptist" beliefs of complete separation of church and state and full religious liberty for all, no matter what their religion. By removing the state-church link and repudiating the infant baptism that was so often the link tying membership in the church to membership in the state, Williams was free to insist upon a regenerate and voluntary church membership, an acceptance of the complete separation of church and state, democracy in both church and state, and the voluntary exercise of religion .

> In regard to the other great doctrines held by the Baptists, liberty of conscience, or soul-liberty, the entire separation of Church and State, the supreme headship of Christ in all spiritual matters, regeneration through the agency of the Holy Spirit, and a hearty belief in the Bible as

---

[107] Walker, *Congregational Churches*, 100.

[108] Thomas Hutchinson, *The History of the Colony of Massachusetts Bay* (Boston: Prince Society, 1865), 1:494.

[109] Richard Baxter, *A Holy Commonwealth; or, Political Aphorisms Opening the True Principles of Government* (London: Underhill and Tyton, 1659), quoted in Radmacher, *What the Church is All About*, 83.

God's divinely inspired and miraculously preserved word and the all sufficient rule for faith and practice, [Roger Williams] was throughout life a sincere believer in them all and an earnest advocate of them, as his letters and published works abundantly show.[110]

For the first time, these principles were given the freedom to develop as never before. Persecution from the institutional church was removed, and the state no longer controlled religion. As a result all the denominations in America eventually came to adhere to many of the principles first espoused by Williams and the Baptists who followed him.

Liberalism and the Church

Prior to the fundamentalist/evangelical debate over the nature of the church, a new view entered the scene, one that had a great impact on fundamentalism. Theological liberalism came from Europe, especially Germany, to America via the educational institutions on both sides of the Atlantic. The liberals took a dim view of the church, a view that was affected by their emphasis on the social gospel. To many liberals, churches were simply social organizations of individuals gathered together because of a common religious and ethical concern. The necessity of the church was purely practical: men are able to do more when organized than as individuals alone.[111]

There was very little interest in what the church was; the real interest was in what the church could do. In one sense the churches were seen as a hindrance to true Christianity, since they often impeded progress by clinging to ecclesiastical dogmas and traditions. "[Liberals] had little faith in the existing organized churches to make any sizable contribution to either the spiritual change of the individual or the radical transformation of society as a whole. In fact, they looked at the churches as elements

---

[110] Reuben A. Guild, librarian at Brown University, and a thorough student of the original sources of information, quoted in Arthur B. Strickland, *Roger Williams: Prophet and Pioneer of Soul-Liberty* (Chicago: Judson, 1919), 61–62.

[111] William Hordern, *A Layman's Guide to Protestant Liberalism* (New York: MacMillan, 1960), 116.

which needed to be overcome before society could be changed."[112] The result was a distinction between the spiritual church and the organized church. Fundamentalism reacted primarily against the liberal beliefs that Jesus was not God, that he did not rise from the dead, that man is not a sinner who needs salvation, and other similar rejection of biblical truth in the late nineteenth and early twentieth centuries. The doctrine of the church was not at the forefront of the fundamentalist-modernist debates, but it did lie under the surface.

Neo-Orthodoxy

Fundamentalism was not alone in its rejection of liberalism. One reaction to liberal theology was Karl Barth's Theology of Crisis, more commonly known as neo-orthodoxy. In 1947 Barth defined the church by his oft-repeated formula: "'Where two or three are gathered together in my name there am I in the midst'—that is the Church."[113] Barth's theology "raised into the forefront in unparalleled fashion the doctrine of the church."[114] Barth defined the church in this way:

> *What the Church is*: the congregation *is*, or *exists*, where and in so far as it dares to live by the act of its living Lord.
> *The danger* menacing the Church: the congregation fails to *exist* when, and in so far as the foundations of its life are shaken by its own sins and errors. . . .

---

[112] Robert Lightner, *Neo-Liberalism* (Chicago: Regular Baptist, 1959), 74. The revival of liberalism (neo-liberalism as Lightner and others call it) brought with it a revival in the interest of the church. Liberals had lost the common consciousness found within a church, but also recognized that the church could not be ignored in ecumenical discussions.

[113] Karl Barth, *Dogmatics in Outline*, translated by G. T. Thomson (New York: Philosophical Library, 1949), 143.

[114] George L. Hunt, ed., *Ten Makers of Modern Protestant Thought* (New York: Associated, 1958), 65.

> The church is not constituted once for all, but . . . it is continually being re-created by renewed divine activity.[115]

Barth believed that the church was not man's organization, nor an act of nature, but the result of the work of the Holy Spirit.

> Woe to us, where we think we can speak of the Church without establishing it wholly on the work of the Holy Spirit. . . . The Christian congregation arises and exists neither by nature nor by historical human decision, but as a divine *convocatio*. Those called together by the work of the Holy Spirit assemble at the summons of their King.[116]

Barth believed in the local church. In fact, he believed that this was *the* church. "By men assembling here and there in the Holy Spirit there arises here and there a visible Christian congregation. . . . If the Church has not this visibility, then it is not the Church. When I say congregation, I am thinking primarily of the concrete form of the congregation in a particular place."[117] He cautioned against the use of the term "invisible." "It is best not to apply the idea of invisibility to the Church; we are all inclined to slip away with that in the direction of a *civitas platonica* or some sort of Cloud-cuckooland, in which Christians are united inwardly and invisibly, while the visible Church is de-valued."[118]

Barth believed that the one, holy, universal church exists in each congregation. Wherever a group of believers join under the leadership of the Holy Spirit, there is the one church.

> The mystery of the Church is that for the Holy Spirit it is not too small a thing to have such forms. Consequently, there are in truth not many Churches but *one* Church in terms of this or that *concrete* one, which should recognise [*sic*] itself as the one Church and in all the others as well. . . .

---

[115] Karl Barth, "The Church—The Living Congregation of the Living Lord in Jesus Christ," in *Man's Disorder and God's Design* (New York: Harper, 1949), 1:67–68.

[116] Barth, *Dogmatics*, 142.

[117] Ibid.

[118] Ibid.

I believe that the congregation to which I belong, in which I have been called to faith and am responsible for my faith, in which I have my service, is the one, holy, universal Church.[119]

When a church ceases to function as a church, no longer fulfills its mission of being the ambassador of Jesus Christ, and ceases to have as its aim the Kingdom of God, it ceases to be a church.[120]

Dispensationalism and the Church

Dispensationalism became the primary hermeneutical approach for fundamentalism. Systematized and popularized by John Nelson Darby in his frequent trips to America in the nineteenth century, dispensationalism spread among fundamentalists through the prophetic conferences held in the late nineteenth and early twentieth centuries.

More than any other single element, however, the *Scofield Reference Bible* contributed to the spread of dispensationalism in the United States. It became the Bible of fundamentalism in the early twentieth century. Scofield emphasized a number of distinctives,[121] but it was his emphasis on a strict division between Israel and the church as two separate peoples of God that would affect fundamentalist ecclesiologies. In his Bible, Scofield declared:

> The word [*ecclesia*] is used of any assembly; the word itself implies no more, as, e.g., the town-meeting at Ephesus (Acts 19. 39), and Israel, called out of Egypt and assembled in the wilderness (Acts 7. 38). Israel was a true "church," but not in any sense the N.T. church—the only point of similarity being that both were "called out" and by the same God. All else is contrast.[122]

Scofield understood the church to exist in four senses. The true church is the whole body of the redeemed during the present

---

[119] Ibid., 143–44.

[120] Ibid., 172.

[121] Such as a strictly literal hermeneutic, a precise scheme for dividing history into epochs or dispensations, and a pretribulational rapture.

[122] C. I. Scofield, *The Scofield Reference Bible* (New York: Oxford University Press, 1945), 1021.

dispensation, composed of every believer of this dispensation. "The true church, composed of the whole number of regenerate persons from Pentecost to the first resurrection . . . united together and to Christ by the baptism with the Holy Spirit . . . is the body of Christ of which He is the Head."[123] This church is part of the kingdom of God, but is not the whole of the kingdom.[124] This church "is formed of regenerate persons, vitally united to Christ and to one another by the baptism with the Spirit, . . . and all true believers of this dispensation are the members."[125]

This becomes evident in the local church, Scofield's second sense of the term. "[The church is] an assembly of professed believers on the Lord Jesus Christ, living for the most part in one locality, who assemble themselves together in His name for the breaking of bread, worship, praise, prayer, testimony, the ministry of the word, discipline, and the furtherance of the Gospel."[126]

A third use of "church" is to designate a group of local churches. This is always found in the plural. He argued against a denominational view of these churches.

> [There was] no form of organization by which they were united together within territorial or doctrinal limitations. All such arrangements are post-apostolical. . . . The Scriptures know nothing of a "church" made up of many local churches united by peculiarities of doctrine, ecclesiastical order, or territorial convenience.[127]

The fourth sense of the word was as the "visible church." This church was different from the local church:

> [It is] distinguished from the local church, and from groups of local churches, in that it is broad enough to include all who profess to believe in Christ; and from "the church which is his body" in that the latter

---

[123] Ibid., 1304.

[124] C. I. Scofield, *The Scofield Bible Correspondence Course* (Chicago: Moody Bible Institute, 1907), 3:420–22.

[125] Ibid., 3:427.

[126] Scofield, *Reference Bible*, 1257.

[127] Scofield, *Correspondence Course*, 3:430–31.

includes only regenerate persons and is invisible as a body, while the former includes profession and is visible.[128]

This "church" is similar to Luther's greater church, of which the true church was the regenerate part.

> [T]hat visible body of professed believers called, collectively, "the Church," of which history takes account as such, though it exists under many names and divisions based upon differences in doctrine or in government. Within, for the most part, this historical "Church" has existed the true Church. . . . The predicted future of the visible Church is apostasy.[129]

This expected apostasy of the institutional church was an important factor in dispensational thought and in the separatism of the fundamentalists. Scofield believed that the "Judaizing" of the church had destroyed her spirituality. This he viewed as the Catholic and Reformed positions of using Old Testament Scriptures to refer to the church. These approaches reduce the purpose of the church to civilizing the world and acquiring wealth, by using an imposing ritual, erecting magnificent buildings, invoking God's blessing upon armed conflicts, and dividing believers into "clergy" and "laity."[130]

Conclusion

Under Cyprian and Augustine, the church was equated with the kingdom of God, under the eventual leadership of the pope. Outside this earthly, visible organization there was no salvation and no hope of forgiveness of sins.

The Reformation partly changed this. The magisterial reformers still maintained a universal church on earth, but with a more purified doctrine. They broke with organizational unity in Romanism and replaced it with sacramental unity. They still, however, maintained the link

---

[128] Ibid., 3:432.

[129] Scofield, *Reference Bible*, 1276.

[130] C. I. Scofield, *Rightly Dividing the Word of Truth* (London: Pickering & Inglis, 1910), 17.

between soteriology and ecclesiology, continuing to believe that there was no salvation outside the church.

The Anabaptists on the continent and the Separatists in England argued for the separation of church and state. The Baptists achieved this in the New World in Rhode Island, but eventually the entire nation adopted this principle. The Baptist church, which led the way for religious liberty, was a voluntary gathered assembly of baptized believers exercising internal discipline. While fundamentalism was interdenominational, this view of the church dominated the movement.

Chapter 2

A BRIEF HISTORY OF FUNDAMENTALISM
AND EVANGELICALISM

Historic evangelicalism/fundamentalism is the movement of American individuals and churches that between the late nineteenth century and the mid-twentieth century strongly opposed and resisted the progress of modernism within the major denominations of America and thus tried to keep those denominations orthodox. It was this opposition to modernism that initially defined the movement. In the middle of the twentieth century fundamentalism and evangelicalism divided, primarily over the means and methodology of resisting the modernist movement and of responding to the culture around them.

The histories of fundamentalism and evangelicalism have been well documented. This chapter is primarily a survey of the events, individuals, and ideas leading up to and continuing through the mid-twentieth century division of fundamentalism and new evangelicalism with a special consideration given to expressions of the doctrine of separation.

Background to the Movements

The fundamentalist/evangelical movement traces its roots back to Puritan, Pietist, Confessional, and Revivalist traditions. This background is essential to an understanding of the theology and practice of fundamentalism.

The seventeenth-century Puritans provide the strongest parallel for the separatism practiced by the fundamentalists. Having failed in their attempts to purify the Church of England of its Romanist tendencies, some Puritans concluded that the only recourse for true believers was to abandon the Church of England and form a new, separate church. The first such church was formed in Norwich, England in 1581. These Separatists established several key themes as the basis for separation. First, unregenerate membership was ruining the church. Second, the only option open to true believers was to come out of the Church of England. Third, the true separatist must denounce the Church of England for its apostasy.[1]

Roger Williams provides an early example of an American separatist. Williams believed that the Church of England had failed and that leaving it was absolutely necessary. He left England to remove himself from its influence, only to discover that the Puritan churches of Massachusetts were "tainted with Roman corruption." This forced Williams to draw a distinction between "godly persons" and "godly persons who had renounced their participation in the Church of England." To worship with a godly person who had not renounced the Church of England was tantamount to worshipping with the unconverted.[2]

The second root of fundamentalism was pietism.[3] The pietist movement of the late seventeenth and eighteenth centuries developed in the context of Enlightenment infidelity and the decline of the Lutheran churches. The basic premise of pietism was the necessity of a radical separation between the converted and the unconverted. A dichotomy between worldliness and spirituality was emphasized and enforced through prohibitions of certain social activities. The avoidance of these prohibited activities became the symbol of personal separation.

The third root was confessionalism.[4] Fundamentalism rejected liberal theology, the movement that rose to importance in the early nineteenth century as European philosophers and theologians began to attack traditional theology. Friedrich Schleiermacher, the German "father of theological liberalism," argued that the Protestant confessions were

---

[1] Leland H. Carlson, ed., *The Writings of Henry Barrowe, 1587–1590* (London: George Allen and Unwin, 1962), 54, 304, 320.

[2] Edmund S. Morgan, *Roger Williams: The Church and the State* (New York: Harcourt, Brace, 1967), 38.

[3] For a thorough understanding of Pietism, see Douglas H. Shantz, *An Introduction to German Pietism: Protestant Renewal at the Dawn of Modern Europe*, Young Center Books in Anabaptist and Pietist Studies (Baltimore: John Hopkins University Press, 2013). Another interesting work on Pietism is Roger E. Olson and Christian T. Collins Winn, *Reclaiming Pietism: Retrieving an Evangelical Tradition* (Grand Rapids: Eerdmans, 2015).

[4] See Annette G. Aubert, *The German Roots of Nineteenth-Century American Theology* (Oxford: Oxford University Press, 2013).

merely historical documents that noted what particular groups believed at particular times. In opposition conservatives such as Charles Hodge and others at Princeton Seminary argued that the Westminster Confession was still the guiding principle for true Presbyterians. Although it was not as authoritative as the Westminster Confession of Faith, the New Hampshire Confession (often modified to reflect a pre-tribulational eschatology), became the standard confession of faith for Baptist churches in the late nineteenth and early twentieth centuries. Nineteenth-century confessionalism primarily affected the Reformed churches, but the belief that a church or denomination coheres by means of its agreement to a confession became a guiding principle for fundamentalism. Differing interpretations or understandings of Scripture, especially those in direct opposition to the commonly held church theology, could not be allowed within a church or denomination.

The fourth root of fundamentalism was revivalism, which Marsden identifies as the most significant heritage of fundamentalism. This revivalism, however, was shaped by dissenting Puritan Calvinism, which embodied a strong inclination to dominate and transform culture, not separate from it. In the nineteenth century Puritanism and revivalism merged, with the ideal of creating a Christian society.[5] Puritanism had failed to change culture from the top down, having tried to use governmental coercion to force change upon the members of the community. Revivalism focused on changing individuals, not the broader culture. The merger of revivalism with Puritanism was an attempt to change culture from the bottom up, without the benefit (or the hindrance) of civil government.

American revivalism was individualistic. Revivalism and individualism came to share the same spirit of democracy and free enterprise. The basic unit in much of early American thought was the free individual, so the revivalists (in spite of their Calvinist heritage) came characteristically to seek from individuals a voluntary decision. Upon the salvation of the individual, the process of sanctification proceeded largely in terms of personal and theological purity, a reflection of pietism and

---

[5] George M. Marsden, "From Fundamentalism to Evangelicalism: A Historical Analysis," in *The Evangelicals: Who They Are, What They Believe, Where They Are Headed*, ed. David F. Wells and John D. Woodbridge (Nashville: Abingdon, 1976), 154–55.

confessionalism. The primary unit of authority was the individual conscience informed by the Bible. Churches were viewed as voluntary associations that individuals were free to join or leave.[6]

Another side of the individualism of revivalism was that, lacking strong concepts of institutional authority, nineteenth century Bible believers emphasized the Protestant principle of the exclusive and infallible authority of Scripture. Revivalism affected by Pietism disposed people to think in terms of dichotomies—saved and lost, truth and error, the spiritual and the worldly. This was reinforced by the Common Sense philosophy prevalent among many Bible believers in the nineteenth century. This mindset believed in the reliability of common-sense judgments concerning morality and reality in general. With Scripture to guide them, Bible believers were confident that they could distinguish between truth and error with a certainty that the most rigorous scientific observation would only confirm. Because they resisted the dominant twentieth-century trends and remained true to the philosophical heritage of what Marsden calls "supernatural positivism," the fundamentalists were viewed by everyone else as obscurantists and their beliefs as anti-intellectual. "Fundamentalists characteristically presented their faith as being the exact representation of biblically revealed matters of fact for which could be claimed the highest positive standards for scientific objectivity."[7] In reality, fundamentalists believed that the Bible was written in a way that allows a normal person to read and understand it. This confidence in the perspicuity of Scripture led to a confidence of faith.

Marsden has suggested four stages in the history of the fundamentalist/evangelical movement. In the first stage, from the mid–1800s to about 1919, conservative Christianity was a unified force. The second stage, from 1919 to 1926, saw defeat on "all fronts." In the third stage, from 1926 to the 1940s, there was withdrawal and regrouping of the fundamentalist forces. In the fourth and final stage, from the 1940s to the 1980s, there was the emergence of new evangelicalism as a movement clearly distinct from the separatist fundamentalism.[8] This chapter will be based on these four stages.

---

[6] Ibid., 155.

[7] Ibid.

[8] Ibid., 122–42. Marsden wrote this in 1987. I suggest that a fifth stage is now present: the separation of conservative evangelicalism from the left wing of

Confrontation
Mid-1800s to 1919

After the Reformation and into the early twentieth century, biblical Christianity saw dramatic growth, but at the same time was attacked on numerous fronts. Confrontation came from philosophy, science, and biblical criticism.

Philosophy at one time had been regarded as the handmaiden of theology; one of its frequent uses was to provide rational proofs for the existence of God. The synthesis of philosophy and theology began to break down under the influence of philosophers such as David Hume and Immanuel Kant. Hume was an empiricist; he argued that it is impossible to prove the existence of God. For Hume this was not simply a presupposition. He argued, philosophically, that an infinite God cannot be inferred from a finite effect, nor can the Christian God be proven from creation. Hume even challenged the concept of cause, arguing that experience cannot deduce the idea of cause as a necessary connection between two events. The transcendent, personal God was replaced with an immanent, impersonal one; miracles were replaced with natural processes. Kant followed the direction established by Hume. Because of his emphasis on epistemology, Kant was convinced that the mind gives form to knowledge, but the content of knowledge is supplied by sense experience. Since no one can experience God, any claim for his existence is empty.

Philosophers such as Thomas Hobbes, René Descartes, Baruch Spinoza, and Gottfried Wilhelm von Leibniz elevated reason and materialism above the objective revelation of the Bible. If rationalism is true, then there is no need of a revealed Scripture. In addition, the Bible was considered to be wrong when it presented man as sinful and helpless before God. In its most ardent form, rational knowledge was possible apart from and without the aid of faith or divine revelation.

Natural science also rejected the traditional biblical concepts of the world and humanity. Darwin rejected the history and theology of Genesis. He did not reject the existence of God; he just felt that God was no longer required as an explanation for the existence of the world. Rather than

---

evangelicalism, along with the reunion of some elements of fundamentalism with the right wing of evangelicalism, but that must be reserved for another book.

viewing humanity in a fallen, sinful state, evolution pictures humanity as progressing forward toward perfection. He saw no need for the supernatural; in fact, the supernatural is not even a possibility. Naturalism argued that truth could be ascertained only by its own self-styled scientific method. Naturalism not only attacked historic Christianity, but also rejected its ability to ascertain truth.

Darwinism had several effects upon theology. If human origins could be explained by evolution, so could the development of religious ideas. Under Darwinism the Bible became merely a record of one people's religious evolution. When the naturalists compared the Bible with other religious writings, they concluded that the Bible could no longer be authoritative and distinct. This became explicitly obvious to Americans in 1893, when the World Parliament of Religions came to Chicago and gave Americans a first-hand taste of non-Christian religions.[9]

The scientific and philosophical attacks came from the outside. Theological attacks, however, came from within Christendom. Historical and literary criticism began to be applied to the biblical text beginning in Germany. Friedrich Schleiermacher (1768–1834) attempted to reinterpret traditional Christianity by the new parameters of the Enlightenment. Religion for him was based on a feeling of dependence on God. God became a mere "experience."[10] By reducing Christianity to an experiential religion, Schleiermacher reduced or entirely removed the importance of biblical authority and the historicity of miracles.[11] Albrecht Ritschl (1822–1889) opposed the individualism of orthodoxy and argued that Christianity was not the rescue of a person from personal sin, but instead an effort to transform society into the kingdom of God. Christ's death on the cross was not a payment for sin, but a moral influence on humanity. Ritschl set the stage for the social gospel, which was anathema to the

---

[9] Kenneth Cauthen, *The Impact of American Religious Liberalism* (New York: Harper, 1962), 23.

[10] Hordern, *Protestant Theology*, 44.

[11] See Friedrich Schleiermacher, *On Religion: Speeches Addressed to Its Cultured Despisers*, translated by Terrence N. Tice (Richmond: John Knox, 1969) and *The Christian Faith*, translated by H. R. Mackintosh and J. S. Stewart (Edinburgh: Clark, 1928).

emerging fundamentalism.[12] He was followed by Adolph Harnack (1851–1930) and in the United States by Walter Rauschenbusch (1861–1918), who became the father of the social gospel in America.

The emergence of higher criticism among German scholars was damaging to conservative Christianity. It was an effort to "read between the lines" of the biblical text.[13] By applying rationalism to the Bible, Julius Wellhausen and others destroyed the authority and authenticity of the Bible. The rationale for changing the order of the Hebrew Bible and reassigning its authorship was based upon an evolutionary concept of religion. The miraculous and prophetic were arbitrarily declared to be impossible and thus had to be rejected. Humanity was held to be basically good, God a benevolent Father, and all humans brothers. The intellectually respectable and spiritually satisfying position became the accommodation of Christian doctrine to the conclusions of science, philosophy, and criticism.[14]

These ideas lent credence to the concept that God's kingdom was something to strive for now through social reform.[15] Denominations formerly committed to orthodoxy began to experience the influence of liberalism. It was in the face of these assaults that conservative believers sought to re-emphasize their task of defending the Scriptures and evangelizing the world.[16]

Fundamentalists developed various forms of defense against the modernism that had invaded America in the 1800s. Some small private Bible conferences were held in the mid-nineteenth century, but "the first official 'Believers' Meeting for Bible Study,' as it was originally called, was held in Swampscott, Massachusetts, in 1876, and for the first time the meeting was opened to the public."[17] This annual meeting was held in

---

[12] Lloyd Averill, *American Theology in the Liberal Tradition* (Philadelphia: Westminster, 1967), 43.

[13] Hordern, *Protestant Theology*, 4.

[14] Erickson, *New Evangelical Theology*, 21.

[15] For instance, see Walter Rauschenbusch, *Christianity and the Social Crisis* (New York: Macmillan, 1910) and *A Theology for the Social Gospel* (New York: Macmillan, 1922).

[16] Marsden, *Fundamentalism and American Culture*, 102–3.

[17] Larry D. Pettegrew, "The Rapture Debate at the Niagara Bible Conference," *Bibliotheca Sacra* 157 (July 2000): 131.

various places until 1883, when the conference met at Niagara-on-the-Lake, Ontario, Canada, and became known as the Niagara Bible Conference. In 1878 the first Bible and Prophecy Conference was held in New York CIty. The importance of the conference movement was that, "rather than developing a hierarchical order from the top down, [fundamentalism] first grew from a network of inter-personal and inter-institutional relationships."[18]

In 1879 Crawford Toy, theology professor at Southern Baptist Seminary in Greenville, South Carolina, was dismissed for his progressive views on the origins of Scripture. Charles Briggs, professor at Presbyterian Union Seminary in New York, created a controversy over his liberal view of inspiration. His heresy trial polarized the Presbyterian Church in the 1890s and resulted in the withdrawal of Union Seminary from that denomination.[19] Walter Rauschenbusch led Rochester Seminary and William Newton Clarke led Colgate Theological Seminary into liberalism. The University of Chicago Divinity School became a bastion of liberalism among Northern Baptists.

Mass evangelism under men like D. L. Moody, R. A. Torrey, and Billy Sunday sought to counteract the criticisms of science, philosophy, and religion and to bring the lost to salvation. Moody united conservatives under an evangelical banner, stressing the "old orthodoxy, or the fundamentals of the old orthodoxy, plus the new emphasis on informality and on the singing of 'human hymns.'"[20] He stood against liberalism. That Moody had no use for these liberals was clear from the dogmatic manner in which he stated his belief in the literal infallibility of the Bible on every occasion. In addition to his attacks on liberalism, he emphasized premillennialism.

> As a premillennialist . . . Moody believed that until Christ returned none of the basic problems of the world could be solved. In his sermons on the imminent Second Coming he discouraged those efforts toward reform which were the distinguishing mark of the social gospel movement after 1890. . . .

---

[18] Marsden, *Fundamentalism and American Culture*, 62.

[19] Ibid., 117.

[20] McLoughlin, *Modern Revivalism*, 193.

Moody utilized the doctrine [of premillennialism] as a convenient handle against the theological liberals who challenged either his revivalism or his social views.[21]

Bible schools were founded to counter the effects of liberal schools such as Andover, Union, and the Divinity School in Chicago.[22] "No analysis of the structure of the fundamentalist movement can proceed very far if the role of the Bible institute is ignored."[23] Most fundamentalists rejected any church organization above the local level, so "the Bible institutes played a major role in giving them some unity."[24] Moody Bible Institute, the best known Bible institute, was founded in 1886 to oppose the apostasy of its time. Periodicals were also started to counter liberal teachings. For instance, Arno C. Gaebelein left the Methodist Church in 1899 and started a militant periodical, *Our Hope*, to fight the inroads of liberalism. George Dollar was undoubtedly correct when he called these nineteenth-century evangelicals, "pioneer fundamentalists."[25] Others used the term "proto-fundamentalists."[26]

The most significant defense against modernism in this early phase culminated in the publication of *The Fundamentals*.[27] This series of twelve books was a defense of historic Christianity and focused on those areas where philosophy, science, and theology had attacked biblical Christianity. Many view the publication of *The Fundamentals* as the starting point of fundamentalism as an identifiable movement.[28] Many of the contributors were outstanding scholars. No articles specifically

---

[21] Ibid., 256, 258.

[22] See S. A. Witmer, *The Bible College Story: Education with Dimension* (Manhasset, NY: Channel, 1962) for a brief history of the early Bible institutes.

[23] Sandeen, *Roots of Fundamentalism*, 241.

[24] Marsden, *Fundamentalism and American Culture*, 128.

[25] Dollar, *History of Fundamentalism*, 2.

[26] The term may have been first used in David Rausch "Proto-Fundamentalism's Attitude toward Zionism, 1878-1918" (PhD dissertation, Kent State University, 1987).

[27] A. C. Dixon and R. A. Torrey, ed., *The Fundamentals: A Testimony to the Truth* (Chicago: Testimony, 1910–1916). There were twelve books issued originally. They were later reprinted in four volumes.

[28] Lightner, *Neo-evangelicalism*, 32. See also Larry Oats, "The Priorities of The Fundamentals," *Maranatha Baptist Theological Journal* 2.1 (2012): 65ff.

attacked modernism; instead, they centered on positive theological themes, such as the inspiration and inerrancy of Scripture and the deity of Christ. The result was a "calm, well-reasoned and well-balanced testimony to Christian truth."[29] While the issue of ecclesiastical separation was not addressed in *The Fundamentals*, the Stewart brothers, who funded the publication and distribution costs, had left the Presbyterian Church because of its liberal tendencies.[30]

Another major publication of this era was the *Scofield Reference Bible*, edited by C. I. Scofield, a Congregationalist minister from Dallas, Texas. The *Scofield Reference Bible*, first published in 1909, became a major reference tool for preachers and teachers throughout the nation. This Bible was characterized by a moderate Calvinism and a pre-tribulational eschatology, two characteristics that came to identify most of later fundamentalism.

By the end of this first stage in the history of fundamentalism, modern assumptions and values had been assimilated into the increasingly liberal Christian tradition. There was an emphasis on God's work through evolution, nature, and history; the growth of Scripture out of natural processes; and a continuing revelation of God in the application of Christian principles to society.

Fundamentalists, for the most part, still remained in the denominations, but were resisting the growing modernism. They attempted to arrest the new trends and emphasized the supernatural origin of Scripture and the supernatural aspects of Christ's person and work. This group generally accepted the pessimistic view of dispensationalism: the apostasy of Christendom in the present dispensation, the imminent return of Christ and rapture of the saints, and the delay of the social and political benefits of Christianity until Christ's return and personal reign.

---

[29] John D. Woodbridge, Mark A. Noll, and Nathan O. Hatch, *The Gospel in America* (Grand Rapids: Zondervan, 1979), 59.

[30] Peter J. Blakemore, "Toward an Honest Portrait of Fundamentalism, 1930–1980: A Historical Study of Progressive Development in the Working Definition of Fundamentalism" (PhD diss., Bob Jones University, 1982), 68.

Conflict
1919 Through 1926

Marsden's second stage, covering the years 1919 until 1926, was one of the most dramatic time periods in the history of fundamentalism. Marsden identifies two dominant factors that precipitated the strong separatist tendencies of fundamentalism: the increasing antagonism towards liberalism and the impact of World War I. The belligerence against the German military carried over into a belligerence against German theology as well. The aftermath of World War I introduced into American society elements alien to a Protestant America. The "Red Scare" captured American politics. Prohibition modified American social life. In spite of some victories, the massive changes in society and religion caused the fundamentalists to feel they were losing control, and they launched a fierce attack on modernism in response.[31]

In 1919 the World Christian Fundamentals Association (WCFA) began, with Bob Jones, Sr., among its early supporters. In 1927 J. Gresham Machen and fellow Princetonian and amillennialist, Robert Dick Wilson, were keynote speakers at the WCFA convention sponsored by William Bell Riley.[32] The Association proclaimed that the Christian's duty was to evangelize the unconverted and prepare the church for Christ's coming.[33] This created a tension that has affected fundamentalism and evangelicalism ever since: holiness requires a separation from the world, while evangelism requires engagement with the world.

In spite of the beginnings of independent organizations, most of the fundamentalists were a loyal opposition in the modernist denominations. The early leaders of the regional strongholds of fundamentalism were faithful members of their denominations. Two such leaders who maintained an allegiance to their denominations while still claiming to be true fundamentalists were Baptist W. B. Riley, who developed his "Empire

---

[31] See Marsden, *Fundamentalism and American Culture*, 141–53 and Hofstadter, *Anti-Intellectualism in American Life,* 133.

[32] Dalhouse, *An Island in the Lake of Fire*, 17.

[33] "Resolutions of the Fundamentalists," *Sunday School Times* 75 (22 July 1933): 472.

of the North," and Presbyterian Mark Matthews, who held the power of his presbytery in Seattle for years.[34]

An example of this loyal opposition surfaced in 1920 in the Northern Baptist Convention. The Northern Baptists were especially hard hit by the modernist-fundamentalist controversy. Conservatives and liberals battled over control of the seminaries, colleges, and mission boards. At the 1919 Baptist Convention in Denver, the denomination had voted to join the ecumenical New World Movement. The support by the modernists of the New World Movement (and its goal of social reform almost to the exclusion of evangelism) was the ultimate expression of liberal theology. Curtis Lee Laws, editor of the *Watchman-Examiner*, attacked this program: "Having fought valiantly for the truth . . . are we now to compromise with error in the name of tolerance, fraternity, and Christian charity?"[35] In writing of the 1920 Baptist Convention held in Buffalo, New York, Laws suggested:

> We here and now move that a new word be adopted to describe the men among us who insist that the landmarks shall not be removed. "Conservatives" is too closely allied with reactionary forces in all walks of life. "Premillennialists" is too closely allied with a single doctrine and not sufficiently inclusive. "Landmarks" has a historical disadvantage and connotes a particular group of radical conservatives. We suggest that those who still cling to the great fundamentals and who mean to do battle royal for the fundamentals shall be called "Fundamentalists." By that name the editor of the *Watchman-Examiner* is willing to be called. It will be understood therefore when he uses the word it will be in compliment and not in disparagement.[36]

---

[34] See William Vance Trollinger, Jr., *God's Empire: William Bell Riley and Midwestern Fundamentalism* (Madison: University of Wisconsin, 1991); C. Allyn Russell, *Voices of American Fundamentalism: Seven Biographical Studies* (Philadelphia: Westminster, 1975), 101–104; and Ezra P. Giobney and Agnes M. Potter, *The Life of Mark A. Matthews, "Tall Pine of the Sierras"* (Grand Rapids: Eerdmans, 1948), 37–74.

[35] Quoted in Joseph M. Stowell, *Background and History of the General Association of Regular Baptist Churches* (Haywood, Calif.: J. F. May, 1949), 13.

[36] Curtis L. Laws, "Convention Side Lights," *Watchman-Examiner* 8 (1 July 1920): 834–35. Donald Tinder notes, however, that the term "Fundamentalist" was used earlier as the name of a British periodical sponsored by the Wesley

Thus the term "fundamentalist" was coined and used to describe the antimodernist crusaders. It was then a broad term, roughly equivalent to a militant conservative. At this same meeting, the Fundamentalist Fellowship of the Northern Baptist Convention was formed by the fundamentalist Baptists.[37] While still a part of the Convention, the Fellowship eventually could boast of its own Northern Baptist Theological Seminary,[38] Eastern Baptist Theological Seminary,[39] Western Baptist Theological Seminary,[40] and the *Watchman-Examiner*, the largest northern Baptist magazine.[41]

Because of the external threats, fundamentalists minimized their differences and maximized their agreements with each other. This fundamentalist union was well represented by one of the best known spokesmen for the movement in those days, J. Gresham Machen. Machen did not like the term "fundamentalist" and preferred not to be called one. Yet he stood with the fundamentalists. His *Christianity and Liberalism* defined the issue as a test between two logically incompatible religions.[42]

Bible Union. Donald Tinder, "Fundamentalist Baptists in the Northern and Western United States" (PhD diss., Yale University, 1972), 5.

[37] Bruce L. Shelley, *Conservative Baptists, A Story of Twentieth Century Dissent* (Denver: Conservative Baptist, 1960), 17–29.

[38] Northern Baptist Theological Seminary was started at Second Baptist Church of Chicago, IL, in 1913 in reaction to the liberalism of the Northern Baptist Convention seminaries.

[39] Eastern Baptist Theological Seminary was formed in 1925 in Philadelphia in reaction to the liberalism of the Northern Baptist Convention.

[40] Portland (Oregon) Baptist Bible Institute began in 1925. Western Baptist Theological Seminary was added two years later.

[41] *The Watchman* was founded in Boston in 1819 as a Baptist paper. It became *The Watchman and Examiner* when the magazine moved to New York. It then became *The Watchman-Examiner*, a union of twenty-three newspapers. Frank Luther Mott, ed., *A History of American Magazines* (Oxford: Oxford University Press, 1930), 138.

[42] Machen's contention was that liberalism and Christianity were two separate religions. He did not like the term "fundamentalist" and was strongly anti-dispensational, but because of the great battles against modernism was closely associated with his co-belligerent fundamentalists. He preferred the term "evangelical," indicating that in his definition of an evangelical church. J. Gresham Machen, *Christianity and Liberalism* (New York: Macmillan, 1923), 168.

The significance of Machen's position is twofold. First, Machen suggested that the separation of orthodox and liberals should take place.[43] Second, he certified that fundamentalism was forged out of a doctrinal controversy. In contrast, when Machen was forced out of the Presbyterian Church, other conservatives (colleagues such as Clarence McCartney and Wilbur M. Smith) refused to depart with him. They argued that separation should be primarily a matter of individual conscience and the appropriate response to liberalism was for conservatives to unite for the cause of traditional evangelicalism while remaining in their denominations.[44]

During the mid-1920s men began to argue for ecclesiastical separation, because they had concluded that reconciliation with the liberals or victory over the liberals within the denominations was impossible.[45] One of the more separatist organizations during this stage was the Baptist Bible Union. It was formed in 1923 by Baptists who were impatient with the Fundamental Fellowship's toleration of error. It was led by Texan J. Frank Norris and Canadian T. T. Shields. Its last meeting was held in 1932, when it was succeeded by the General Association of Regular Baptist Churches.[46]

The major concluding event of this period was the Scopes Monkey Trial. The state of Tennessee had passed a law that required that only

---

[43] Machen plainly stated, "If the liberal party, therefore, really obtains control of the Church, . . . evangelical Christians must be prepared to withdraw no matter what it costs." Machen, *Christianity and Liberalism*, 166.

[44] Ned B. Stonehouse, *J. Gresham Machen: A Biographical Memoir* (Grand Rapids: Eerdmans, 1954), 496–500.

[45] The first instance of fundamentalists separating from liberalism is when, in 1914, a majority of the Baptist pastors in Grand Rapids refused to continue fellowship with the liberal Fountain Street Church and formed the Grand Rapids Association of Regular Baptist Churches. This, however, was a remote event. Separation did not become common for another two decades. Sheldon Quincer, "A History of the Grand Rapids Association of Regular Baptist Churches," an unpublished paper presented at the annual meeting of the Grand Rapids Association of Regular Baptist Churches, Grand Rapids, Michigan, 23–25 September 1958, 2–8; quoted in Joel A. Carpenter, *The Renewal of American Fundamentalism, 1930–1945* (PhD diss., John Hopkins University, 1984), 47.

[46] Stowell, *Background and History,* 1–37. See also Robert Delnay, *A History of the Baptist Bible Union* (ThD diss., Dallas Theological Seminary, 1963).

creationism could be taught in the public schools. The American Civil Liberties Union sought to overthrow the law and after some searching found a teacher who would be willing to teach evolution. In 1925 John Scopes, a high school biology teacher, was arrested for teaching evolution in Dayton, Tennessee. Clarence Darrow, a leading attorney with the American Civil Liberties Union, served on Scopes' defense team. William Jennings Bryan, a staunch Presbyterian, a three–time Democratic candidate for President of the United States, Secretary of State, and committed Bible believer, aided the prosecuting attorney. The first part of the trial was comparatively simple: Scopes had clearly broken the Tennessee law. In the second part of the trial, however, Darrow sought to show that evolution was not incompatible with the Biblical account of creation. Bryan allowed himself to be put on the witness stand in defense of biblical creationism. Bryan's confessed ignorance to what would happen physically if the earth really had stood still, what the civilizations of the world believed, how many languages there were in the world, the age of the earth, or the exact date of the flood made Bryan seem to be too ignorant to argue against evolution.[47] While fundamentalism won the actual trial, it lost in the eyes of the public. This trial was viewed as the "final desperate outcry of an outdated and intellectually repressive religious establishment."[48] The fundamentalists had lost the battles on all fronts.

Under cultural, philosophical, and theological attack, fundamentalism began to concentrate on core doctrines, the "fundamentals." Some of those who would eventually form the new evangelical movement began to criticize fundamentalism for leaving other doctrines scarcely touched upon, because they believed that the organic unity of revealed truth was being neglected and the relationship of the underlying theology was being ignored.[49] In reacting against the social gospel, fundamentalism was accused of overreacting and neglecting the social application of the gospel. "The fundamentalist stressed increasingly the salvation of the soul, and bypassed the care of the material needs of man. To the observer, the fundamentalist appeared to be somewhat callous."[50]

---

[47] Erickson, *New Evangelical Theology*, 27.

[48] Marsden, "From Fundamentalism to Evangelicalism," 147.

[49] Erickson, *New Evangelical Theology*, 28.

[50] Ibid.

During this time fundamentalism began losing its influence in society. Its power waned within the denominations, as can be seen in the lost battles of especially the Presbyterian and Baptist denominations. There were far more positive developments taking place, however. Fundamentalism was effective in evangelism and church growth. For all the liberals' concern for alleviating social ills, it was the fundamentalists who were on the foreign mission field, doing not only direct evangelism, but also medical work, literature production and distribution, and education.[51] Fundamentalists were engaged in the relief of the poor in America and the support of rescue missions for the indigent. Fundamentalism maintained an interest in aiding the needy, especially those affected by the sins of alcohol and drug use. Many of the early rescue missions had strong fundamentalist support.[52]

This stage was a period of disintegration for the fundamentalist coalitions, losses in the denominations, problems in fundamentalism's contact with society, but growth in individual churches and organizations and outreach around the world.

Consolidation
1926 Through the 1940s

The third stage lasted from 1926 to the 1940s. It was a time of fundamentalist withdrawal and regrouping. In the previous stage fundamentalism had been primarily a movement within the mainstream of Protestantism. In this stage, fundamentalism left the mainstream denominations and the doctrine of separation became a test of fidelity. In the 1920s and 1930s the fundamentalists had three choices with respect to most of the major denominations in the north: to be content as a minority in denominations dominated by the liberals, to separate from the old denominations and form new ones, or to leave all denominational connections and become independent.[53] During this stage some fundamentalists simply left their denominations and formed independent

---

[51] Ibid., 30.

[52] Preston Mayes, "Fundamentalism and Social Involvement," *Maranatha Baptist Theological Journal* 2 (Spring 2012): 31–68.

[53] Larry Dean Sharp, *Carl Henry: Neo-Evangelical Theologian* (DMin thesis, Vanderbilt University, 1972), 9.

churches, but many more established new denominations or fellowships. It was also during this stage that the key individuals and organizations who were involved in the fundamentalist/evangelical controversy began their ministries.

Fundamentalism had been rejected by the large denominations. The common outsider perception was that it was "split and stricken."[54] Its critics were certain that the movement was finished.[55] There is, however, a difference between the death of a movement and merely losing the respect of the elite, the scholars and the historians. Popular movements are often built on dissent. They thrive on an "outsider" status.[56] The fundamentalists were not a defeated movement. Indeed, while the modernists spoke of a vanishing fundamentalism, it was actually the modernist churches that were in the decline.[57]

A bastion of fundamentalism was Bob Jones College, begun in 1927 by evangelist Bob Jones, Sr.[58] Jones was born in Shipperville, Alabama, on October 30, 1883. After his conversion at the age of eleven in a Methodist church, he became known as the "Boy Preacher." At age twelve he became the Sunday School superintendent at the Methodist Episcopal Church in Brannon's Stand. At age thirteen he held a "brush arbor" meeting and started a church. At fifteen he was licensed by the Alabama Conference and became a circuit rider with five churches under his charge, including the one he started.

---

[54] Sandeen, *Roots of Fundamentalism*, 269.

[55] In 1926 *Christian Century* described the movement as "an event now passed" ("Vanishing Fundamentalism," *Christian Century* 43 [June 24, 1926], 799). Stewart G. Cole, a liberal Baptist educator who published the first history of the movement in 1931, predicted that progressive religious education would remove its last vestiges (Cole, *The History of Fundamentalism*, 324–328). In 1931 H. Richard Neibuhr referred to fundamentalism exclusively in the past tense (Niebuhr, "Fundamentalism," 526–27).

[56] Luther P. Gerlach and Virginia H. Hine, *People, Power, Change: Movements of Social Transformation* (Indianapolis: Bobs and Merrill, 1970), 183–86.

[57] Robert T. Handy, "The American Religious Depression, 1925–1935," *Church History* 29 (March 1960): 1–29.

[58] Biographical material for the Joneses is found in Ed Reese, *The Life and Ministry of Bob Jones, Sr.,* Christian Hall of Fame Series (Glenwood, Ill.: Fundamental Publishers, 1975); Dalhouse, *An Island in the Lake of Fire*; Johnson, *Builder of Bridges*; Jones, Jr., *Cornbread and Caviar*; and Wright, *Fortress of Faith*.

He attended Southern University (later called Birmingham Southern) at Greensboro, Alabama, from 1901 to 1904. He married Bernice Sheffield in 1905, but she died of tuberculosis ten months later. He then married Mary Gaston Stollenwerck, who was converted in one of his meetings. Their only child was Bob Jones, Jr., born in 1911. "Senior" worked full time in evangelism until he started Bob Jones College in 1927 near Panama City, Florida, although he continued to hold evangelistic meetings regularly even after becoming a college president.[59] The crash of 1929 devastated Florida, so in 1933 the college moved to Cleveland, Tennessee. In 1947 four major events took place at Bob Jones College: the college moved to Greenville, South Carolina; it changed its name to Bob Jones University; Bob Jones, Jr., became president; and Bob Jones, Sr., became Chairman of the Board.[60] When Junior took over the presidency of Bob Jones University, he broke fellowship with the NAE, Youth for Christ, and nearly every other major evangelical organization in the country.

Jones' years as an evangelist coincided with that period of time during which tremendous religious transitions took place in American history. Morality was being lost, America's cities were growing at a phenomenal rate, and a flood tide of immigrants changed the complexion of American cities. It was the wave of Roman Catholic immigration that especially troubled Protestants.

Bob Jones, Sr., represented a more interdenominational version of fundamentalism. He came from a Methodist background, but his evangelistic ministry crossed broad denominational lines. He had been a participant in the modernist–fundamentalist battles of the early twentieth century. In the summer of 1920, he and William Biederwolf sponsored a resolution at the Winona Conference stating that evangelists associated with the conference would not preach under the auspices of theological liberals.[61] Jones, and his son, Bob Jones, Jr., became a part of the NAE because of its emphasis on evangelism.[62] In 1943, Jones, Sr., decried the division between the NAE and the ACCC: "If England, America and Russia can get together on how to win the war and each nation retained its own form of government, it would seem to me that our

---

[59] Reese, *Bob Jones, Sr.*, 5–10.

[60] Ibid., 11.

[61] Johnson, *Builder of Bridges*, 106.

[62] Dalhouse, *An Island in the Lake of Fire*, 62.

fundamental groups, since we believe the same doctrines, could get together."[63]

In the spring of 1947 Jones, Jr., was elected to a three-year term on the NAE's board of administration. During the next few years, however, a rift developed between the NAE and the Joneses. The Association refused an offer to hold the 1949 annual meeting in Greenville, South Carolina, where Bob Jones University had relocated. The NAE had also rejected a plan for evangelism suggested by Bob Jones, Sr. In addition there were elements within the NAE who were uncomfortable with the Joneses. The identification of the NAE with the "New Evangelicalism" defined by Harold Ockenga in 1947 created a problem for the Joneses. In 1950 Jones, Jr., was elected vice president of the NAE, but in his memoirs, he indicated that he believed he was being used by the Association to "deceive the fundamentalists" into thinking the NAE was a fundamentalist institution.[64] In June 1951 Jones severed his connections with the Association.[65]

In 1929 Princeton Theological Seminary began to include liberals on its faculty. In reaction a conservative group led by J. Gresham Machen left and founded Westminster Theological Seminary in Philadelphia. Four years later Machen and others formed the Independent Presbyterian Board of Foreign Missions to provide an alternative to the more liberal Presbyterian Board of Foreign Missions; Machen was its first president. The denomination's General Assembly ruled that this was an unlawful move. Machen and others were defrocked or resigned from the denomination and formed the Orthodox Presbyterian Church (originally called the Presbyterian Church of America) in 1936.[66] The very next year this group split, with the formation of the Bible Presbyterian Church led

---

[63] Bob Jones, Sr., to Rev. E. G. Zorn, 23 July 1943, Fundamentalism Collection, Mack Library, Bob Jones University, Greenville, SC.

[64] Jones, *Cornbread and Caviar*, 103–4.

[65] Bob Jones, Jr., to Gertrude Clark, 13 June 1951, Fundamentalism Collection, Mack Library, Bob Jones University, Greenville, SC.

[66] John Fea notes, "Most interpretations of fundamentalist Presbyterianism stop chronologically after 1936, the year J. Gresham Machen was ousted from the denomination for violating his ordination vows. . . . Yet such an interpretive practice neglects the fact that a fundamentalist current . . . continued to exist not only into the 1940s, but beyond" (Fea, "McIntire," 253).

by Carl McIntire of Collingswood, New Jersey and Oliver Buswell of Wheaton College. Other fundamentalist Presbyterians, while sympathetic to the separatists, remained in their denomination, forming a "loyal opposition."[67]

The separation issue divided friends and colleagues. Fellow Westminster graduates and close associates Harold J. Ockenga and Carl McIntire divided. Ockenga retained his ordination in the Presbyterian denomination, while McIntire became a separatist and founded the militantly-separatistic ACCC.[68] McIntire's departure from the Presbyterian Church was expensive. "[Separation] involves loss of friendships, pensions, stained glass windows, family ties, manses, position and ecclesiastical standing. Separation involves controversy—hard grueling controversy. It involves attacks—personal attacks, even violent attacks. It involves salaries, food, houses; it tests faith."[69]

Carl McIntire was born on May 17, 1906, in Ypsilanti, Michigan, into the home of a Presbyterian minister, but grew up in Durant, Oklahoma.[70] He graduated from Park College, Parkville, Missouri, in 1927 and in 1928 enrolled at Princeton Theological Seminary, which was then embroiled in the fundamentalist-modernist controversy. He became one of Machen's most active student participants in the fight with modernism. In 1929 McIntire left with Machen and graduated from Westminster Seminary in 1931.[71] McIntire said of this time, "The principles espoused then and the stand taken have led inexorably on through the years in the struggle for the gospel and the purity of the Church."[72]

---

[67] Edwin H. Rian, *The Presbyterian Conflict* (Grand Rapids: Eerdmans, 1940), 151–247.

[68] See Lindsell, *Park Street Prophet*, 30–31, 113–17; and Carl McIntire, "N.A.E., Fuller Seminary Championed by Ockenga," *Christian Beacon* 16 (10 May 1951): 1, 4–5, 8.

[69] Carl McIntire, *Testimony of Separation* (Collingswood, NJ: Christian Beacon, 1944), 44.

[70] Biographical information on McIntire can be found in Laman, *God Calls a Man* and Morris, *The Preachers*.

[71] Fea, "Carl McIntire," 255.

[72] Carl McIntire, "A Generation that Knew Not Machen," *Christian Beacon* 41 (July 1976): 3, 5, 7.

Following a brief pastorate in Atlantic City, New Jersey, McIntire was called to the Collingswood Presbyterian Church in Collingswood, New Jersey. Machen preached his installation sermon. In 1936 he was suspended from the Presbyterian ministry because of his affiliation with Machen's Independent Board of the Presbyterian Foreign Missions. Forced out of the Presbyterian Church-USA, he joined Machen's Presbyterian Church of America.

McIntire, Machen's ecclesiastical lawyer Charles Woodbridge, and Wheaton President Oliver Buswell began calling for greater theological liberty than Machen was willing to allow. These dissenters pressed for total abstinence from alcohol and more openness toward dispensational premillennialism, since McIntire had adopted the premillennialism advocated by C. I. Scofield.[73] After Machen's death, McIntire spearheaded the new Bible Presbyterian Church, with a modified Westminster Confession which allowed for premillennial dispensationalism.[74]

> While McIntire saw the church as the purest form of Presbyterianism, the organizational structure, theology, and ethical concerns that the church championed evidenced a denomination that might be called "Presbyterian" in name only. In reality McIntire's "true Presbyterianism" was supported by a great deal of fundamentalist leaven.[75]

Because of McIntire's defection from the denomination, the West Jersey Presbytery took possession of McIntire's church building. The resultant move of the church into a circus tent drew national media coverage.[76] From these experiences came his belief in a pure church and that "separating from the church was the only way to avoid what he believed to be the corrupting influence of modernism."[77]

---

[73] Fea, "Carl McIntire," 257.

[74] Carl McIntire, "Bible Presbyterian Fellowship Formed," *Christian Beacon* 2 (June 1937): 1, 8 and "Proposed Changes to Confession of Faith" *Christian Beacon* 3 (August 1938): 1, 2.

[75] Fea, "Carl McIntire," 258.

[76] For instance, "In a Tent," *Time* 31 (11 April 1938): 46–47.

[77] Fea, "Carl McIntire," 256.

McIntire developed a network of fundamentalist organizations he labeled "The Twentieth Century Reformation Movement."[78] He started the *Christian Beacon* in 1936, the weekly newspaper that would unite his followers until it ceased publication in the 1990s. While its circulation was less than the *Sword of the Lord*, the *Christian Beacon* received virtually all the attention of the secular and non-fundamentalist religious press. McIntire and the *Christian Beacon* became the prime example of American fundamentalism to the public eye. Faith Theological Seminary opened in 1937 with Allen McRae as president. The ACCC was formed on September 17, 1941. Beginning with just the Bible Presbyterian Church and a few other Bible Protestant churches, the ACCC grew with the addition of the Independent Fundamental Churches of America and the General Association of Regular Baptist Churches. The ACCC was clear in its position: "God's people cannot support or be a part of a fellowship with unbelievers, such as is represented in the modernist Federal Council."[79] Members of the American Council could not work even with other fundamentalists who persisted in staying in the Federal Council of Churches. In 1955 he began his daily radio broadcast, "Twentieth Century Reformation Hour" (which was carried by 600 stations by 1958).[80]

In 1923 twenty-four men formed the American Conference of Undenominational Churches (ACUC) at a meeting in Arnold Park, Iowa. Seven years later a group of mostly Congregational pastors from Chicago joined the ACUC and at the same time changed the name of the organization to the Independent Fundamental Churches of America (IFCA). J. Oliver Buswell, president of Moody Bible Institute, was part of this new organization. Until 1945 churches and individuals could be part of the IFCA and any other denomination. Some of the early members were Billy McCarrell, pastor of Cicero (Illinois) Bible Church, at whose desk the IFCA took shape; M. R. DeHaan of the Radio Bible Class and *The Daily Bread*; Louis Talbot, president of BIOLA; John Walvoord and Charles Ryrie of Dallas Theological Seminary; and numerous other well-known

---

[78] See Carl McIntire, *Twentieth Century Reformation* (Collingswood, NJ: Christian Beacon, 1944).

[79] McIntire, *Twentieth Century Reformation*, 179.

[80] Clabaugh, *Thunder on the Right*, 91.

individuals.[81] The IFCA became a part of McIntire's ACCC, while maintaining its own identity.

McIntire's strong leadership and heavy-handed practices created enemies even among his own followers. In 1955 the Bible Presbyterian Church split, with the disgruntled forming the Evangelical Presbyterian Church. In 1965 Carl McIntire's school, Shelton College, lost its ability to grant degrees. In 1968 McIntire was voted out of the leadership of the ACCC. In 1970 he was voted out of the membership of the ACCC, which then withdrew from the McIntire-controlled ICCC. In 1971 McRae and all but two of the faculty at McIntire's Faith Seminary left and formed Biblical Theological Seminary in Hatfield, Pennsylvania.[82]

While the NAE formed a rallying point for the emerging new evangelicalism, there was no similar format for the fundamentalists. The ACCC was a relatively small organization. Rice and Jones, Sr., would never align themselves with the organization. On December 26, 1958, the only formal meeting of the separatists took place when Rice and Jones, Sr., called for such a meeting. Nearly twelve hundred separatist pastors and leaders from various factions gathered together. McIntire was not present, but he did send representatives from his movement. This group agreed that they would not accept invitations to speak at non-fundamentalist activities, that they would not support or encourage churches that were not aligned with fundamentalism, that doctrine was the basis of unity, and that unity even in evangelism could only come between those who were saved in Christ, sound in doctrine, unwilling to quarrel in minor matters, and completely separate from modernism.[83]

The Baptist movement had gained a large following in the 1800s. The Baptists of the South had organized the Southern Baptist Convention in 1845, but the North had no centrally-organized "convention" during this time. "Anniversaries" were held in the North, usually in May, when church delegates would meet for preaching and mutual encouragement. These gatherings were cooperative meetings held jointly by the independent societies devoted to the work of missions and promotion

---

[81] See J. O. Henry, *For Such a Time as This* (Westchester, IL: Independent Fundamental Churches of America, 1983) for a history of the IFCA.

[82] Marsden, *Reforming Fundamentalism*, 43–44.

[83] John R. Rice, "Christian Leaders December 26 in Chicago Restate the Historic Position of Bible Believers," *Sword of the Lord* 25 (16 January 1959): 1, 5.

among the Baptists of the North.[84] These independent societies were the American Baptist Foreign Mission Society (founded 1814), the American Baptist Publication Society (founded 1824), and the American Baptist Home Mission Society (founded 1832), along with various state and local associations.

A sentiment began to grow among northern Baptists for the creation of a central organization. The impetus for the formation of the Northern Baptist Convention came from a resolution developed by Ernest DeWitt Burton and Shailer Matthews, professors at the University of Chicago Divinity School and part of the Chicago Baptist Association. The initial steps toward organization took place at the meeting of the American Baptist societies in May 1907, in Washington, DC, although it was not until 1909 that all the legal work was completed and the Northern Baptist Convention officially came into existence. The convention was formed under the impetus of liberals and "from the very beginning the modernists had control of it."[85]

This liberal control was made very evident at the 1919 meeting of the Northern Baptist Convention in Denver. Losses in membership during the Great War and financial problems caused by post-war inflation created the need for change.[86] Five significant actions were taken by the convention that year that alarmed the fundamentalists within the convention: 1) the convention invited liberal Harry Emerson Fosdick to be the principal speaker, 2) it voted to enter the liberal Inter-Church World Movement, 3) it established a denominational paper, *The Baptist*, under liberal leadership, 4) it authorized the establishment of the General Board of Promotion, centralizing the authority of the convention, and 5) it adopted a report of the Resolutions Committee, which called for a socially-centered Christianization of the world.[87]

Almost from the inception of the convention, the fundamentalists recognized that some form of organized protest had to be inaugurated

---

[84] Robert G. Delnay, "Background Struggles of the Conservative Baptist Movement," *Central Conservative Baptist Quarterly* 7 (Summer, 1964), 33.

[85] Ibid., 34.

[86] Shelley, *Conservative Baptists*, 12.

[87] Chester E. Tulga, *The Foreign Missions Controversy in the Northern Baptist Convention* (Chicago: Conservative Baptist Fellowship, 1950), 10–11; Shelley, *Conservative Baptists*, 21.

among conservatives to check the powerful influence of the liberals. William B. Riley, an early fundamentalist leader from Minneapolis, expressed this concern in a letter written in 1910. "We have without a struggle surrendered the denomination into the hands of the higher critics. Their plan of operation is outlined: ours is not; they are a unit: we do not even have any meetings. The program for the coming Convention is in their hands from its chairman down. We will not be heard regarding it."[88]

It was not until 1920, however, that the fundamentalists acted decisively. A call went out to any interested members of the Northern Baptist Convention to attend a fundamentalist conference prior to the Buffalo, New York, meeting of the convention in May, 1920. The immediate occasion for this pre-convention conference was the launching at Denver in 1919 of the ecumenical New World Movement and that movement's goal of raising one hundred million dollars.[89]

> [A]ware of the steady inroads of modernism, the gradual abandonment of Baptist polity for a centralized system of ecclesiastical authority and complete capture of its strongest seminaries by liberalism, one hundred and fifty ministers and laymen signed the call which brought forth the Fundamentalist Fellowship of the Northern Baptist Convention at Buffalo in 1920.[90]

For the next twenty-seven years the Fundamentalist Fellowship, as a part of the Northern Baptist Convention, would struggle to turn the denomination to a position of biblical conservatism.

One leader among the fundamentalists in the Northern Baptist Convention was Robert T. Ketcham.[91] Ketcham was converted at the age

---

[88] Robert G. Delnay, "A History of the Baptist Bible Union," *Central Conservative Baptist Quarterly* 7 (Fall, 1964), 7–8. Riley, to a limited extent, sought to fight against liberalism when he founded the World Christian Fundamentals Association in 1919, although this had little effect upon the Northern Baptist Convention. "Dr. Riley Reaches 85th Milestone," *The Christian Fundamentalist* 3.4 (December 1946), 5.

[89] Delnay, "Background Struggles," 37.

[90] *Why the Conservative Baptist Association of America* (Chicago: The Conservative Baptist Association of America, n.d.), 3.

[91] The biographical information on Ketcham is from Murdoch, *Portrait of Obedience*.

of twenty-one in a Northern Baptist Convention church in Pennsylvania. Despite his lack of education (no high school diploma and no college education), he began to pastor in Roulette, Pennsylvania, at the age of twenty-three. When the Northern Baptist Convention began its "New World Movement" in 1918 (calling on its churches to raise $100,000,000 for a variety of causes, including modernistic ones), Ketcham protested. His pamphlet, "A Statement of the First Baptist Church Butler, Pennsylvania, with Reference to the New World Movement and the $100,000,000 Drive," thrust him into the national spotlight. After numerous losses in the Northern Baptist Convention, Ketcham left the convention and helped establish the General Association of Regular Baptist Churches (GARBC) in 1932. This Association began with twenty-two churches, but within twenty years there were nearly 650 churches.[92] Ketcham became the second president of the Association in 1934; in 1938 he became editor of *The Baptist Bulletin*, the official journal of the Association. Ketcham later assumed a leading role in the ACCC, becoming its president in 1944. It was the Ketcham-McIntire alliance that represented the opening salvo in the separatist war against new evangelicalism. The leaders of the GARBC were certain that the Northern Baptist Convention was so permeated with liberalism that it was beyond recovery. They charged the leaders of the Fundamentalist Fellowship, such as Earle V. Pierce and Curtis Lee Laws, with helping the "inclusive policy" and defying the scriptural injunctions to come out and be separate.[93] Ketcham wrote a series of pamphlets called "Facts for Baptists to Face," which delineated the modernism of the Northern Baptist Convention. These were not written as much to attack the convention as they were to convince men in organizations like the Fundamentalist Fellowship that they needed to withdraw from the convention.

---

[92] R. T. Ketcham, "The Doctrine of Separation," *The Baptist Bulletin* 18 (December 1952): 10.

[93] Three articles concerning the perceived disloyalty of the Fundamentalist Fellowship leaders to the Word of God appeared in the *Baptist Bulletin*, the official journal of the General Association of Regular Baptist Churches: H. G. Hamilton, "Secretary Lerrigo Struggles Hard to Explain," *Baptist Bulletin* 1 (August 1933): 2; O. W. VanOsdel, "How About It?" *Baptist Bulletin* 1 (November 1933): 2; and "An Open Letter to Dr. W. B. Riley from Dr. R. T. Ketcham," *Baptist Bulletin* 2 (November 1936): 3–4.

In 1943 the conservatives still in the Northern Baptist Convention formed the Conservative Baptist Foreign Mission Society to provide a means of supporting theologically-conservative missionaries. In 1947 most, but not all, of the remaining fundamentalists left the Northern Baptist Convention and formed the Conservative Baptist Association (CBA). The Fundamentalist Fellowship changed its name to the Conservative Baptist Fellowship, but still maintained a quasi-independence from the CBA. However, the Conservative Baptist Association, unlike the General Association of Regular Baptists, never required its member churches to separate from the Northern Baptist Convention. Chester E. Tulga was a Baptist pastor in Ohio, Pennsylvania, Nebraska, South Dakota, and Illinois. More important to the current discussion, he served as the Executive Secretary for the Conservative Baptist Fellowship for 12 years. His ministry was spent mostly during the modernist/ fundamentalist debates, but he concluded his ministry during the debates between fundamentalism and evangelicalism. In 1957 he preached "The Fundamentalism of Yesterday, the Evangelicalism of Today, and the Fundamentalism of Tomorrow," at the Silver Anniversary Conference of the General Association of Regular Baptist Churches; this was an early critique of new evangelicalism.[94]

Not all of these Bible believers were separatists. Some remained in the denominations as a loyal opposition. John W. Bradbury, pastor and associate editor of the *Watchman-Examiner*, saw ulterior motives in the separatists. He argued that it made neither good sense nor good Christianity to wreck the Northern Baptist Convention and that instead the fundamentalists should work to unify and strengthen the conservatives in the Convention.[95] One of the most powerful of the

---

[94] Tulga wrote numerous short works. Many of them were part of his "Case" series: *The Case Against Neo-Orthodoxy, The Case Against Modernism in Foreign Missions, The Case Against the National Council of Churches, The Case Against the Federal Council of Churches, The Case Against the World Council of Churches, The Case Against the Social Gospel, The Case Against Modernism in Evangelism, The Case for Separation in These Times, The Case for the Virgin Birth of Christ, The Case for the Resurrection of Jesus Christ, The Case for the Atonement by Christ, The Case for Jesus the Messiah,* and *The Case for Dispensationalism.* He also wrote *The Doctrine of Separation in These Times.*

[95] John W. Bradbury, "The N.B.C. Fundamentalists," *Watchman-Examiner* 25 (12 August 1937): 916–18.

loyalists was W. B. Riley. Although involved in the Baptist Bible Union, he did not leave the Northern Baptist Convention until the year of his death. He stayed, he said, because he could not bear to see the liberals inherit a vast denominational enterprise which had been built by evangelicals.[96]

While the Fundamentalist Fellowship was an important alliance of fundamentalists in the North, an important fundamentalist journal in the South (which also had a significant influence on the North) was the *Sword of the Lord*, the most widely-circulated and influential fundamentalist publication during this stage. John R. Rice[97] began the *Sword* on September 28, 1934, primarily to give firsthand information to readers of his revival crusades and to keep the readers informed on modernistic tendencies in the Southern Baptist Convention.[98] The paper grew from an initial circulation of 5,000 to 135,000 in 1980, when Rice retired from his function as editor. In the initial issue, Rice declared, "The First Baptist Church in Oak Cliff, of which I am the pastor, is greatly interested in this paper but I alone am responsible for the paper. . . . We have no board of directors to consider about the policy of this paper."[99] Subject matter ranged from gambling and horseracing to abortion to organ playing during church prayer. More importantly, it also dealt with theological issues such as modernism, neo-orthodoxy, and eventually the new evangelicalism.

Rice was born and raised in Gainesville, Texas, the son of conservative Southern Baptists. After graduating from Decatur Baptist College in 1918 and Baylor University in 1920, he entered Chicago University to obtain an education degree, but soon withdrew and attended Southwestern Baptist Theological Seminary. In 1926 he entered full-time evangelism, ministering primarily among the Baptists of Texas. He moved to Ft. Worth where he came into contact with J. Frank Norris, an independent Baptist fundamentalist. Under Norris's influence, Rice began to attack his alma

---

[96] W. B. Riley, "The Denominational Division Among Baptists," *The Pilot* 20 (January 1940): 104–105.

[97] Two biographies of Rice are Sumner, *A Man Sent From God* and Walden, *John R. Rice*.

[98] John R. Rice, "The New Paper and Its Policies," *Sword of the Lord* 1 (28 September 1934): 1. Marsden called Rice "the most influential fundamentalist publicist of the era" (Marsden, *Reforming Fundamentalism*, 159).

[99] Rice, "The New Paper and Its Policies," 1.

mater, Baylor University, because of modernist tendencies. He soon separated from the Southern Baptists. He planted and pastored the Fundamentalist Baptist Church of Oak Cliff from 1932 until 1940, when he returned to full-time evangelism. In 1939 Rice changed the name of his church from Fundamentalist Baptist Church to Galilean Baptist Church. This name change had less to do with his concern over being a "fundamentalist" as it did the connection the term had in Texas with J. Frank Norris. Norris, a leading fundamentalist in Fort Worth, had been accused of murder, arson, failure to pay his employees, slander, and libel. Rice declared, "An atmosphere of suspicion, insinuation, charges and counter-charges has grieved the Spirit, has injured Christian fellowship and done much harm."[100] This affected his position on separatism in later years, for he was concerned with an over-emphasis on separation among some segments of fundamentalism.

Rice served on the board of trustees at Bob Jones University. He praised the University for doing a "magnificent work of training young people for Christ, rearing up Christian leaders in these terrible and apostate days."[101] When the university was criticized by Dr. J. Oliver Buswell, he rushed to the school's defense.[102] Rice and Jones, Sr., preached together frequently in evangelistic meetings. Jones, Sr., required ministerial students at the university to read and review the

---

[100] John R. Rice, "Name Changed: Fundamentalist Baptist Church Becomes Galilean Baptist Church," *Sword of the Lord* 5 (December 1939): 4.

[101] John R. Rice, "Editor Visits Bob Jones College," *Sword of the Lord* 7 (8 June 1945): 1.

[102] John R. Rice, "Dr. J. Oliver Buswell's Charges against Bob Jones University Answered," *Sword of the Lord* 10 (8 June 1948): 2. In the 1920s, Buswell, as the president of Wheaton College, believed that one conservative college was sufficient to meet the needs of the nation and discouraged Bob Jones from starting or enlarging Bob Jones College. In the 1930s, when Buswell and other Christian educators formed a Christian accreditation society, Bob Jones refused to join them. In 1940, when BJU began to perform Shakespearean plays and Greek tragedies, Buswell was at the forefront of the criticism. In 1949, Buswell, president at Shelton Bible College at that time, again criticized Bob Jones for its theatrical productions. http:// recollections.wheaton.edu/?p=287.

sermons in the *Sword*. In 1959 Jones, Sr., invited Rice to preach on separatism in the university chapel.[103]

In the mid–1950s Rice and other fundamentalists had begun to call themselves evangelicals, until the new evangelicals made it clear that this new movement was heading in another direction. On May 18, 1956, Rice opened his attack on new evangelicalism.

> There are doubtless honest, noble, good Christian men, but all of them are enlisted in a left-wing movement to bring in a "new evangelicalism." They sneer at fundamentalists, deride the motto "earnestly contend for the faith," talk about the "reactionary antischolasticism" of the fundamentalists of the past generation. . . . The truth is the same in all of the articles [of *Christianity Today*] with the tendency to playdown fundamentalism and the defence [*sic*] of the faith, to poke fun at old-time fundamentalists and to quote with glowing terms of appreciation the weighty pronouncements of infidel scholars.[104]

Rice had defended Billy Graham early in his evangelistic ministry, frequently reporting on his campaigns. In November, 1957, Rice published a letter to Graham in which he accepted Graham's resignation from the Board of the *Sword of the Lord*, because they were going in different directions.[105] From then on, Rice and other contributors to the *Sword of the Lord* routinely critiqued Graham's ministry.

Fundamentalism had survived and played a prominent role in the religious resurgence in the decades after World War 2. There had been defeat in the antimodernist controversies in the denominations. The movement had splintered and there was little hope of mounting a public campaign of any kind. During the 1930s fundamentalism nearly disappeared from the national scene, shifting its energies to evangelism and building its own churches and schools. During this time the movement grew. "[It] had the popular support, structural strength, innovative

---

[103] This was later printed as a tract entitled "Christian Cooperation and Separation." John Rice, *Come Out or Stay In?* (Nashville: Thomas Nelson, 1974), 177.

[104] John R. Rice, "Our Beloved 'Intellectuals' Again!" *Sword of the Lord* 22 (18 May 1956): 1, 12.

[105] John R. Rice, "Which Way, Billy Graham?" *Sword of the Lord* 22 (23 November 1956): 2.

flexibility and reproductive potential to maintain its vitality during the depression years and by the 1940s to seek once again to win America— this time by revival."[106]

The fundamentalists saw separation as a clear demonstration of their obedience and faith. They believed God would reward their obedience. They were completely willing to leave the security of their denominations in exchange for the life of a separatist and denominational pioneer. As McIntire stated, "They knew not where the battle against modernism would lead them, but they knew that wherever they ended, Jesus Christ would be there."[107]

Fundamentalism came to be characterized by two elements: an unshakable fidelity to doctrinal purity and a penchant for separating from anything or anyone that might compromise that purity. They had been defeated in their attempts to rescue the denominations from modernism. They were thrust negatively into the national limelight with the Scopes trial. Fundamentalists responded by withdrawing and, further, by erecting a fundamentalist subculture.[108] Out of this subculture a network of fundamentalist agencies developed.

The fundamentalists left the liberal denominations and founded new ones or became completely free of any form of binding external affiliations. While a dispute developed over the implications and extent of separation, and a wedge which would grow eventually into a permanent split developed, there was agreement over the "separated life": patterns of devotion, life-style habits, and an outlook that would mark fundamentalists as a separated people.[109] This separatist impulse and concurrent withdrawal from society would seem to have marked the demise of fundamentalism; instead it was the opposite. The separatists saw that the church's purity and Christianity itself were at stake. Their defeats had only confirmed their dispensational vision of the demise of the worldly culture.

---

[106] Joel Carpenter, "From Fundamentalism to the New Evangelical Coalition," in *Evangelicalism and Modern America,* ed. George Marsden (Grand Rapids: Eerdmans, 1984), 4. See also Carpenter, *Revive Us Again.*

[107] Carl McIntire, "Discussing the Issues of the Present Hour," *Christian Beacon* 8 (11 February 1943): 1, 2, 5.

[108] Dalhouse, *An Island in the Lake of Fire*, 19.

[109] Carpenter, *Renewal of American Fundamentalism*, 38.

Challenge
1940s to the 1980s

After the battles with modernism subsided, a portion of fundamentalists became dissatisfied with the separatist, culture-denying aspects of fundamentalism. Calling themselves "new evangelicals," they precipitated a major split in the ranks of fundamentalism. In Marsden's view, fundamentalism became a coalition of dispensationalists and separatists, while new evangelicalism sought to retain its essential commitment to evangelical orthodoxy and anti-modernism while getting rid of "these more recent aspects of fundamentalism."[110]

Disorder within liberalism and growth among the fundamentalists convinced the fundamentalists that perhaps not all was lost, but that they were in a position to influence the theological world and society at large. One such fundamentalist was James Murch. Murch was part of the Disciples of Christ and served at the Standard Publishing Company, co-founded the Cincinnati Bible Seminary, was co-founder the NAE and editor of its *United Evangelical Action* magazine, was a managing editor of *Christianity Today*, and served in numerous other areas. He observed that there existed "a tremendous constituency accomplishing great things for the Lord but without cohesion, or means of united action."[111] J. Elwin Wright was in agreement. Wright's father was a Free Will Baptist, turned Free Methodist, and then Pentecostal. Wright graduated from Missionary Training Institute (now Nyack College) in 1921 and joined his father's ministry. In 1929 he created the New England Fellowship, which was designed to bring various evangelicals together at summer conferences. Wright was concerned that too many fundamentalists were "hypercritical and intolerant."[112] In 1937 and 1940 the New England Fellowship had passed resolutions calling for some kind of united action. In the winter of 1940–41 an interested group of ministers called for a national meeting.

At the same time, Carl McIntire was calling for a national organization to rise up in opposition to the Federal Council of Churches (now the National Council of the Churches of Christ in the USA). McIntire was

---

[110] Marsden, *Reforming Fundamentalism*, 10.

[111] Murch, *Cooperation with Compromise*, 48.

[112] J. Elwin Wright, "A Few Observations," *New England Fellowship Monthly* (April 1937): 8.

strongly opposed to modernism, particularly in the Federal Council. On September 17, 1941, separatists joined together under McIntire's initiative at the National Bible Institute in New York City to form the American Council of Christian Churches.[113] Early leaders were Will Houghton, president of Moody Bible Institute, and evangelists Bob Jones, Sr., and Jack Wyrtzen.[114] By 1944 the council consisted of fourteen denominations, totaling approximately 1.2 million members.[115]

On October 27 and 28, 1941, a group of prominent evangelical leaders met at the Moody Bible Institute to discuss the possibility of a national organization. McIntire, with his associates H. McAllister Griffiths and Harold Laird, stated the case for these men joining the ACCC. However, it was quickly apparent the two groups were on divergent paths. Wright and others believed that the ACCC was completely negative; they envisioned something larger and more positive.[116] Ralph Davis summed up the impossibility of unity between the forming NAE and the ACCC when he wrote of that organizational meeting:

> After many hours of discussion, we found ourselves in disagreement on two points. The American Council felt it advisable to state as a major doctrine their determination to fight the Federal Council of Churches of Christ in America. While our group is not

---

[113] John Albert Stroman, "American Council of Christian Churches: A Study of Its Origin, Leaders and Characteristic Positions" (ThD diss., Boston University, 1966), 94.

[114] Carl McIntire, "American Council of Christian Churches Organized in New York," *Christian Beacon* 6 (19 September 1941): 1. Jones and Houghton would also be involved in the beginning of the NAE.

[115] The council consisted of the Bible Protestant Church, Bible Presbyterian Church, American Bible Fellowship Association, General Association of Regular Baptist Churches, Independent Fundamental Churches of America, Methodist Episcopal Church, Old Evangelical Catholic Church, Union of Regular Baptist Churches of Ontario and Quebec, Tioga River Christian Conference, Conference of Fundamentalist Churches, United Christian Church, National Fellowship of Brethren Churches, Methodist Protestant Church, and the Ohio Independent Baptist Churches (McIntire, *Twentieth Century Reformation*, 183). Because of restrictions on voting privileges, the American Council of Christian Churches was constantly criticized concerning the accuracy of its membership statistics (Gasper, *The Fundamentalist Movement*, 31–37).

[116] McIntire, *Twentieth-Century Reformation*, 192.

favorable to the Federal Council, we did not feel it advisable to establish an organization upon a negative basis. . . . A second point of disagreement was that they felt the A.C.C.C. . . . did not represent all evangelicals.[117]

These men set the stage for the founding of the NAE in St. Louis on April 7, 1942, followed by a Constitutional Convention in Chicago, May 3-7, 1942.[118] The purpose of the Association was to preserve a larger ethos of conservative Protestantism and to "organize an Association which shall give articulation and united voice to our faith and purposes . . . while not considering ourselves as an executive or legislative body in any wise controlling constituent members nor proposing to initiate new movements and institutions."[119] The ethos of the early members of the NAE was not far from that of fundamentalism. The themes of anti-

---

[117] Open Letter from Ralph T. Davis of The Committee of United Action Among Evangelicals, 2 March 1942, Records of the African Inland Mission, Collection 81, Box 14, Folder 27, Billy Graham Center Archives, Wheaton, Illinois.

[118] The organizational meeting included leaders such as Robert Ward Ayer (Calvary Baptist Church, New York City), Ralph T. Davis (African Inland Mission), William Horace Dean (Philadelphia College of the Bible), William Erdman (Wheaton College), Charles Fuller (Old Fashioned Revival Hour), Harry Ironside (Moody Memorial Church, Chicago), Stephen Paine (Houghton College), Will Houghton (Moody Bible Institute), and J. Elwin Wright. Wright stated that the following were interested in the possibility of formation of a national organization, but were unable to attend the initial meeting: Lewis Sperry Chafer (Dallas Theological Seminary), Walter Ferrin (Providence Bible Institute), Harold J. Ockenga, William Bell Riley (First Baptist Church, Minneapolis), and William Holdcroft (Independent Board of Presbyterian Foreign Missions, an organization heavily supported by McIntire). Also present were three representatives from the ACCC, Carl McIntire, Harold S. Laird (Faith Theological Seminary), and McAllistar Griffiths (Bible Presbyterian pastor). "Minutes of the Committee for United Action Among Evangelicals," (27–28 October 1941, Chicago), Records of the African Inland Mission, Collection 81, Box 14, Folder 27, Billy Graham Center Archives, Wheaton, Illinois.

[119] J. Elwin Wright, "An Historical Statement of Events Leading Up to the National Conference at St. Louis," in *Evangelical Action: A Report of the Organization of the NAE for United Action*, compiled and edited by the Executive Committee (Boston: United Action, 1942), 3–16.

Catholicism and anti-liberalism were common.[120] The Statement of Faith adopted by the Association was readily acceptable by any fundamentalist. In spite of this theological and practical similarity, the differences that would define the split into "fundamentalist" and "evangelical" were already present.

An important feature of new evangelicalism was its emphasis upon and effort toward unity.[121] To many new evangelicals, the division among fundamentalism, often over minor doctrines, was deplorable. These men called for a biblically-based union. They rejected the Federal Council of Churches as too liberal and the ACCC as too narrow. Ockenga made it clear that those who formed the NAE preferred the term "evangelical" to "fundamentalist."[122] There was, however, a strong tie between fundamentalism and evangelicalism, in terms of doctrine, institutions, and people, during the 1940s and 1950s.

Harold John Ockenga was born to a godly Methodist mother and an unregenerate father on July 6, 1905, in Chicago, Illinois.[123] He was baptized as an infant in the Austin Presbyterian Church and grew up in the Olivet Methodist Church, but it was not until his teenage years that he was truly regenerated. He attended Taylor University, a Methodist school, and graduated in 1927. An indicator of his studious mind was his rejection of the doctrine of sinless perfection taught at Taylor and his acceptance of the eternal security of the believer. He then went to Princeton Seminary; after his second year, the struggle in the Presbyterian Church broke open and Westminster Theological Seminary

---

[120] John W. Bradburn, "Co-operation Among Evangelicals," in *United . . . We Stand: A Report of the Constitutional Convention of the NAE, LaSalle Hotel, Chicago, Illinois, May 3–6, 1943* (Boston: NAE, 1943), 16–20.

[121] Erickson, *New Evangelical Theology*, 41. An important work on this theme at the time was Murch, *Co-operation Without Compromise*.

[122] Harold John Ockenga, "Editorial," *United Evangelical Action* 2 (January 1943): 1. See also "What the N.A.E. is and What It is Doing," *United Evangelical Action* 7 (15 April 1948): 5–6. However, James Leo Garret has argued that the American press and people were hardly aware of any distinctions between the fundamentalists of the ACCC and the evangelicals of the NAE during the 1940s, 50s, and 60s. James Leo Garret, *Are Southern Baptists "Evangelicals"?* ed. James Leo Garret, E. Glenn Hinson, and James E. Tull (Macon: Mercer, 1983), 53.

[123] Biographical information on Ockenga comes from Lindsell, *Park Street Prophet*.

began. Still viewing himself a Methodist and thus having no active part in what he deemed to be a Presbyterian problem, Ockenga left Princeton to attend Westminster under the men whose reputation had been responsible for his attending Princeton in the first place. In spite of his Methodist background, he entered the Presbyterian ministry upon his graduation. After two short ministries, he became the assistant pastor at the First Presbyterian Church in Pittsburgh; the senior pastor was Clarence Edward Macartney, a leading conservative voice in Presbyterianism. Macartney was allied with J. Gresham Machen in his battles but refused to break with the denomination.[124] In 1936 Ockenga became pastor of the Park Street Congregational Church in Boston, where he spent the remainder of his life. In 1944 Ockenga received a Doctor of Humanities degree from Bob Jones College. In 1947 Fuller Theological Seminary opened its doors, with Ockenga as president *in absentia*. Ockenga, while arguing against the separatist strategy, joined with other churches to separate from the ecumenically-oriented United Church of Christ (after the merger of 1957-61) and helped organize the Conservative Congregational Christian Churches.[125]

From 1946 to 1948 several of the fundamentalists began to criticize the fundamentalist position and attitude and called for a renewal of influence on society. A significant work came from the pen of Carl F. H. Henry.[126] Henry's *The Uneasy Conscience of Modern Fundamentalism* is universally cited as an example of the dissatisfaction of the new evangelicals with fundamentalism and the trumpet call for a new movement. Henry's book, while short in length, was long in effect as a milestone of the new evangelical identity. Essentially a political manifesto, *The Uneasy Conscience* provided an ideological blueprint for socially-inclined evangelicals. Henry deplored the lack of fundamentalist social involvement. "Fundamentalism, although heir-apparent to the

---

[124] Marsden, *Reforming Fundamentalism*, 42.

[125] Sharp, *Carl Henry*, 21–22.

[126] See especially his *Remaking the Modern Mind* (Grand Rapids: Eerdmans, 1946) and *The Uneasy Conscience of Modern Fundamentalism* (Grand Rapids: Eerdmans, 1947). See also Ockenga's article, "Can Fundamentalism Win America?" which concluded "not as presently constituted." Harold Ockenga, "Can Fundamentalism Win America?" *Christian Life and Times* 2 (June 1947): 13–15.

supernaturalist gospel of the Biblical and Reformation minds, is a stranger, in its predominant spirit, to the vigorous social interest of its ideological forbears."[127]

He still considered himself a "fundamentalist," although he used the term "evangelical" as well. Henry received sharp barbs from the fundamentalists because of his book. It must be kept in mind that Henry's book was not a guide to general new evangelical concerns of the 1940s, but it was instead an expression from the cutting edge of the community, from one of its most educated and articulate leaders.

Henry was born in New York in 1913 into a nominal Christian home.[128] With a Lutheran father and Roman Catholic mother, Henry grew up going to an Episcopalian church. In 1933, while editor of the Smithtown Star, Henry was converted. He entered Wheaton College, graduating in 1938. A study of the Scriptures while he was at Wheaton led him to become a Baptist. It was the historical distinctives of the Baptists, especially the autonomy of the local church, that impressed him.[129] His Wheaton education was followed with an MA, BD, and ThD by 1943. He completed a PhD at Boston University in 1949. In 1947 Henry joined the faculty of the newly-founded Fuller Theological Seminary, joining Wilbur M. Smith, Everett F. Harrison, and Harold Lindsell. In 1949 he became an active leader in the organization of the Evangelical Theological Society. In 1956 he was chosen by Billy Graham and L. Nelson Bell (Graham's father-in-law and executive editor of Christianity Today) to become editor of Christianity Today. When Graham's 1957 New York crusade threatened to divide evangelicals and fundamentalists, Henry rose to the defense of Graham and his cooperative evangelism.

Fuller Seminary began in 1947. The faculty members developed a strong apologetic for the faith. They believed that the fundamentalists had lost the battle with modernism because they had not persuasively presented their case. Consequently, new evangelicalism placed a great emphasis on education. The Fuller faculty were scholars in their own right. Wilbur Smith, an author, editor, and bibliophile, taught Bible and

---

[127] Henry, The Uneasy Conscience, 61.

[128] Biographical information is from Henry, Confessions. Another helpful biographical work is Patterson, Carl F. H. Henry.

[129] Carl F. H. Henry, "Twenty Years a Baptist," Foundations 1 (January 1958): 47.

apologetics. Everett Harrison from Dallas Seminary taught New Testament and Greek. Harold Lindsell came from Northern Baptist Theological Seminary and taught missions. Carl Henry was professor of systematic theology and philosophy of religion.

In his inaugural address at Fuller Seminary, Harold John Ockenga, with a recent trip to war-ravaged Germany fresh in his mind, argued that it was imperative that the church not "withdraw itself to a separated community again."[130] Also in the inaugural address, perhaps to placate the Presbytery of Los Angeles who had voted not to allow its candidates to the ministry to attend Fuller, Ockenga declared that Fuller would be "ecclesiastically positive." This was also a direct attack on the fundamentalists and their belief that separatism was foundational to genuine Christianity.[131] Harold Ockenga was Fuller's first president, serving from 1947 to 1954, although he remained in Boston as the pastor of the Park Street Church. Edward John Carnell was the second president, serving from 1954 to 1959; he far preferred the classroom and was uncomfortable in the leadership role as president. Ockenga returned as the third president, from 1960 to 1963. Ockenga was replaced by David Allan Hubbard who served as president for the next thirty years.

Carnell was born in Antigo, Wisconsin, on June 28, 1919.[132] He grew up in the home of a conservative Baptist minister. Carnell complained "about the cultic mentality of fundamentalism." He viewed it as "rigid, intolerant, and doctrinaire."[133] Although a Baptist, he "studiously avoided identification with any denominational expression of Christianity."[134] His first book, *An Introduction to Christian Apologetics*, was published while he was still a graduate student at Harvard and member of Ockenga's Park

---

[130] Marsden, *Reforming Fundamentalism*, 46.

[131] Ibid., 64.

[132] Biographical information is found in John A. Sims, *Edward John Carnell: Defender of the Faith* (Washington, DC: University Press of America, 1979) and Nelson, *The Making and Unmaking of an Evangelical Mind*.

[133] L. Joseph Rosas, III, "The Theology of Edward John Carnell," *Criswell Theological Review* 4 (1990): 353.

[134] Ibid., 365.

Street Church.[135] Carnell joined the faculty at Fuller in 1948, but remained a member of Ockenga's church. In 1955 Carnell became the first resident president of Fuller Seminary. After declaring himself an administrative misfit, he left the presidency and resumed full-time teaching in 1959. A self-confessed barbiturate addict, he underwent extensive psychiatric counseling and electroshock treatment. On April 14, 1967, he was found dead in his hotel room while attending a Catholic ecumenical workshop in northern California. No collection of Carnell papers exists. Shortly after his death, his widow sold the family home, gave away his books, and destroyed all his correspondence and personal papers, assuming that they were of no value to anyone.[136]

While Carnell was president of Fuller, he had a problem with Charles Woodbridge, who he felt was undermining the seminary. He declared to Ockenga:

> The issue, of course, is the struggle between dispensationalism and the new evangelicalism. Dr. Woodbridge is a straight-line fundamentalist. He has been an enemy of your philosophy of the new evangelicalism from the very inception of the institution. My being appointed president crushed his hope of seeing the institution coming under the control of his position.[137]

The new evangelicals maintained an emphasis on evangelism. Billy Graham became the popularizer of their message. Graham had grown up in fundamentalism. For a time he was president of Northwestern College, founded by fundamentalist W. B. Riley.[138] With his evangelistic campaigns, he carried the message to the masses. He showed a desire to work with ministers of varying theological stripes, both liberal and conservative.[139] Billy Graham's style of evangelism was not new. The modern roots of Graham's evangelism are found in John Wesley and

---

[135] Edward John Carnell, *An Introduction to Christian Apologetics* (Grand Rapids: Eerdmans, 1948). This book established Carnell's reputation as a rising star of the new evangelical movement.

[136] Nelson, *Evangelical Mind*, ix.

[137] Letter from Edward John Carnell to Harold J. Ockenga, probably in late 1956, quoted in Nelson, *Evangelical Mind*, 104.

[138] See Trollinger, *God's Empire*.

[139] Erickson, *The New Evangelical Theology*, 32–38.

George Whitefield. Graham continued the long tradition of calling men and women to repentance and faith in Christ, while eschewing separation from unbelievers, including liberal theologians and Roman Catholics.[140]

Graham both shaped and was shaped by the larger evangelical movement. He was born in 1918 into a strongly Presbyterian family. He was converted under the preaching of Mordecai Ham in 1934 and attended Bob Jones College in Cleveland, Tennessee, for one semester. He indicated to a biographer that he did not have the slightest idea what Bob Jones College was all about. "I never did fit in. . . . I couldn't believe the rules there. . . . [T]here were demerits for just about everything."[141] He attended Florida Bible Institute near Tampa from 1937–40. He then went to Wheaton College, where he enrolled as a freshman. He was concerned about his unaccredited degree from Florida Bible Institute and chose to start college all over again. From that time on he was shaped by northern fundamentalism. His admirers argue that Graham was what the fundamentalism of that time might be expected to produce as the latest expression in a long succession of evangelical awakeners, revivalists, and more recent professional evangelists.

Graham became pastor of the Village Church, a Baptist fellowship, in Western Springs, Illinois, in 1943; was a field representative for Youth for Christ from 1944 to 1949; and served as the president of W. B. Riley's Northwestern Schools in Minneapolis from 1948 to 1952. While at Northwestern, Graham attempted to reconcile with the Joneses. In three letters written after he assumed the presidency of Northwestern, he declared, "We are trying to do here in the great Northwest what Bob

---

[140] For a history of revivalism in general, see William Warren Sweet, *Revivalism in America: Its Origin, Growth and Influence* (New York: Charles Scribner's Sons, 1944); Bernard A. Weisberger, *They Gathered at the River: The Story of the Great Revivalists and Their Impact upon Religion in America* (Boston: Little, Brown, 1958); and two works by William G. McLoughlin, Jr., *Modern Revivalism: Charles Grandison Finney to Billy Graham* (New York: Ronald, 1959) and *Revivals, Awakenings, and Reform: An Essay on Religion and Social Change in America, 1607–1977*, Chicago History of American Religion Series, ed. Martin E. Marty (Chicago: University of Chicago, 1978).

[141] Frady, *Billy Graham*, 96. Bob Jones, Jr., took note of him as a promising leader. He was extremely disappointed when Graham informed him of his decision to leave Bob Jones College for Trinity Bible Institute in Florida (Jones, *Cornbread and Caviar*, 153).

Jones University has done 1200 miles away." After his Los Angeles campaign, he called Jones, Sr., the "model toward which we are patterning our lives." In an apparent attempt to make amends with Jones, Jr., he mailed a request to Jones, Sr. "Give my love to Dr. Bob Jr., as there is no man in the world that I love more than I do him. You may rest assured that if the Lord should take you Home first, I shall stand by Bob with everything I have."[142] In 1950 Graham held a campaign in Columbia, South Carolina. He was invited to Greenville in conjunction with that meeting and held a rally for 6,000 people in the Rodeheaver Auditorium on the campus of Bob Jones University.

Graham entered the limelight when he was "discovered" in 1949 in his Los Angeles revival campaign.[143] He had had earlier campaigns in cities such as Grand Rapids, Michigan; Charlotte, North Carolina; Augusta, Georgia; Modesto, California; and Birmingham, England. It was the Los Angeles campaign, however, that brought him into the national spotlight. While at Northwestern he incorporated the Billy Graham Evangelistic Association in 1950, and when he left Northwestern in 1952, he went full time into evangelism.

As early as 1950, Ketcham had privately questioned Graham concerning rumors that modernists had been on the executive committees of some of his crusades, and by 1952 Ketcham was making public criticisms.[144] Rice had initially supported Graham, giving running accounts of each of his crusades in the *Sword of the Lord*. When Graham came under criticism from some segments of fundamentalism, Rice supported him.[145] In 1952 Graham attempted to calm any fears Rice had over his lack of separation: "Contrary to any rumors that are constantly

---

[142] Billy Graham to Bob Jones, Sr., 19 February 1949; 29 December 1949; and 23 October 1950, Bob Jones University Archives, Greenville, SC.

[143] Newspaper publisher William Randolph Hearst ordered his publicists to "puff Graham," insuring his status in the public eye. McLoughlin, *Modern Revivalism*, 480, 489.

[144] Billy Graham/Robert T. Ketcham correspondence, Palmer Muntz Papers, Collection 108, Box 1, Folder 1, Billy Graham Center Archives, Wheaton, Illinois. See also Robert T. Ketcham, "The Billy Graham Controversy," *Baptist Bulletin* 18 (December 1952): 6, 23–24.

[145] See, for instance, John R. Rice, "Billy Graham and Revival Critics," *Sword of the Lord* 17 (2 March 1951): 6–8.

floating about, we have never had a modernist on our Executive Committee and we have never been sponsored by the Council of Churches in any city except Shreveport and Greensboro—both small towns where the majority of the ministers are evangelical."[146] In 1955 after he spent a week at the Scotland Crusade and a weekend with Graham at his home in Montreat, North Carolina, Rice could boldly declare, "I am an out and out defender of Billy Graham."[147]

Within months, however, Rice acknowledged that he and Graham were going in different directions and accepted Graham's resignation from the board of the *Sword of the Lord*. Graham already had begun preparations for the 1957 New York crusade, which would identify him as an "ecumenical evangelist." The New York crusade severed whatever fragile relationship was left between fundamentalists and the new evangelicals. Prior to that crusade, Graham had usually been sponsored by Bible-believing pastors in the area.[148] In this crusade, Graham had not only included modernists in his advance campaign, he had rejected the invitation of the fundamentalists and required that the New York City ministerial alliance invite him to the city.[149] The split between fundamentalism and new evangelicalism was confirmed. Graham declared at the NAE national convention in Buffalo, "I am not a Fundamentalist" and "God has bypassed extreme fundamentalism."[150] Bob Jones, Sr., believed that Graham was "prostituting the office of the

---

[146] John R. Rice, "Billy Graham Seattle Campaign Reviewed," *Sword of the Lord* 18 (6 June 1952): 9.

[147] John R. Rice, "Questions Answered About Billy Graham," *Sword of the Lord* 21 (17 June 1955): 9.

[148] See McCune, *Promise Unfulfilled*, 47–55 for a detailed discussion of declarations from Graham and his associates prior to the New York Crusade that Graham had never been sponsored by liberals and the contrasting pattern of including select liberal pastors and leaders that had been developing in earlier Graham crusades.

[149] The alienation of Graham and the fundamentalists is documented in Butler F. Porter, Jr., *Billy Graham and the End of Evangelical Unity* (PhD diss., University of Florida, 1976).

[150] John R. Rice, "Billy Graham Openly Repudiates Fundamentalism," *Sword of the Lord* 23 (17 May 1957): 2, 10.

evangelist" and was giving "recognition to the anti-Christ."[151] So significant was this division that at the grass roots level one's allegiance to fundamentalism or new evangelicalism was often reduced to a single question, "Are you for or against Billy Graham?"[152]

In 1956 the first major presentation of the theological views of the new evangelicals appeared in an article in *Christian Life* magazine entitled "Is Evangelical Theology Changing?" The contributors included Edward J. Carnell and Carl F. H. Henry.[153] The article identified seven characteristics of this new evangelicalism: a friendly attitude toward science, a re-examination of the work of the Holy Spirit, a move away from dispensationalism, an emphasis on scholarship, more emphasis on social responsibility, a re-examination of the doctrine of Biblical inspiration, a more tolerant attitude toward varying views of eschatology, and a dialogue with liberal theologians.[154] The fundamentalists were highly disappointed with this article. They viewed the leadership of new evangelicalism as a group of compromisers who were abandoning the fundamentals of the faith in order to be accepted by the larger theological world.[155]

In 1957 *Christianity Today* began with Carl H. F. Henry as editor. It was designed to insert a conservative viewpoint into the mainstream of American and European theology. Fundamentalists saw it otherwise. Ketcham identified four specific problems with the new magazine: no separatists were included in the organization; the magazine cast a favorable light on neo-orthodoxy, especially Karl Barth; the magazine

---

[151] Bob Jones, "About Billy Graham's New York Crusade: Dr. Bob Jones Says," *Sword of the Lord* 23 (3 May 1957): 12.

[152] Ernest Pyles, "Bruised, Bloody and Broken: Fundamentalism's Internecine Controversy in the 1960s," *Fides et Historia* 18 (October 1986): 50.

[153] "Is Evangelical Theology Changing?" *Christian Life* 8 (March 1956): 16–19.

[154] Ibid. See also Vernon Grounds, "The Nature of Evangelicalism," *Eternity* 7 (February 1956): 12–13, 42–43.

[155] For samples of fundamentalist reactions see John R. Rice, "Can Theology Change?" *Christian Life* 8 (May 1956): 3; Chester Tulga, "More Than Evangelicals," *Sword of the Lord* 22 (27 July 1956): 1-5; and Robert Ketcham, "A New Peril in our Last Days," *Christian Beacon* 21 (17 May 1956): 2, 6–7.

"slapped" the separatists in articles such as "The Perils of Independency"; and the magazine only mildly criticized the World Council of Churches.[156]

By 1959, when Edward J. Carnell's *The Case for Orthodox Theology* first appeared, fundamentalism and new evangelicalism were split. Carnell's book hardened both positions further. In an attempt to present a positive portrayal of his idea of biblical Christianity, Carnell attacked fundamentalism for its militancy and "cultic" attitude.[157] Rice's response was representative of the broader fundamentalist reaction: "We believe that Christians should avoid those who cause doubts about the historic Christian faith, those who attack fundamental Bible believers, those who set out to slander and demean those who contend for the faith."[158]

The lines of separation were not always clear and men often moved from one camp to the other. In the 1940s McIntire's Faith Seminary produced men like Kenneth Kantzer, Vernon Grounds, Francis Schaeffer, and Douglas Young, men who in the 1950s would become leaders in new evangelicalism. On the other hand, J. Oliver Buswell (former president of Wheaton College and nominee for the Agenda Committee at the first NAE meeting in 1942) became president of the National Bible Institute (later Shelton College), which was affiliated with the ACCC. John R. Rice had been an active member of the NAE in the 1940s and encouraged other fundamentalists to join.[159] Billy Graham, Harold Ockenga, J. Elwin Wright, and Vernon Grounds wrote articles for the *Sword* in the 1940s and early 1950s. Billy Graham was part of the *Sword's* Cooperating Board. Bob Jones, Sr., was one of the original signers of the proposed agenda at the 1942 NAE meeting and helped direct the program for religious broadcasting.[160] In 1950 he was nominated as the second vice-president

---

[156] Robert Ketcham, "Christianity Today—An Analysis," *Baptist Bulletin* 22 (March 1957): 8–9, 21. See also John R. Rice, "New Magazine: 'Not Anti-Anything,'" *Sword of the Lord* 22 (13 July 1956): 2; and Carl McIntire, "Christianity in Eclipse," *Christian Beacon* 21 (25 October 1956): 1, 8.

[157] Edward J. Carnell, *The Case for Orthodox Theology* (Philadelphia: Westminster, 1959).

[158] John R. Rice, "Fuller Seminary's Carnell Sneers Fundamentalism," *Sword of the Lord* 22 (30 October 1956): 7, 11.

[159] John R. Rice, "National Association of Evangelicals Convention: Columbus, Ohio, April 12–17," *Sword of the Lord* 10 (24 March 1944): 1, 3.

[160] Murch, *Cooperation without Compromise*, 77, 113.

of the association.[161] He was a frequent contributor to the *United Evangelical Action*, the official journal of the NAE.

Until 1945 Rice and Jones had maintained their membership in the NAE, but also maintained close friendships with McIntire and Ketcham. Both Rice and Jones were evangelists and undoubtedly looked to the NAE as an impetus for revival in America. In 1945, however, the NAE denied both Rice and Jones the right to organize nationwide conferences on evangelism under the aegis of the NAE. Rice soon left the organization.[162]

Likewise, the Jones family struggled with their involvement in the NAE. As early as 1944, NAE secretary Ralph T. Davis indicated "it is going to be very hard to recommend [Bob Jones College] in the future."[163] In 1950 the Association refused to include Bob Jones University in their annual list of "NAE Approved Schools." The Joneses' concern over the openness of the young NAE leaders such as Ockenga and Henry was growing, and they called such men as those two "traitors" who turned the association into a "bridge to liberalism."[164] When elected vice-president of the NAE in 1950, Jones, Jr., felt he was being used as a political pawn by the more progressive members of the association in an attempt to deceive separatists. He refused the position and left the organization.[165]

---

[161] "New Officers and Commissions," *United Evangelical Action* 9 (1 May 1950): 6.

[162] John R. Rice, "Our Life Long Fight Against Modernism," *Sword of the Lord* 24 (2 May 1958): 11; and John R. Rice, "If We Compromise What Happens?" *Sword of the Lord* 24 (9 May 1958): 12.

[163] Ralph T. Davis to Harry Ironside, 28 April 1944, Records of the African Inland Mission, Collection 81, Box 8, Folder 61, Billy Graham Center Archives, Wheaton, Illinois.

[164] Jones, *Cornbread and Caviar*, 103.

[165] Ibid., 104, 108. In a letter to James Murch and a later letter to the NAE, Bob Jones, Sr., withdrew officially from the NAE (Bob Jones, Sr., to James DeForest Murch, 26 July 1950, Bob Jones, Sr., to NAE, 6 September 1950, Records of the Evangelical Foreign Mission Association, Billy Graham Center Archives, Wheaton, Illinois).

Conclusion

Early fundamentalism was an amalgamation of forces that had developed in opposition to theological liberalism. Men such as D. L. Moody had popularized the conflict between conservatives and liberals. The prophetic Bible conferences united the conservatives across denominational lines. These conferences bequeathed to fundamentalism an attitude of cooperation, a premillennial eschatology, lists of "essentials" (although there was never a single, definitive list), and the start of the fundamentalist organizations. The denominational warriors waged the conflict. Later fundamentalists resolved the conflict; they left or were driven out of the denominations.

Fuller Seminary had been formed, Ockenga had called for a "new evangelicalism" different from the old evangelicalism or fundamentalism of the previous decades, and Carnell and Henry had attacked the various negatives of fundamentalism. This division culminated in 1957 when Billy Graham joined forces with the modernists in his New York crusade. From that time on, the fundamentalism represented by McIntire, Jones, Rice, and numerous others clearly understood itself as continuing the line of militant, anti-modernist fundamentalism of the 1920s and 30s. The new evangelicals associated with the National Association of Evangelicals, Fuller Seminary, and *Christianity Today* sought to return to the irenic evangelicalism of the nineteenth century, although the culture and worldview of the nineteenth century were never to return.

Chapter 3

FUNDAMENTALIST
VIEWS OF THE CHURCH

The ecclesiology of fundamentalism was characterized by the American emphasis on individualism and volunteerism and by a dispensational hermeneutic. Fundamentalists demonstrated greater dispensational thought than evangelicals but still had those who held to covenant theology among them. Most fundamentalists accepted the doctrine of a universal and/or invisible church, although their emphasis was on the local, visible church. They emphasized the purity of the local church (and, in an extension of that, the purity of the denomination or association to which the church belonged). It was their common belief that the purity of the church or denomination took precedence over the unity of that individual church, denomination, or even Christianity as a whole. This adherence to purity was a core distinctive of fundamentalism.

The doctrine of the church was intrinsic to the fundamentalist movement. In his 1923 attack on liberalism J. Gresham Machen wrote:

> But what is the trouble with the visible Church? What is the reason for its obvious weakness? There are perhaps many causes of weakness. But one cause is perfectly plain—the Church of today has been unfaithful to her Lord by admitting great companies of non-Christian persons, not only into her membership, but into her teaching agencies. . . . What is now meant is not the admission of individuals whose confessions of faith may not be sincere, but the admission of great companies of persons who have never made any really adequate confession of faith at all and whose entire attitude toward the gospel is the very reverse of the Christian attitude.[1]

While Machen was concerned with the unfaithfulness of the Presbyterian denomination as a whole, he was also concerned with the potential sin of schism. As a loyal Presbyterian, he struggled with the difficulty of separating from his denomination.

---

[1] Machen, *Christianity and Liberalism*, 159.

If anything was clear to Machen it was that schism is sin. But he also knew that there were those in the church of his youth who in effect denied the Christ on whom the church is founded. When the church no longer proclaimed the substitutionary death of Christ as central to its preaching, it was no longer the church of Christ.[2]

This attitude expanded among the next generation of fundamentalism. The fundamentalists did not make separation their primary function; separation for them was a result of their desire to maintain obedience to the Word of God and the purity of the church.

It was not the fundamentalists alone who saw a distinctive ecclesiology to be at the heart of the division between fundamentalism and the new evangelicalism. At his inaugural address during Fuller Seminary's first year of operation, Ockenga decried fundamentalist ecclesiology.[3] He undoubtedly had reference to the premillennial, dispensational view of the church so common to the fundamentalist movement. While not all fundamentalists were thoroughgoing dispensationalists, the movement drew support from a premillennial pessimism about the future of the church.[4] The dispensational teaching regarding the apostasy of the church was important in the development of fundamentalist views of the church.[5] Fundamentalists generally taught that apostasy had set in early in church history. Passages such as 2 Timothy 3:1–7, interpreted from a dispensational point of view, taught that the last days would be preceded by large-scale apostasy, eventually led by the Antichrist who would use apostate churches and denominations to carry out his purposes. The result would be the total

---

[2] Cornelius Van Til, *The New Evangelicalism*, photocopy (Philadelphia: Westminster, n.d.), 10.

[3] Ockenga, "Foreword," 11.

[4] Most of the fundamentalists were premillennialists; the Scofield Reference Bible was their common Bible. Scofield described the visible church as "that visible body of professed believers called, collectively, 'the Church.' . . . The predicted future of the visible Church is apostasy (Lk. 18. 8; 2 Tim 3. 1–8)." Scofield, *Scofield Reference Bible*, 1276.

[5] "It is impossible to overestimate the importance of this ecclesiology for the history of Fundamentalism." Sandeen, "Toward a Historical Interpretation," 69.

leavening of professing Christendom and the rise of the Babylon church of Revelation 17 and 18.[6]

The fundamentalists' viewpoint required them to separate from the apostate church and preserve the purity of the true church until the Lord returned. An emphasis on personal holiness, predicated by the dispensational view of an imminent Second Coming, demanded removing oneself from worldly practices on a personal level and from doctrinally-corrupt churches and denominations on an ecclesiastical level.[7] Fundamentalists believed they could separate without being schismatic. By rejecting the universal church as the only or primary church, they refused to identify separation as schism. They believed that faithfulness to the Word of God took precedence over faithfulness to any human organization or any human fellowship.

The early fundamentalists struggled to define clearly what they meant by the term "separation," although they frequently used it, repeated numerous biblical texts favoring separation, and even illustrated how they would apply separation to particular situations. They did not initially establish definitive limitations of the term, nor did they very frequently clearly distinguish whether they meant personal separation or ecclesiastical separation. As time went by, however, they more carefully clarified and refined their view of fellowship and separation.

The doctrine of the church was part (although certainly not all) of the rationale for ecclesiastical separation. While there was no absolute agreement in the ecclesiologies of the leading fundamentalists, there was an identifiable core to their combined ecclesiology, a central concept of

---

[6] McIntire argued that "Babylon the Great" would be the World Council of Churches. *The Testimony of Separation*, 101. See also Carl McIntire, *Servants of Apostasy* (Collingswood, NJ: Christian Beacon, 1955), 257–58. The more common position was expressed by Scofield, who spoke of "ecclesiastical Babylon which is apostate Christendom, headed up under the Papacy" (Scofield, *Scofield Reference Bible*, 1346). Bob Jones, Jr., believed the "Roman Catholic Church is described in the seventeenth chapter of the book of The Revelation, where she is depicted as the 'great whore'" (Campbell, *Spectrum of Protestant Beliefs*, 89). Fundamentalists of that time were convinced the World Council would lead Protestant Christianity back to the fold of the Roman Church.

[7] Timothy Weber, *Living in the Shadow of the Second Coming: American Premillennialism, 1875–1925* (New York: Oxford, 1979), 58.

the church which helped inform the character of the separatism of fundamentalism.

It is the purpose of this chapter to delineate, as far as possible, the identifying characteristics of the ecclesiology of the fundamentalists. The areas of significance among fundamentalists centered on the meaning of *ekklesia*, the church's authority, the membership of the church, the relationship between the visible, invisible, universal, and local churches, and the relationship between unity and purity within the church

The Meaning of "Church"

Fundamentalists agreed that the New Testament used the word *ekklesia* in a minimum of three ways: first, of Israel in the wilderness; second, of a mob of idolaters in Ephesus; and third, of local assemblies of Christians (the most common use of the term). Some, but not all, added a fourth use, that of a universal church. Among those who held to a universal church, some, like C. I. Scofield, believed the universal church had a present existence, while others, such as many in the General Association of Regular Baptist Churches, saw the universal church only as an eschatological reality.[8] Rice distinguished between the first two uses of *ekklesia* as "churches" (perhaps "assemblies" or "congregations" would be more appropriate) and the last two as "Christian churches."[9]

John Rice was typical of most fundamental Baptists and dispensationalists when he rejected any concept of a "Christian Church" in the Old Testament. He wrote in response to a letter concerning Reformed theology, "I think you need not take seriously the rather foolish

---

[8] This was the position promoted by some early members of the General Association of Regular Baptist Churches and a portion of the Conservative Baptist Association. "There will be no way to come into the full realization of the 'bride' aspect of the Church until our Lord comes back for His bride. . . . There will be a day when all the *redeemed* will be molded into one united whole." R. L. Powell, "My Church," *Baptist Bulletin* (December 1954): 25.

[9] John R. Rice, "'Churches' and 'The Church,'" in *Twelve Tremendous Themes* (Wheaton: Sword of the Lord, 1943), 149. This chapter appeared in the *Sword of the Lord* under the same title in 1935, 1941, and 1956. John R. Rice, "'Churches' and 'The Church,'" *Sword of the Lord* 1 (7 June 1935): 1–3; 7 (30 May 1941): 1–4; 22 (19 October 1956): 7, 11–12.

'claim' that the church is Israel because Stephen called Israel the church in the wilderness." The "church" is a called-out assembly and thus Israel was a "church," but not the "Christian" church.[10]

Carl McIntire based his theological positions on the standard Presbyterian confessions.

> The Twentieth Century Reformation is doctrinal, not sociological. It is based on teaching, not eccentric behavior or some hysterical hybrid of evangelicalism. It is fundamental because it is based on the very fundamentals of the Christian faith. . . . It is dedicated to reforming the church in the same way the sixteenth-century Reformation reformed the church. It is therefore a Twentieth Century Reformation. It proclaims the evangelical Gospel; but its chief concern is not evangelistic crusades—therefore it prefers being called fundamentalist to being called evangelical. . . .
>
> Fundamentalism is confessional Christianity. Evangelicalism, many times, is not. . . .
>
> Doctrine, then, its purity and preservation, is basically the fundamental cause.[11]

The Westminster Confession defined the visible church as that which consists of all those in the world who profess the true religion and the invisible church as the whole number of the elect. Oliver Buswell, a close associate of McIntire and a fellow Presbyterian confessionalist, agreed: "Through the invisible Church the Spirit moves to express the redemptive program of God in the visible Church."[12] He, like McIntire, accepted the Westminster definition of the catholic (universal), invisible church, which "consists of the whole number of the elect that have been, are, or shall be gathered into one, under Christ the Head thereof."[13] While Buswell was influenced by dispensational thought, this view of the church is in keeping with the more typical covenant concept of a church in both

---

[10] John R. Rice, "Reformed and Covenant Doctrine," *Sword of the Lord* 20 (5 November 1954): 3.

[11] Carl McIntire, "Twentieth Century Reformation," *Christian Beacon* 31 (23 June 1966): 3.

[12] J. Oliver Buswell, Jr., "The American and International Councils of Christian Churches," *Christianity Today* 9 (29 January 1965): 429.

[13] James Oliver Buswell, *A Systematic Theology of the Christian Religion* (Grand Rapids: Zondervan, 1962), 2: 216.

biblical testaments. He realized that the visible church would never be perfect in this world, but he did insist on a regenerate membership.

While the Presbyterian fundamentalists maintained the typical Presbyterian Church organization, the ease with which they left one presbytery and started another showed their acknowledgement of a more autonomous Presbyterian church. The churches were free to leave one denomination and join another based on theological purity and belief.

Bob Jones, Sr., argued that no ecclesiastical organization, be it Lutheran, Roman Catholic, Methodist, or Baptist, was *the* church of the Scriptures. Jones rejected the ecumenical movement because he believed it was an attempt to build a unity of apostate ecclesiastical organizations. While he did not write a significant amount on the doctrine of the church, his actions spoke loudly. Jones had been a member of the Methodist-Episcopal Church, South, and served as an evangelist for that denomination. In spite of modernist inroads, he decided "to remain in the denomination . . . supporting that which is orthodox and . . . refusing to support that which is not."[14]

In the 1930s, however, a problem developed between Jones and his denomination. The Secretary of the Home Department, General Work, wrote to Bob Jones, Sr., about complaints concerning meetings in places where the pastors of the local Methodist-Episcopal churches objected to his coming.[15] In keeping with the fundamentalist belief in individualism, Jones emphasized the autonomy of his own ministry. He told the Secretary, "Because of the interdenominational part of our program it has been impossible for us to follow the usual routine of organization. . . . I am perfectly willing to hand in my resignation at any moment you wish it."[16] Although Jones remained an authorized Methodist-Episcopal evangelist for a few more years, there was continuing friction between him and his church authorities.

---

[14] Bob Jones, Sr., to Rev. M. A. Stephenson, 5 September 1939, Bob Jones University Archives, Bob Jones University, Greenville, SC.

[15] J. W. Perry to Bob Jones, Sr., 31 March 1932, Fundamentalism Room, Mack Library, Bob Jones University, Greenville, SC.

[16] Bob Jones, Sr., to J. W. Perry, April 2, 1932, Fundamentalism Room, Mack Library, Bob Jones University, Greenville, SC.

In 1939 the Joneses left the Broad Street (Methodist) Church in Cleveland, Tennessee (where Bob Jones College was located at the time), because the pastor allowed a modernist to preach.[17] Shortly thereafter, the *Alabama Christian Advocate* refused to carry advertisements for Bob Jones College, arguing that the college was in reality a slap at Methodist schools.[18] Jones was not yet ready to leave the Methodist denomination; instead, he sought to find a church with a fundamentalist pastor and place his membership there. Bob Jones, Jr., stated, in reference to his and his father's position on ecclesiastical separation, "Our position—both mine and my father's—was that as long as we had a pastor who preached the Word of God and tried to drive away strange and erroneous doctrine, we would try to stay in but not support the program and do what we could to encourage that pastor."[19] This attitude began to change as they developed a later militancy for the necessity of complete separation from all forms of apostasy.[20] Eventually they left Methodism and joined the Christian Missionary Alliance, but soon left that denomination and joined an independent Baptist church, remaining members there the rest of their lives.

The General Association of Regular Baptist Churches formed in 1932 in reaction to the liberalism of the Northern Baptist Convention. These Baptists viewed each local church as totally independent. The decisions of the Association were not binding on the churches in the Association.

> [N]o church *must* cooperate or lose its place in the Fellowship. No matter how good and right the "common task" might be, each local church is the sole judge as to the measure and extent of its cooperation. Baptist churches must always be left free to determine their own program. We believe the GARBC offers a Scriptural and Baptistic

---

[17] Jones, *Cornbread and Caviar*, 73–74.

[18] *Little Mody's Post*, Spring 1940, Bob Jones University Archives, Bob Jones University, Greenville, SC; quoted in Dalhouse, *Island in the Lake of Fire*, 51.

[19] Jones, *Cornbread and Caviar*, 1–2. There is very little theological information from Bob Jones, Jr. He stated about theology: "I find most of it [theological reading] deadly dull and try to avoid it. The Bible and the great preachers I listened to in Bob Jones College chapel and Bible Conferences taught me my theology" (Jones, *Cornbread and Caviar*, 44).

[20] See, for instance, Bob Jones, Jr., *Scriptural Separation: First and Second Degree Separation* (Greenville, SC: Bob Jones University, 1971).

program of advance and common interest, but each church is ever free to say how much it will help. There should be cooperation. There will be no coercion. The GARBC offers to all its churches a constraining motive but never degenerates into a compelling machine. It is not a dictatorship. It is a partnership.[21]

The fundamentalists were agreed in viewing the meaning of *ekklesia* to be that of solely, or at least primarily, the New Testament local church, with the individual freedom to join the church of one's choice and the church's freedom, but not necessity, of being part of a larger organization which has no control of or authority over the independent churches. That the Baptists among fundamentalism should insist on autonomous local churches and their freedom from denominational influences should not be surprising. That the Presbyterian wing of fundamentalism should exercise a similar type of autonomy shows that the individualism of fundamentalism took precedence over the authority of any larger group outside the local church.

When the Church Began

An important consideration in the fundamentalist definition of *ekklesia* was the determination concerning when the church began. Because of the influence of dispensationalism, most fundamentalists viewed Pentecost as the starting point of the church. Not all fundamentalists, however, were thoroughgoing dispensationalists.

John Rice was a "soft" dispensationalist. While he used and appreciated the *Scofield Reference Bible*, he rejected Scofield's belief that the church began at Pentecost.

Rice's belief that Pentecost was not the beginning of the church (or the new dispensation) was based on several arguments. First, Rice believed that the Holy Spirit indwelled and filled believers prior to Pentecost. Second, Rice believed that Christ was discussing a present reality in Matthew 16:18. "'I will be building, indicat[es] a continuous process. The Lord is *not* discussing the *origin* or *beginning* of His church,

---

[21] Robert T. Ketcham, "What Is the General Association of Regular Baptist Churches?" General Association of Regular Baptist Churches Archive Collection, 2. http://wprnd.net/ garbc/ wp-content/ uploads /2007/01/what_is_garbc.pdf.

but the process of its growth." Third, Rice argued that the Bible never declared that the church began at Pentecost. Acts 2, Acts 11, and Hebrews 2:4, all of which refer to Pentecost, do not state that it began then. Fourth, Rice viewed Matthew 18:17 as indicative that the church existed before Pentecost, since Christ would not give instructions for discipline in the church unless it already existed. Finally, the universal church could not have been born at Pentecost because of its very nature. The image of the church as a building shows that it is not born, but it is being built. If the beginning of a house is the laying of the first stone, then the universal church began when the first soul was saved.[22]

Oliver Buswell, a Presbyterian fundamentalist, also believed that the church started in the Old Testament. He did not argue the position but simply assumed it. Basing his definition of *ekklesia* on the Westminster Confession, he focused his attention on how the church in the Old Testament functioned.[23]

Most fundamentalists, however, separated the church from Israel and argued that the church started at Pentecost. Lewis Sperry Chafer gives a typical argument. "Things cannot be the same in this age as they were in the past age, after the death of Christ has taken place, His resurrection, His ascension, and the advent of the Spirit on Pentecost."[24] He then presents four arguments for starting the church at Pentecost. First, there could be no church without the death of Christ. The church's "relation to that death is not a mere anticipation, but is based wholly on His finished work and she must be purified by His precious blood." The second argument is that there could be no church without Christ's resurrection. Third, there could be no church until Jesus had ascended on high to become the head of the church. This argument has two points: Christ is the head of the church based on the federal headship of the resurrected Christ, and the church could not survive without Christ's intercession in heaven. The final argument that Chafer raised is that there can be no church without the advent of the Holy Spirit, for whom the church is the temple. The church is regenerated, baptized, and sealed by the Spirit.

---

[22] John R. Rice, "Christ Builds His Church," *Sword of the Lord* 22 (13 January 1956): 3.

[23] Buswell, *Systematic Theology*, 1:418-19.

[24] Lewis Sperry Chafer, *Systematic Theology* (Grand Rapids: Kregel, 1976 reprint), 45.

Chafer concluded, "A Church without the finished work on which to stand; a Church without resurrection position or life; a Church which is a new humanity, but lacking a federal head; and a Church without Pentecost and all that Pentecost contributes, is only a figment of theological fancy and wholly extraneous to the New Testament."[25]

Fundamentalism, then, was divided in its arguments concerning when the church began. While the majority of fundamentalists were dispensational and therefore argued that the church began at Pentecost, there was an element of fundamentalism that argued for an Old Testament church. The difference between evangelical and fundamentalist ecclesiology cannot, therefore, be simply a difference between dispensationalism and covenant theology.

The Universal and Local Church

Another issue of concern for the fundamentalists was the relationship between the universal church and the local church. This has been a problem historically and has never been fully resolved in the various approaches to the doctrine of the church. Fundamentalists placed their emphasis on the local church. Some denied the existence of any other church but the local church, while others accepted, but downplayed the importance of, a universal or invisible concept.

Local churches are the entities through which God works in the New Testament era. Local congregations are made up of people who profess faith in Christ as their Savior. Local congregations baptize converts, receive people for membership, celebrate the Lord's Supper, and maintain their own positions on independence from or connections with any other local congregation. Local churches have elders or pastors and deacons or servants to minister in a variety of fashions.

For fundamentalists, the emphasis of Scripture is clearly on the local church. This is the most common use of the term *ekklesia*, with at least ninety such occurrences in the New Testament.

> [A] local congregation of Christians was never called *a part* of the church. . . . The Holy Spirit did not speak of "the church" in the province of Galatia, but of "the churches of Galatia." He did not speak of "the

---

[25] Chafer, *Systematic Theology*, 45-46.

church" in the cities of Asia, but of the seven "churches" of Asia. Every local congregation is a separate church, and these congregations are never put together to form one body called a church in Bible terminology.[26]

There is a difference in how a person becomes a member of the local church and how one becomes a member of the universal church. A person becomes a member of a local congregation by a voluntary act of the individual in choosing a church and the church in bringing that individual into its membership. That same person becomes a member of the universal church by the baptism of the Holy Spirit at salvation.[27]

For Rice, there was a genuine use of *ekklesia* to refer to the "great assembly of Christians to be called out at the second coming to meet Christ in the air and to be assembled in Heaven."[28] Hebrews 12:22, 23 is the key passage for this belief. This gathering met his definition of a church as a called-out assembly. It would be composed of all the saved of all ages. Rice believed this assembly would not be an aggregate of local churches, but of individual Christians, "without respect as to whether they were members of any local congregation or church."[29]

Buswell placed more emphasis on the connection between the local church and the universal church, in keeping with a more Presbyterian ecclesiology. His discussion of the church in his systematic theology is focused almost entirely on the universal church.[30] His discussion on the local church, interestingly, is placed in his section on Anthropology.[31] His basic conclusion is that the invisible church *is* pure; the local or visible church *should be* pure.

Fundamentalists generally made no distinction between the local and visible church and no distinction between the invisible and universal church. They viewed the visible church to be the individual local church and the invisible church to be the body of Christ or the universal church,

---

[26] Rice, "'Churches' and 'The Church,'" 151.

[27] Rice, "Questions and Answers on 'The Church,'" 2.

[28] Rice, "'Churches' and 'The Church,'" 152.

[29] Ibid., 153.

[30] Buswell, *Systematic Theology*, 2:216ff.

[31] Ibid., 1:418ff.

whether that body exists in the world at the present time or whether it is some future entity.

Fundamentalists occasionally accused the new evangelicals of making the invisible church a substitute for visible churches resulting, claimed Tulga, in theological weakness. "[Christians] can claim membership in the true church, while refusing to face up to their responsibility to be a part of a local New Testament church. Belonging to the true church, they say, justifies holding membership in false local churches."[32]

The Church and the Scriptures

Foundational to the fundamentalist ecclesiology was the belief that the Bible, and especially the New Testament, was not merely a starting point for an ongoing development of the doctrine of the church but was instead the required pattern for all times. This was a result of the literal interpretation commonly practiced by dispensationalists.

On December 26, 1959, under the leadership of Bob Jones, Jr., and John R. Rice, about one hundred fifty fundamentalists met in Chicago to reaffirm the fundamentals of the faith. The fundamentals they laid down were common themes from the earlier fundamentalist conferences and writings: the inspiration, authority, and infallibility of the Scriptures; the deity, virgin birth, atoning death, resurrection, and future return of Jesus Christ; man's fallen nature and thus the need for regeneration; salvation by grace through faith; and the Great Commission.[33] There was no willingness to accept the possibility of the development of new doctrines but only an emphasis on the historic doctrines of the past.

Rice believed that a person should be a member of a church that "demands the new birth before membership, a local church that controls its own affairs."[34] In spite of a frequent nondenominational spirit, Rice was a Baptist. As such, there were some issues concerning church polity

---

[32] Chester Tulga, "Fundamentalism: Past and Future," *Sword of the Lord* 23 (4 October 1957): 12. Tulga, a Baptist, was one of the more theologically inclined of the fundamentalists. He wrote frequently for the *Sword* during its battles with new evangelicalism.

[33] Rice, "Christian Leaders Dec. 26," 5.

[34] Rice, "The Editor Answers: Bible Questions," 2.

on which he took a strong stand based on his understanding of the New Testament. For instance, he believed in baptism by immersion. "I do not approve nor accept any kind of baptism except baptism by immersion and of saved people only. . . . I cannot approve or endorse baptism which is not right in Bible doctrine otherwise."[35]

McIntire also believed that the Bible was the only authority for the church. He believed that there were core evangelical doctrines common to all Protestant churches.

> One of them is that the Bible is the infallible, inerrant word of God. Another, which has always been recognized, is that the church must maintain its own purity and integrity. This is the reason men take vows of ordination and installation.[36]

McIntire declared that the "one message and mission of the church is to hold before men the Word of God, the Bible, nothing more, nothing less—the whole counsel of God."[37] This was a major theme in McIntire's writings. He made constant comparisons between the International Council of Christian Churches and the World Council of Churches, but one of the main distinctives was their basis of authority.

> The World Council of Churches includes the modernists and neo-orthodox who accept the conclusions of the higher critics. The International Council of Christian Churches includes only those who stand by the historic position of the church, believing that an infallible, inerrant Bible is not only defensible from a scholarly and critical standpoint, but that it is also the truth of God.[38]

Bob Jones, Sr., also believed that the Bible was the sole authority for the church. He divided Scripture into essentials and non-essentials. In a veiled critique of new evangelicalism, Jones stated:

> In speaking of a divided church, I do not refer to divisions that have arisen concerning the non-essentials; I refer to the divisions that have come about with regard to eternal essentials of Christianity. Practically

---

[35] Rice, "The Orthodox Baptist Tradition," 2.

[36] McIntire, *The Testimony of Separation*, 5.

[37] Carl McIntire, *Modern Tower of Babel* (Collingswood, NJ: Christian Beacon, 1949), 85.

[38] Ibid., 126–27.

all Protestant denominations are supposed to believe what we call the fundamentals of the Faith. The house is divided, however, because of some leaders who repudiate the creeds they are supposed to believe. Strangely, some people are pleading for harmony in spite of the division. Jesus warns that "a divided house or kingdom will have desolation."[39]

Jones defined the essential doctrines to be the Bible as the verbally-inspired Word of God and Jesus Christ as God incarnate, who gave up his own life freely and rose from the dead. For Jones, there was no salvation outside of Christ; "these are the eternal essentials of the faith."[40] He argued that no one who believed these essentials could support a denomination that rejected them. Such a person "is violating the clear teaching of the Word of God by bidding Godspeed to those who deny the doctrines of Christ."[41] Biblical unity for Jones was "good, sound, Bible-believing, orthodox Christians . . . working together *as individuals,* regardless of their ecclesiastical affiliation."[42]

Tulga argued that before the development of modernism, Christians were almost universally convinced that there was a definite body of truth delivered to the church (Jude 3), although they did not always agree on exactly which of their various interpretations constituted that body of truth. They did agree, however, on the source of that truth: the Scriptures. This truth was to be defended and preserved; it also served as the basis for fellowship. In the early twentieth century, modernism had sought to invalidate Scripture as the rule of authority and therefore had concluded that the teachings of Scripture could not be used to limit fellowship. Experience became the source of truth and basis for fellowship. In the middle of the twentieth century, fundamentalism became concerned that evangelicalism was following the same path modernism had taken. The fundamentalists believed especially that the new birth was being interpreted so loosely and broadly that it had come to mean almost any kind of religious experience. Because of this,

---

[39] Bob Jones, Sr., "Comments on here and hereafter," *Faith for the Family* 3 (May/June 1975), 39.

[40] Bob Jones, Sr., "Dr. Bob Jones Says," *Sword of the Lord* 22 (14 September 1956): 10.

[41] Ibid.

[42] Ibid.

evangelicals could consider almost all modernists as Christians on the basis of their experience, no matter what their doctrine was.[43]

Fundamentalists were also concerned that evangelicals were replacing dispensational hermeneutics with a historical approach, abandoning "that biblical literalism which opens the Word of God to the average man or woman, and [making theology] a field for specialists for which it was never intended."[44]

Fundamentalism was convinced that the church must be subordinate to the Scriptures. The Bible, and the Bible alone, was the church's authority. Fundamentalists separated from those who placed tradition, experience, or any other human authority over or beside Scripture.

The Membership of the Church

Fundamentalists were agreed that only believers should be members of the church. They agreed with the evangelicals that the universal church was composed only of believers, but they went a step further, arguing that there should be no unbelievers in the membership of a local or visible church or denomination.

Jones, Sr., believed that the church is for believers only. "The *ecclesia* is composed of the 'called out' ones—those who have been born of the Spirit of God through faith in Jesus Christ."[45] He declared that they are "out of every kindred, and tongue, and people, and nation," quoting from Rev 5:9.

Rice believed that there should be no one in the church who was not already a born-again child of God. He noted that in the New Testament model no one could be accepted for baptism or any other Christian rite or into church membership until that person had trusted Christ as Savior. He argued against those who believed that church membership could include not only the saved, but also those who hoped to be saved and the children of the saved.[46] He rejected infant baptism, since to his way of

---

[43] Tulga, "More Than Evangelicals," 4.

[44] Ibid., 5.

[45] Campbell, *Spectrum of Protestant Beliefs*, 75.

[46] Rice, *Come Out or Stay In*, 42.

thinking this would only populate the church with unregenerate members.[47]

The one hundred and fifty fundamentalists that met in Chicago in 1959 declared:

> We believe that with brotherly love, Christians, as individuals, may properly co-operate with all who (1) claim and evidence in life saving faith in Christ as Saviour, (2) firmly believe and profess the above essentials of the faith, and (3) though they may differ on lesser matters of faith, do not make "doubtful disputations."[48]

The concern of the fundamentalists, however, was that evangelicalism was modifying the definition of the new birth, thus giving up the expectation that all church members be believers. In an obvious attack on Billy Graham, but without naming him, Rice argued:

> [A]ny evangelist who calls unbelievers Christians, who has enemies of the Bible lead in prayer, or who sends new converts or inquirers to churches which do not believe and preach the Bible as the perfectly revealed Word of God, and where their faith is likely to be destroyed, does wrong, whether his motives are good or bad.[49]

This, they believed, was a violation of 2 Cor. 6:14–18.

McIntire's denunciation of ecumenism and the World Council of Churches was based on his belief in a regenerate church membership. This requirement was so obvious to McIntire that he never actually defended it; it just seemed logical to him that those who refused to believe the Bible could not be part of the church. Beyond that, however, he also believed that fundamentalists alone had the right to be called "Christian," for anyone who rejected the historic doctrine of the church had given up that right.[50] In *Modern Tower of Babel, The Death of a*

---

[47] "No human proxy has a right to speak for a baby to have him baptized" (Rice, "Bible Doctrine of the Church," 12).

[48] Rice, "Christian Leaders," 5.

[49] Ibid.

[50] McIntire, *Twentieth Century Reformation*, 7. The reader needs to keep in mind that McIntire began writing in the 1940s, when the division in Christendom was between liberals and fundamentalists. The fundamentalist/evangelical division took place in the latter portion of his ministry. *Twentieth Century Reformation* was written in 1944.

Church, and *Twentieth Century Reformation*, McIntire documented the unregenerate state of the leaders of the World Council of Churches and the ecumenically-minded denominations in the United States. He argued time and again that modernism cannot be Christian.[51]

> There is what is called the modernist and fundamentalist groups and the modernist-fundamentalist controversy. We are a fundamentalist. . . . One is said to be a modernist Christian and another is said to be a fundamentalist Christian. Here is where the terminology is so disastrous. A man who calls himself a modernist is not a Christian. He cannot be. The things that he believes and teaches deny the very essentials of the Christian faith.[52]

McIntire's concern with the Federal Council of Churches was based on a simple fact: "The Federal Council asks unbelievers to join in such an intimate, holy union [discussing the union of Christ and the believers in John 17], without first even asking them to become believers in the Lord Jesus Christ."[53]

Concern over the issue of a regenerate church membership carried over to the evangelistic efforts of fundamentalism. In one sense, the issues raised by the doctrine of ecclesiastical separation did not come into any sharper focus than in evangelism. Fundamentalists insisted that winning souls was the domain of the churches. "The American Council brethren believe that evangelism is primarily the function of the

---

[51] In the *Twentieth Century Reformation*, McIntire explicated the theologies of men such as Henry Sloane Coffin, Francis McConnell, and Harry Emerson Fosdick, calling them "Men Who Deny the Faith" (McIntire, *Twentieth Century Reformation*, 29–56). In his *Modern Tower of Babel*, McIntire explored the theologies of men such as John C. Bennett, G. Bromley Oxnam, William B. Pugh, Henry P. Van Dusen, and other leaders of the ecumenical church, calling them "Angels of Light" (McIntire, *Modern Tower of Babel*, 137–206). In both of these books, McIntire delineated the departure of modernists and ecumenical churches from traditional Christianity and argued that they had no right to represent Christianity and no right even to claim the name Christian. For instance, McIntire stated, "Without the resurrection there is no Christianity. What Dr. Bennett offers is not Christianity at all. It is another religion." McIntire, *Modern Tower of Babel*, 141.

[52] McIntire, *Twentieth Century Reformation*, 4–5.

[53] Ibid., 23.

church."[54] Rice and Jones were both evangelists. They both held what they called "union meetings." While Rice was a Baptist and Jones a Methodist, they routinely crossed denominational lines in their meetings. Jones, for instance, spoke of Baptist, Presbyterian, and Methodist preachers visiting his meetings.[55] However, he insisted that "Christian cooperation never means compromising with modernism."[56]

Fundamentalists contrasted this with Graham's cooperative evangelism, an important issue in the controversy with the new evangelicals. Robert O. Ferm wrote a defense of Graham's evangelistic methods, using a variety of practical, biblical, and theological arguments.[57] Rice critiqued Ferm's book in a number of areas, but his main criticism was Graham's use of modernists who rejected the Bible, the historic Christian faith, the blood atonement, and whose "churches and pastors . . . are definitely unchristian."[58] Rice argued that the real issue between Graham and fundamentalists like himself was whether Christians and non-Christians could associate as sponsors, whether Bible-believers and infidels could serve together to promote revival campaigns, and whether converts could be turned over "to Christians and infidels alike."[59]

The fundamentalists were united in their belief that only the regenerate could be members of the churches and hence of the denominations. Since the unregenerate could not be members of a church, they likewise could not be involved in the ministry of a church, a denomination, or an evangelistic endeavor of any kind.

---

[54] McIntire, *The Testimony of Separation*, 86.

[55] Bob Jones, Sr., "Evangelism Today—Where Is It Headed" in *Do Right!* (Murfreesboro, Tenn.: Sword of the Lord, 1971), 193.

[56] Jones, "Evangelism Today," 188.

[57] Ferm, *Cooperative Evangelism*.

[58] John R. Rice, "Cooperative Evangelism," *Sword of the Lord* 24 (20 June 1958): 5.

[59] Ibid., 5.

Unity and Purity in the Church

The discussion of the relationship between unity in the churches (or unity in *the* church) and purity within the churches (or within *the* church) was a natural outcome of the preceding issues.[60] It was at this point that fundamentalism and evangelicalism developed strongly divergent views. Fundamentalism placed its emphasis on the purity of the church (and of the denomination), even at the price of unity, and criticized new evangelicalism for their "almost total lack of interest in purity of doctrine in the church of God."[61] Fundamentalists believed this was a direct result of "affirming the inspiration of the Word of God and disregarding its authority."[62] Tulga argued that "the fundamentalist watchword is 'Ye should earnestly contend for the faith.' The evangelical emphasis is 'Ye must be born again.'"[63]

The fundamentalist emphasis on doctrinal purity was not taken lightly. They believed that the custody of the faith was a sacred trust. The purity of this faith was more important to the cause of Christ than any institution. "Since the church was founded to spread the true faith, when this faith is corrupted and compromised, the reason for any church's existence is destroyed."[64] Not only was it important for fundamentalists to maintain their own doctrinal purity; they believed that "the founding of true New Testament churches is our God-given task."[65]

McIntire's view of purity was affected by Machen, who had influenced many in the generation of fundamentalists who followed him. McIntire declared of his relationship to Machen: "The principles espoused then and the stand taken have led inexorably on through the years in the

---

[60] It must be noted at this point that all too often the discussion of unity and purity was not the *result* of the preceding arguments, but the *cause*. In some instances the belief in ecclesiastical separation drove the theological discussions, instead of growing out of them. Theology frequently develops in this manner, however. Much of theology historically has grown out of crises.

[61] Tulga, "Fundamentalism: Past and Future," 12.

[62] Ibid.

[63] Ibid., 4.

[64] Chester Tulga, "The Christian and the Problem of Religious Unity," *Sword of the Lord* 25 (2 January 1959): 11.

[65] Ibid., 12.

struggle for the gospel and the purity of the church."[66] While McIntire always claimed to be a true Presbyterian, "many of his theological commitments and ecclesiastical practices were more akin to a broader fundamentalist movement that transcended denominational lines." Fea calls this a move from "fundamentalist Presbyterian" to "Presbyterian fundamentalist."[67] This fit the individualism, autonomy, and doctrinal purity inherent in fundamentalism.

McIntire was influenced by New School Presbyterianism, an Americanized version of Presbyterian theology and practice. The New School was strongly influenced by the revivals of the nineteenth century and adopted some of Nathaniel Taylor's "New Haven Theology."[68] There was an emphasis on volunteerism, interdenominationalism, millennialism, and the visible signs of faith, especially a conversion experience and a separated life.[69] McIntire rejected Machen's pure Reformed Presbyterianism, preferring instead a broader fundamentalist version of the church. He was also committed to his own modification of a dispensational interpretation of Scripture.[70]

McIntire and those who associated with him were so concerned about the purity of the church that they expressed no reluctance in leaving their denominations. In a 1936 editorial, McIntire rejected a plea

---

[66] Carl McIntire, "Dr. Machen," *Christian Beacon* 2 (7 January 1937): 4.

[67] Fea, "Carl McIntire," 257. He adds that McIntire appears several times in Marsden's *Reforming Fundamentalism*, but only for the purpose of contrasting his separatist brand of fundamentalism with the more open-minded new evangelicals at Fuller. Fea, "Carl McIntire," 154.

[68] Taylor graduated from Yale University and was influenced by its president, Timothy Dwight, the grandson of Jonathan Edwards. Taylor became the pastor at New Haven in 1812 and returned to Yale as professor in 1822. Appreciative of what was taking place in the Second Great Awakening, he developed a theology that merged Calvinism with Revivalism. See Douglas Sweeney, *Nathaniel Taylor, New Haven Theology, and the Legacy of Jonathan Edwards,* Religion in America Series (Oxford: Oxford University Press, 2002).

[69] See George Marsden, *The Evangelical Mind and the New School Presbyterian Experience* (New Haven: Yale University, 1970) and Marsden, "The New School Heritage," 129–147.

[70] Carl McIntire, "Premillennialism," *Christian Beacon* 1 (1 October 1936): 4.

for fundamentalists to remain in the Presbyterian Church and fight the modernists.

> "Nothing would suit the Modernists better than that the Conservatives in the Church should withdraw and leave them in peace," said Dr. Macartney [a fundamentalist in theology, but opposed to separation]. We believe the reverse to be true, "Nothing would suit the Modernists better than for the conservatives to remain in the church to be a smoke screen in this hour of the church's dethroning of Jesus Christ."
>
> If there are thousands of Bible believing Presbyterians of whom he speaks, then they should be fully informed of what is taking place and that they are remaining in the hulk of an old ship which has had the boiler room taken out and which is sinking; or, to change the figure, the ship which Dr. Macartney does not want to give up is the ship which has thrown overboard its only true captain, Jesus Christ, and has placed at the helm of the ship the will of the majority, to flounder the ship in the sea of naturalism.
>
> Such a ship is as good as sunk.[71]

Placing purity over unity, McIntire separated from the Presbyterian Church and joined Machen's Orthodox Presbyterian Church, only to later leave that denomination to start his own Bible Presbyterian Church. "Separation must take place in one of two ways, either the unbelievers must be put out or the Bible believers must withdraw; else the church ceases to be the church."[72]

Buswell also spoke of his work with J. Gresham Machen to purify the Presbyterian Church of theological liberals, particularly those who signed the Auburn Affirmation, which rejected the inerrancy of Scripture and declared that belief in the Virgin Birth, miracles, substitutionary atonement, and the bodily resurrection of Christ was not necessary for the Presbyterian ministry. When Machen and his disciples failed to purify their denomination, some were forced out for failing to submit to the authority of the synod and others left because of the unbelief. Buswell was disappointed with the NAE because he believed they were following the same path the Presbyterian Church had taken. They "did not see the

---

[71] Carl McIntire, "The Ship is Sunk," *Christian Beacon* 1 (2 July 1936), 4.

[72] McIntire, *The Testimony of Separation*, 4–5.

doctrine of the purity of the visible Church as we believe the Bible sets it forth."[73]

McIntire's opposition to the NAE was also based on a belief in the necessity of a pure church. In 1955 McIntire published an article by F. Ockenden that had been published earlier in the *Bible League Quarterly*. In that article, Ockenden stated:

> The position of the American Council of Christian Churches is that the Bible believer should separate from the modernist. This takes place either by removing the modernist from the church and preserving the purity of the church, or, if that be impossible, by withdrawal and the establishment of true churches.[74]

The Constitution of the American Council of Christian Churches stated:

> No national church or association which is a member of the National Council of Churches of Christ in the U.S.A. is eligible for membership in this Council so long as he retains connection with that body, nor shall local churches or individuals connected with national bodies holding membership in the said National Council be eligible for constituent membership.[75]

As early as 1944, McIntire accused the NAE of "expediency and compromise."[76] This accusation was based on the fact that the NAE would allow its member churches to remain in the Federal Council of Churches (although it would not allow denominations still in the Federal Council of Churches to join the NAE). McIntire's concern was based on his belief that the Northern Baptist Convention, the Methodist Church, the Presbyterian Church, USA, and the Federal Council of Churches were all apostate.[77]

---

[73] Buswell, "American and International Councils," 430.

[74] F. Ockenden, "Why I am a Fundamentalist," *Christian Beacon* 20 (4 August 1955): 4.

[75] Quoted in Pickering, *Biblical Separation*, 123. The International Council of Christian Churches started in 1948. Both councils also excluded Pentecostals and holiness groups. This was a major difference with the NAE from its beginning.

[76] McIntire, *Twentieth Century Reformation*, 191.

[77] Carl McIntire, "The National Association of Evangelicals and Separation," *Christian Beacon* 13 (7 October 1948): 4.

The fundamentalists were not isolationists, however. They were willing to accept differences in minor or non-essential doctrines in order to work together. Jones, Jr., stated:

> Neither Dad nor I were eager to split with the brethren [written in the context of Sr. and Jr. leaving the Methodist Church], break with organizations, or become involved with needless controversy. Our policy always was to stay in an organization and do what we could to get it straightened out until it became apparent it is not going to get straightened out, and then break with it and come out of it.[78]

James Oliver Buswell, a close associate of Carl McIntire and one-time professor at McIntire's Faith Theological Seminary, encouraged fundamentalism to express a clear ecclesiology. The doctrines of the purity of the church on one hand and of the unity and fellowship of believers on the other hand were critical to a valid ecclesiology. He sought to strike a balance between these elements. He proposed a rejection on one extreme of a formal, established religion that had grown cold and worldly and on the other extreme of those who pursued independency for independency's sake.[79]

Rice, particularly in his discussions of the Southern Baptist Convention, stressed fellowship with all true Bible believers, in or out of the convention. "In fact, we should prefer cooperation to isolation whenever we could cooperate and be true to the Word of God as we see it."[80] Rice did not believe that absolute obedience to every Scriptural command was necessary for fellowship to occur between believers.

> The Bible never hints anywhere that absolute uniformity in minor matters of belief is to be demanded even in local church fellowship. And if I demanded such uniformity in a union campaign, I would be

---

[78] Bob Jones, Jr., "Response to Mark Taylor Dalhouse, 'Bob Jones University and the Shaping of Twentieth Century Separatism, 1926–1991,'" Fundamentalism Collection, Mack Library, Bob Jones University, Greenville, SC.

[79] Buswell, *A Systematic Theology*, 2:226.

[80] John R. Rice, "Fellowship with Convention Brethren: How Far to Go? What We Want: Some Reservations," *Sword of the Lord* 3 (8 April 1937): 3.

demanding what you yourself do not demand in your local church fellowship, and I would be wrong.[81]

Fundamentalism placed a strong emphasis on the purity of the church and any denomination or association to which it may belong. Fundamentalists did not reject fellowship with believers who were faithful to the Bible, but they did reject fellowship with unbelievers and with believers who failed to obey Scripture.

Conclusion

The church is a special creation of God. While not all fundamentalists were dispensationalists, most believed that the church began at Pentecost and that it was specifically, or at least especially, a New Testament institution. This, however, was not at the heart of the differences, since some of the new evangelicals were also dispensationalists. A more important difference was a common emphasis on the primacy of the local church that included the belief that the universal or invisible church was distinct from the local or visible churches. Apostasy was the expected result of the visible church, and apostasy requires separation. Fundamentalism, in general, was not eager to separate. It was a costly tactic in the world's eyes. They gave up buildings, pensions, friends, and position. The belief in the necessity of a pure church, however, left them no options. The previous generation had failed in its attempts to remove modernism from the great denominations. That left the next generation with no choice but separation or compromise.

---

[81] John R. Rice, "Co-operation Among Christians—Is it Baptistic? Scriptural?" *Sword of the Lord* 25 (21 August 1959): 5.

Chapter 4

EVANGELICAL
VIEWS OF THE CHURCH

A system of thought is not simply a set of ideas, held abstractly from one's life and character. The theology and practice of the new evangelicals developed out of the lives of its leaders. The early new evangelicals had come from conservative and even fundamentalist backgrounds. Their undergraduate training was frequently in fundamentalist schools, although they often went on to leading secular or liberal institutions to complete their education. They had concluded, however, that fundamentalism was insufficient to meet the needs of the hour.[1]

The new evangelicals in the middle of the twentieth century came to consider themselves no longer fundamentalists. The evangelicals often worked through organizations separate from the mainline denominations, but they did not insist on separatism. While they opposed modernism, they did not require a militant exposure of its errors. Many moved away from dispensationalism in favor of covenant theology but did not necessarily reject premillennialism. Evangelism, along with missionary endeavors, was a central activity. They insisted that Christianity had a significant social aspect. There was an emphasis on scholarship that replaced the perceived anti-intellectualism of fundamentalism.

Harold J. Ockenga, in the first convocation address at Fuller Seminary in 1948, affirmed his agreement with the essential theology of fundamentalism. "Evangelical theology is synonymous with fundamentalism or orthodoxy. In doctrine the evangelicals and the fundamentalists are one. . . . It is a mistake for an evangelical to divorce himself from historic fundamentalism as some have sought to do."[2] At the same time

---

[1] Erickson, *New Evangelical Theology*, 43.

[2] Ockenga, "Resurgent Evangelical Leadership," 13. John Walvoord differed with Ockenga, however: "An evangelical is free to believe all that fundamentalists believe theologically . . . or, if he prefers, he can deny all the fundamentals and still claim the same name, as does Cecil John Cadous in his *The*

that Ockenga reaffirmed the theology of fundamentalism, he also issued a "ringing call for a repudiation of separatism" and rejected fundamentalism's "ecclesiology and its social theory."[3] He declared, "Doctrinally, the fundamentalists are right, and I wish to be classified as one. In ecclesiology, I believe they are wrong and I cannot follow them."[4] Ockenga, and those who joined him in the rejection of fundamentalist ecclesiology and its concurrent separatism, realized that the issue was critical.

> Shall we contend against these unbelievers who are now in our churches and often in positions of great power, or shall we just quietly and unobtrusively withdraw from the church, giving up the buildings, the endowments, the great name and heritage of that particular local congregation or that denomination? Or should these adopt something which they call Christianity but is not Christianity at all when it is judged by either the history of the church, the creed of the church, or the incorporation papers of the church? . . . Unless we understand the nature of the church, we will never know how we should withdraw ourselves or separate ourselves from those who are not in the church.[5]

The fundamentalists and evangelicals differed in their answers to this

---

Case for Evangelical Modernism. In a word, the designation *evangelical* only declares one in favor of the evangel, or the gospel, but it does not in itself define the term theologically. Its meaning depends upon the one who uses the term." John F. Walvoord, "What's Right About Fundamentalism," *Eternity* 8 (June 1957): 35.

[3] Ockenga, "Foreword," 11. New evangelicalism's rejection of separatism was related partially to its conception of the cultural roles of fundamentalism and evangelicalism. The evangelicals saw themselves as closer to the heritage of the Puritans like John Winthrop, governor of Massachusetts, rather than the dissident Roger Williams, who demanded a pure and separatist church and saw the state as thoroughly secular. Marsden also indicates that the early ideals of new evangelicalism were based on three models: the scholarship of Machen, the ecclesiology of Macartney and the evangelism of Fuller. Marsden, *Reforming Fundamentalism*, 7, 261.

[4] Harold Ockenga, "From Fundamentalism, Through New Evangelicalism, to Evangelicalism," in *Evangelical Roots*, Kenneth Kantzer, ed. (New York: Thomas Nelson, 1978), 40.

[5] Harold John Ockenga, *The Church in God: Expository Values in Thessalonians* (Westwood, NJ: Revell, 1956), 326–27.

question. The differences created the separation between the two movements.

The debate between fundamentalism and evangelicalism was not waged over whether to accept or reject separation. Evangelicals were, at least to some extent, separatists. The NAE separated from the National Council of Churches. Fuller Seminary was separate from the mainline denominations, although its purpose was to send its graduates back into those denominations. The real issue was to what extent and on what basis a person, church, or denomination should *practice* separation.

One reason for Ockenga's disagreement with fundamentalism was its "shibboleth of having a pure church, both as a congregation and a denomination." He was critical of their exegesis of 2 Corinthians 6:14–18 and the parable of the tares, which he viewed as the basis of their ecclesiology. "The sad practice called 'come-outism' developed."[6] The evangelical "differentiates his position from theirs in ecclesiology."[7] Fundamentalist ecclesiology required separation, and the new evangelicals saw this as a faulty strategy.

> The cause of the fundamentalist defeat in the ecclesiastical scene lay partially in fundamentalism's erroneous doctrine of the Church which identified the Church with believers who were orthodox in doctrine and separatist in ethics. Purity of the Church was emphasized above the peace of the Church.[8]

Ockenga argued that a change in strategy was necessary for the new evangelicalism to prosper.

> An up-to-date strategy for the evangelical cause must be based upon the principle of infiltration. . . . It is time for firm evangelicals to seize their opportunity to minister in and influence modernist groups. Why is it incredible that the evangelicals should be able to infiltrate the denominations and strengthen the things that remain, and possibly resume control of such denominations? Certainly they have a responsibility to do so unless they are expelled from those denominations.[9]

---

[6] Klaas Runia, "When Is Separation a Christian Duty?" *Christianity Today* (23 June 1967): 942.

[7] Ockenga, "Resurgent Evangelical Leadership," 13.

[8] Ibid., 12.

[9] Ibid., 14–15.

The new evangelicals were a generation away from the battles of the 1920s that had informed separatist thought. The early theme of new evangelicalism was "Cooperation without Compromise."[10] The fundamentalists viewed this theme itself as compromise.

In 1967 a *Christianity Today* article explained the difference between schism, separation, and separatism. Schism referred to a division within a church that is "due to causeless differences and contentions between its members." Separation is the departure of a group from the main body "because that body has become unfaithful to the Word of God."

> [Separatism] denotes the ecclesiology and practical attitude of those who leave their church prompted by a wrong spirit. Separatists make no attempt to reform the church from within, nor do they have any understanding of or concern for the visible unity of the church; instead, they are motivated by some form of ecclesiological perfectionism that compels them to abandon the existing church and establish a new one.[11]

Carl Henry also rejected the separatism of the fundamentalists. When the Conservative Baptist Association began as a break-off from the Northern Baptist Convention, Henry stayed in the convention, demonstrating his preference for a strategy of influencing the major denominations from within rather than from without. Although he sympathized deeply with the cause of the separatists, he rejected separatism itself.[12]

It is the purpose of this chapter to delineate, as far as possible, the identifying characteristics of the ecclesiology of the new evangelicals. The areas of significance among evangelicals centered on the meaning of *ekklesia*; the church's relationship to Scripture; the membership of the church, the relationship between the visible, invisible, universal and local churches; and the relationship between unity and purity within the church.

---

[10] James DeForest Murch used this as the title of the first history of New Evangelicalism: *Cooperation Without Compromise: A History of the National Associations of Evangelicals.*

[11] Runia, "When is Separation a Christian Duty?" 939–41.

[12] Marsden, *Reforming Fundamentalism*, 46.

The Nature of the Church

Fundamentalism was shaped by its dispensational view of the church. Although many of the early new evangelicals came out of a dispensational background and carried some dispensational thinking with them, new evangelicalism as a movement was heavily influenced by covenant theology. It is not sufficient, however, to argue that the distinction between fundamentalism and evangelicalism was simply the difference between covenant and dispensational theologies. Numerous fundamentalists had some covenant thinking in their view of the church, while numerous evangelicals had some dispensational thinking in their view of the church.

Dispensational thought among some of the new evangelicals was particularly evident in their discussions of the start of the church. A good example is Harold John Ockenga. In an exposition of Romans 11, Ockenga declared:

> Note from this that the Church is not Israel and Israel is not the Church. This illustration of the olive tree makes this clear. . . . The Church as the bride of Christ was initiated at Pentecost. The promises of Israel do not transfer to the Church which has specific blessings and privileges of its own.[13]

The branches in Romans 11 are Israel; they are removed, and the grafted branches are individual Jews and Gentiles who believe. "The nation of Israel has no special place in God's redemptive scheme today. . . . Yet God has a future for Israel and it will as a nation be grafted into the olive tree."[14] However, Ockenga also believed the saved of all ages would be part of the church: "We must insist that Abraham, David, and Paul were redeemed as we are through Christ and therefore that we are one in the church (Gal. 3:7, 14, 29)."[15] For Ockenga, that church exists now. The framework for the church was laid in the death and resurrection of Christ.

---

[13] Harold John Ockenga, *Everyone That Believeth: Expository Addresses on St. Paul's Epistle to the Romans* (New York: Revell, 1942), 170.

[14] Ockenga, *The Church in God*, 99–100.

[15] Ibid.

God was now to work in a new economy... called the dispensation—if you please—of the Holy Spirit, or of the Church. . . . The Church today is the present form, I think, of the Kingdom of God. But the Church, remember, is in the world for a testimony. And the Church has a part to play in the economical and political and social order.[16]

Graham also revealed a measure of dispensational thought. He believed that Christ himself founded the church and that Christ was the cornerstone upon which the church is built (1 Cor 3:11).[17]

Carl F. H. Henry, on the other hand, was clearly covenant in his ecclesiology. He believed that the fundamentalists had neglected the doctrine of the church, except in discussions of ecclesiastical separation.

This failure to elaborate the biblical doctrine of the Church comprehensively and convincingly not only contributes to the fragmenting spirit of the movement but actually hands the initiative to the ecumenical enterprise in defining the nature and relations of the churches.[18]

He firmly believed that the evangelicals needed to emphasize the spiritual unity of the church.[19] He himself did not write extensively on the church, but he did approve articles for *Christianity Today* and *Basic Christian Doctrines: Contemporary Evangelical Thought*, which he edited.[20]

J. I. Packer, who wrote a chapter for Henry's *Basic Christian Doctrines*, argued that the "church is not simply a New Testament phenomenon. An

---

[16] Harold John Ockenga, *The Church God Blesses* (Pasadena: Fuller Missions Fellowship, 1959), 11, 15.

[17] Charles G. Ward, *The Billy Graham Christian Worker's Handbook* (Minneapolis: World Wide, 1984), 58. This is a systematic collection of articles from a variety of Billy Graham publications.

[18] Carl F. H. Henry, "Dare We Renew the Modernist-Fundamentalist Controversy? Part 2. The Fundamentalist Reduction," *Christianity Today* 1 (24 June 1957): 24.

[19] Carl F. H. Henry, "Dare We Renew the Modernist-Fundamentalist Controversy? Part 4. The Evangelical Responsibility," *Christianity Today* 1 (22 July 1957): 24.

[20] Carl F. H. Henry, ed., *Basic Christian Doctrines: Contemporary Evangelical Thought* (New York: Holt, Rinehart, and Winston, 1962).

ecclesiology which started with the New Testament would be out of the way at the first step."[21] He based his argument on Paul's image of the olive tree, which he viewed as the church, from which the Jews were essentially removed and replaced with Gentiles. He also argued that Paul called the Gentile believers "Abraham's seed" and "the Israel of God" (Gal 3:29; Rom 4:11–18; and Gal 6:16). For Packer, the fundamental idea of a biblical ecclesiology was of "the church as the covenant people of God."[22] Christ was the link between the Mosaic church and the Christian church, and baptism was the New Testament correspondent to circumcision.[23] The New Testament adds to the Old Testament notion of a covenant people the picture of a new creation in Christ, raised with Him from death, and possessed of a new life from the Holy Spirit.[24]

> The church must reject trying to politicize an unregenerate world into the kingdom of God; it must also reject interpreting evangelical conversion devoid of active social concern as fulfilling Christian responsibility. God works through the Christian community to change the world; its members are to mirror the precepts and practices to be preserved while at the same time deploring, remedying or rejecting those inimical to God's purposes. The church thus ministers in the world as a servant for Christ's sake and bears a good conscience in view of its calling. Its task is not to force new structures upon society at large, but to be the new society, to exemplify in its own ranks the way and will of God. In view of the risen Lord's presence and power in the life and community of his followers, the community of faith convicts and hopefully attracts the unredeemed multitudes (John 17:21). But whether society at large takes notice or not, the fellowship of believers is to be the new community. Even this new society will be less than

---

[21] James I. Packer, "The Nature of the Church," in *Basic Christian Doctrines: Contemporary Evangelical Thought*, ed. Carl F. H. Henry (New York: Holt, Rinehart, and Winston, 1962), 242.

[22] Ibid.

[23] Packer also believed baptism "represents primarily union with Christ in His death and resurrection, which is the sole way of entry into the church." Ibid., 244.

[24] 2 Cor 5:17; Eph 2:14–22; Rom 8:9–14. Ibid.

perfect (Rom. 8:18–25) until the Lord's return (1 John 3:1–3), but it nonetheless bears the moral fortunes of a renegade humanity.[25]

Baptist historian Timothy George noted that while Henry wrote about 3000 pages in his six-volume collection *God, Revelation and Authority,* he spent very little time on the church. This demonstrated that "evangelical scholars have been preoccupied with other theological themes such as biblical revelation, religious epistemology and apologetics" and had little opportunity to construct an ecclesiology.[26] Al Mohler has been critical of Henry because the "most glaring omission in his theological project is the doctrine of the church (ecclesiology)."[27]

Edward John Carnell also held a covenant view of the church. "The church is a fellowship of all who share in the blessings of the Abrahamic covenant."[28] He believed that the church was a continuation of Israel, the "spiritual Israel" of the New Testament.[29] He viewed the Old Testament church as the bud, the New Testament church as the flower. "The two phases differ in glory but not in substance. The church is one because the prophets and apostles spoke one Word. The church is the seed of Abraham."[30] He defined the church in keeping with the Apostles' Creed: "True believers are a fellowship in Christ. This fellowship is not an

---

[25] Carl F. H. Henry, *God, Revelation, and Authority* (Waco: Word, 1979), 4:530.

[26] Timothy George, "What I'd Like to Tell the Pope about the Church," *Christianity Today* (15 June 1998), 41–42.

[27] R. Albert Mohler, Jr., "Carl F. H. Henry," in *Baptist Theologians,* ed. Timothy George and David S. Dockery (Nashville: Broadman and Holman, 1990), 530.

[28] Carnell, *Case for Orthodox Theology*, 21. This book was written in response to a request to help produce a trilogy of books expounding the conservative, liberal, and neo-orthodox theological positions. His problem was, "could he conscientiously write the case book without probing orthodoxy's weaknesses? And if he probed the multiple weaknesses subsumed under the label fundamentalism, could he do so without unleashing the Furies? The answer to both questions was no" (Nelson, *Evangelical Mind*, 107).

[29] Carnell, *Case for Orthodox Theology*, 115.

[30] Ibid., 21.

external society whose rights dissolve when the corporation dissolves; it can exist without any organization at all."[31]

Carnell's view of the church can be seen most dramatically in his discussion of the reform initiated by J. Gresham Machen.[32] Machen was a faithful Presbyterian who taught at Princeton Seminary from 1906 to 1929. He adhered to the Westminster Confession and its teaching on the church. He viewed schism as sin, but he also knew that there were those in his denomination who rejected the Christ on whom the church was founded. Hence he viewed his church as no longer a true church.[33] This led Machen and others to leave Princeton and begin Westminster Seminary in 1929 and eventually to create the Orthodox Presbyterian Church in 1936. Carnell concluded, "Ideological thinking prevented Machen from seeing that the issue under trial was *the nature of the church*, not the doctrinal incompatibility of orthodoxy and modernism."[34] Carnell believed that the departure of fundamentalist Carl McIntire from Machen's denomination was a fitting judgment on Machen's theories.

> Machen . . . honored Reformed doctrine, but not the Reformed doctrine of the church. This inconsistency had at least two effects: First, it encouraged Machen's disciples to think that the conditions of Christian fellowship could be decided by subjective criteria; secondly, it

---

[31] Edward John Carnell, "The Government of the Church," in *Basic Christian Doctrines*, ed. Carl F. H. Henry (New York: Holt, Rinehart, and Winston, 1962), 249.

[32] See Carnell, *The Case for Orthodox Theology*, 115.

[33] This concept was not new to Presbyterians. Charles Hodge had declared earlier: "One of the greatest evils in the history of the Church has been the constantly recurring efforts to keep men united externally who were inwardly at variance. Such forced union must be insincere and pernicious. It leads to persecution, to hypocrisy, and to the suppression of the truth. Where two bodies of Christians differ so much either as to doctrine or order as to render their harmonious action in the same ecclesiastical body impossible, it is better that they should form distinct organizations." Charles Hodge, "The Unity of the Church," *Eternity* 9 (June 1958): 27.

[34] Carnell, *The Case for Orthodox Theology*, 115. Carnell declared, "While Machen was a foe of the fundamentalist movement, he was a friend of the fundamentalist mentality, for he took an absolute stand on a relative issue, and the wrong issue at that" (Carnell, *The Case for Orthodox Theology*, 26).

planted the seeds of anarchy. . . . The result was a subtle reversion to the age of the Judges: each man did what was right in his own eyes.[35]

This raises the question, however, of what objective criteria could be used for determining what constitutes a true church. If acceptance or denial of the gospel was one of the "subjective" criteria, how could the church be biblically defined?

Graham spoke of the church in sociological terms. "Man is a social animal, gregarious by nature, and finds his greatest sense of security and satisfaction in the company of others who share his interests and attitudes."[36] Of all the groups that men have organized, Graham notes that none is as powerful or universal as the church.[37] What was lacking in his discussion was any declaration that God had ordained the institution of the church, although Graham undoubtedly believed this.

Lewis Smedes argued that the Greek *ekklesia* was used to translate the Hebrew *qahal* ("assembly" or "congregation"), both referring to the people called of God for his service. The *qahal* continued its existence in the *ekklesia*, but there was a difference: in the former Christ is promised, in the latter Christ has come. "The new relationship to Jesus Christ creates the fuller realization of the nature of the Church." The church in the Old Testament was still the church of the New Testament.[38] He then argued that becoming a Christian and joining the fellowship of a church were two sides of the same coin. A Christian and the church are essentially the same. The institutional church is the tangible embodiment of the spiritual church. The externals (dogma, ministry, mission, and ordinances) are no less essential than the inner life of the body. "They are the Body in its outward manifestation. Paul never makes a clear distinction between the spiritual life and its tangible expression. He never divides the inner, organic life from the outward, institutional life of the Church. There is only one *ekklesia*."[39] Whether the church at Jerusalem,

---

[35] Ibid., 117.

[36] Billy Graham, *Peace with God* (Waco: Word, 1953), 188.

[37] Ibid.

[38] Lewis B. Smedes, "The Essence of the Church" *Christianity Today* 4 (26 Oct 1959): 51.

[39] Ibid.

or the church at Ephesus, or the churches of Judea, they "all are equally *the* Church because all share equally in the whole of Christ."[40]

The emphasis of the evangelicals was on one church and the unity found in that one church. They believed in the local church, but the universal church held greater significance for them.

The Church and the Scriptures

The authority of the church for both the evangelicals and fundamentalists was the Bible. The early evangelicals were fairly united in their belief in the inerrancy and authority of Scripture. Graham, for instance, believed that the Bible was "truly authoritative."[41] Henry declared, "Evangelical scholars are fully aware that the doctrine of the Bible controls all other doctrines of the Christian faith."[42] He realized, however, that this was not universal among evangelicals. "[N]ot all evangelicals, although insisting that the Bible is infallible in matters of theology and ethics ('faith and morals'), were ready to espouse inerrancy in all scientific and historical statements."[43] This was not the case with Henry himself, however. "Inerrancy is the evangelical heritage, the historic commitment of the Christian church."[44]

Fundamentalism was unwilling to add to the New Testament when it came to determining the nature and practice of the church. Carnell, however, was willing to allow the church to go beyond the New Testament in organization. "[T]he ministry of rule, like other auxiliary ministries in the Church, is free to develop its office according to the needs of the times. . . . When a fellowship reaches vast proportions, however, expedience may dictate that a separate office of rule be

---

[40] Ibid.

[41] Ward, *Christian Worker's Handbook*, 34.

[42] Carl F. H. Henry, *Frontiers in Modern Theology* (Chicago: Moody, 1966), 138.

[43] Campbell, *Spectrum of Protestant Beliefs*, 85.

[44] Henry, *God, Revelation and Authority*, 4:367. Much of Henry's writing dealt with the issue of the authority of Scripture in the life of the individual, the church, and even the nation.

created."[45] This office could be a bishop, archbishop, superintendent, state secretary, or a council of pastors.

The Membership of the Church

Most, but not all, evangelicals agreed with the fundamentalists that only believers should be members of the church. Those evangelicals who opened the doors of the church to the unregenerate created an area of major division between fundamentalism and evangelicalism.

Graham defined the "true Church, or the Church universal," as "the family of believers, the Body of Christ, the heirs of the kingdom, along with Jesus (Romans 8:17)." He went on to say that "the Church is composed of those who have repented of sin and have been born again."[46] Once a person accepts Christ as Savior, he becomes a member of "the great universal church."[47]

Ockenga believed the gospel produces a "holy Christian community of born-again ones, a colony from heaven, a called-out people."[48] He argued that the church is one—one body (1 Cor 12:12), one bride (Eph 5:24–27), one house (Eph 2:21, 22; 1 Pet 2:4–8), and one communion in the Holy Spirit (1 Cor 10:16, 17, 12:13). Into this one body comes every believer upon regeneration. This results in a relationship that is first to Christ and then to each other. "Hence, all Christians are united in Christ."[49] The key to the understanding of this unity is found in John 17:21. The redeemed of every age are brought into the body as a result of Calvary, for there the prayer of Christ for unity was answered. This unity is a historic reality.[50]

According to Henry the precondition of anyone's participation in the kingdom "is a change of nature, a new nature . . . regeneration by the Spirit of God."[51] Henry rejected the sacraments and church membership

---

[45] Edward John Carnell, "The Government of the Church," *Christianity Today* 6 (22 June 1962): 931.

[46] Ward, *Billy Graham Handbook*, 42.

[47] Graham, *Peace with God*, 176.

[48] Ockenga, *The Church in God*, 13–14.

[49] Harold John Ockenga, "The Body Christ Heads: A Symposium," *Christianity Today* 1 (19 Sept 1957): 10.

[50] Ibid., 10–11.

[51] Carl F. H. Henry, *The God Who Shows Himself* (Waco: Word, 1966), 101.

as means of salvation.[52] He did, however, express his concern that the churches of his day were "overrun with members who remain outside the door of Christ's Kingdom."[53]

Evangelicalism and fundamentalism both agreed that membership in the universal church (if they accepted the universal church) was based on salvation alone. It was in the discussion of the membership of the local church or the visible church that a difference appeared.

The believer was expected to join with others in the worship of God in the local church. Graham stated, "When Jesus founded the church, He intended His followers to join it and remain faithful to it."[54] He viewed the various denominations as ways in which people could find the greatest possible opportunity to be of service to others and to worship God.

> Churches have different backgrounds, different traditions, different customs, different emphases. . . . Some people find it easier to draw closer to God in magnificent buildings and with some form of ritual. Others find they can seek God only in stark simplicity. Some people find themselves in sympathy with one kind of service, others feel more at home in a different atmosphere. The important thing is not *how* we do it, but the sincerity and depth of purpose *with which* we do it, and we should each find and join the church in which as individuals we can best accomplish this.[55]

This concept fit with Graham's view of cooperative evangelism. Graham did not focus his attention on what the Bible said about a true church. Doctrinal differences for him were minor variations of interpretation. Converts from his crusades would not be told what kind of church theologically they should attend. Instead they were told, "each Christian should select his church because he is convinced that within its particular structure he will find the greatest opportunities for spiritual growth, the greatest satisfactions for his human needs, and the greatest chance to be of helpful service to those around him."[56] In addition, Graham declared, "The all-important thing is to belong to the one true

---

[52] Ibid.

[53] Ibid., 102.

[54] Graham, *Peace with God*, 176–78.

[55] Ibid., 193.

[56] Ibid., 193–94.

Church. . . . What local congregation one should join is a matter that the individual must decide."[57]

An important defense of Graham's evangelistic methods came from Robert O. Ferm. Ferm raised a series of arguments, primarily through historical and biblical examples of Graham-like cooperative evangelism. With reference to ecclesiology, Ferm argued that "Billy Graham has worked to make mass evangelism Church-centered."[58] Ferm believed that "[t]he mission of the Church is to make the truth known, not just to preserve and protect it. . . . But unless it is proclaimed to those whose need is greatest, the Church will have failed."[59] Graham was willing to work alongside the unregenerate as well as the regenerate in order to be sure that the church did not fail in its work of evangelism.

Ferm recognized that this was a problem. "Having these nominal Christians in the churches has convinced Dr. Sweaze as well as many others that 'the evangelizing of church membership is our first duty.'"[60] He acknowledged that this was not the proper situation but had no recommendation for change; rather, he accepted the situation as the norm. Graham agreed with him: "The visible Church is the present-day universal Church, composed of local groups of Christians. In it are both the 'wheat and tares' (Matthew 13:25–40)—the truly redeemed, and many who are not."[61] Graham's emphasis was on winning the lost, whether they were in or out of the church. His cooperative methods were rejected by the fundamentalists, but defended by the evangelicals.

In *The Case for Orthodox Theology* Carnell criticized the peculiarities of the various denominations as divisive. He noted that one example of "cultic mentality" was that "Baptists often limit fellowship to those who have been immersed." He concluded, "This is unfortunate."[62] Carnell did argue, however, that certain persons should be removed from the

---

[57] Ward, *Billy Graham Handbook*, 42–43.

[58] Ferm, *Cooperative Evangelism*, 13.

[59] Ibid., 22.

[60] Ibid., 27.

[61] Ward, *Christian Worker's Handbook*, 58.

[62] Carnell, *The Case for Orthodox Theology*, 59. It might be noted that Carnell, having come out of a Baptist background, had little use for Baptist theology. At the end of each chapter in *The Case for Orthodox Theology*, he listed suggested reading material; no Baptist sources are cited in any list.

church. Those members guilty of gross immorality "must be excluded from the fellowship" until they repent.[63] From Carnell's point of view, the New Testament was not as clear when church members follow false doctrine. He noted that Judaizers (Acts 15:1–5) and deniers of the resurrection (1 Cor 15:12), among others who held wrong beliefs, were never excommunicated from the church.

> When church members follow false teaching, however, the New Testament is not so clear.... [T]hey are not told precisely what doctrines are essential to fellowship, nor are they told precisely what to do with errorists.... [I]t is only natural that the church will be divided on how far to go when confronting errorists with the evil of their ways.[64]

While fundamentalists were concerned that the church be pure and worked hard at maintaining that purity, the evangelicals expressed their expectation that it would not be. The evangelicals were sure that the local church cannot be perfect; "the church is but turning a blind eye toward itself when it claims infallibility or perfection for itself or any of its members."[65] Carnell expressed his willingness to accept the unregenerate into a church (actually a denomination in this case), when he asked:

> Does the church become apostate when it has modernists in its agencies and among its officially supported missionaries? The older Presbyterians knew enough about Reformed ecclesiology to answer this in the negative. Unfaithful ministers do *not* render the church apostate.[66]

Fundamentalists and evangelicals differed in their beliefs concerning requirements for membership in a church. Evangelicals were more tolerant of error and expected unregenerate individuals to be members of the visible church and denominations.

---

[63] Carnell, "Government," *Christianity Today*, 931.

[64] Carnell, "Government," in *Basic Doctrines*, 252–53.

[65] Graham, *Peace with God*, 176.

[66] Ibid., 115.

The Universal and Local Church

Fundamentalism placed its emphasis on the local, visible church. Although it did not necessarily reject a universal or invisible form of the church, it relegated it to a minor role. Evangelicalism, on the other hand, placed a much greater emphasis on the universal or invisible church.

Graham's organization defined the church as both visible and invisible. "The invisible Church is that larger body of believers who, down through the ages, have sincerely trusted Jesus Christ as Lord and Savior. . . . The visible Church is the present-day universal Church, composed of local groups of Christians."[67]

Graham viewed the purpose of the local church as first, "to glorify God by our worship"; second, for fellowship; third, for the strengthening of faith; and fourth, to be a medium of service. "A virile Christian has never existed apart from the church." The fifth purpose was to be a means of channeling funds for Christian work. The sixth purpose was for the spreading of the gospel. "The basic and primary purpose of the church is to proclaim Christ to the lost. . . . The mission of the church is to throw the life line to the perishing sinners everywhere." The final purpose was to provide a means for the widest expression of humanitarianism.[68]

Graham believed there was only one church, but there were also "any number of local churches formed into various denominations and societies or councils."[69] There may have been a variety of divisions but only one true church of which Jesus Christ was the head. The "hair-splitting and apparent lack of unity" were superficial conflicts that came from varying interpretations of scripture.

> Study the underlying beliefs of the various denominations and you will find that basically and historically they are almost identical. They may differ widely in ritual, they may seem to lock horns over theological technicalities; but fundamentally they all recognize Jesus Christ as God incarnate, who died upon the cross and rose again that man might have salvation—and that is the all-important fact to all humanity.[70]

---

[67] Ward, *Christian Worker's Handbook*, 58.

[68] Graham, *Peace with God*, 178–82.

[69] Ibid., 174.

[70] Ibid., 176.

Ockenga also identified two kinds of churches—the universal church and the local church. He identified the universal church as "the ecumenical church, the catholic church, the church which constitutes His body." This church is identified by several characteristics. The first is that of apostolicity. Apostolicity does not require organic continuity; instead, it means "a spiritual continuity, for the church of Jesus Christ universal is a spiritual entity." The second characteristic is purity. "It is a holy, universal, catholic church and there must be a semblance of purity of holiness which is attached to that church." A third characteristic is unity. There are to be no divisions in the body of Christ. This church is intangible, a universal, spiritual body made up of those who are born of God. "It is not identified and coterminous with any organization as such which exists." This church was not Rome, for Rome was not doctrinally pure. Neither was it the World Council of Churches for that was not doctrinally pure, although there certainly would be members of each of these organizations who would be included in the universal church.[71]

Ockenga believed that the counterpart to the universal church is the local church. Matthew 16 and Ephesians were written for and to the universal church, but Matthew 18 and Corinthians were written for and to the local church. Acts records the activities of several local churches. The characteristics of a true local church were "the preaching of God's Word, the worship in the sacraments, and also Christian action founded upon that Word."[72] Local churches had a responsibility "to exclude on the ground of heresy or aberration of conduct."[73] These characteristics are not found in the universal church.

Ockenga rejected an "invisible" church. While some would say that the invisible church was the same as Ockenga's universal church, Ockenga himself firmly believed that there was no evidence in Scripture for an invisible church. "There is no validity to the distinction between the visible and invisible Church. Wherever the Church militant exists it must be visible. It is concerning the unity of the Church militant that we are writing."[74] The "Church militant" consists of those believers who are still

---

[71] Ockenga, *The Church in God*, 328–29.

[72] Ibid., 330.

[73] Ibid.

[74] Harold John Ockenga, *Our Evangelical Faith* (New York: Revell, 1946), 67. *Our Evangelical Faith* was a series of sermons preached by Harold Ockenga at

on earth, as contrasted to those who died and entered into the "Church triumphant."[75] For Ockenga the universal church was a visible church, composed of all believers since Pentecost. It was not simply the local church, since both the local and universal churches are visible.[76]

Ockenga drew a distinction between the universal and local church by distinguishing between the church as an organism (the universal church) and the church as an organization (the local church). Christ's declaration in Matthew 16:18 concerned the church as an organism. Matthew 18 was given to the church as an organization, "in which there must be discipline, public teaching and prayer."[77] This organizational church was in view in Paul's admonition to the Corinthians to correct their problems and produce an organizational unity. For Ockenga, therefore, there was both a particular church and a universal church, both of which were visible and scriptural. "The Church is the Church universal, but the church at Boston or Pittsburgh or Chicago is an individual assembly, a particular congregation, still called a 'Church.'"[78]

Packer dealt more at length with the universal church. His position was a more traditional covenant ecclesiology. He viewed the universal church as more than an aggregate of local churches. Speaking of any time two or three believers would meet in Christ's name, Packer declared, "[T]hey *are* the church in the place where they meet. Each particular gathering, however small, is the local manifestation of the church universal, embodying and displaying the spiritual realities of the church's supernatural life." He viewed the local church as the body *in* Christ and the universal church as the body *under* Christ.[79]

Park Street Congregational Church. These were "discourses which give his elaboration of the doctrinal witness of the National Association of Evangelicals. . . . Dr. Ockenga has poured into these pages his own emphatic personality and has high-lighted them from his own doctrinal angle" (Ockenga, *Our Evangelical Faith*, Preface). The important chapter for this study is "The Unity of the Church."

[75] Ibid., 67.

[76] Ockenga, *The Church in God*, 331.

[77] Ockenga, *Our Evangelical Faith*, 67.

[78] Ibid.

[79] Packer, "The Nature of the Church," 246.

Packer also accepted the Reformation distinction between the visible and invisible churches. The invisible church is the church on earth as God sees it over against the visible church, which is the church on earth as man sees it. The church in God's view is composed only of believers. The two are closely related, for when the church meets it becomes visible. However, the visible church is a mixed body. "Some who belong, though orthodox, are not true believers. . . . The Reformers' distinction thus safeguards the vital truth that visible church membership saves no man apart from faith in Christ."[80] This was important in the issue of ecclesiastical separation.

In another article in Henry's *Fundamentals of the Faith*, Marcus Loane defined the invisible church as "the blessed company of all faithful people" and the visible church as "the society of all professing Christians, organizing for worship, orthodox in doctrine, and open to observation by all."[81] Loane saw a theological development in Scripture from the local church in the home (Acts 2:42; Rom 16:5) to a city church (Acts 13:1; 1 Cor 1:2) to a national or regional church (Gal 1:2; 2 Cor 8:1; 1 Cor 16:19) to finally a universal church (Acts 20:28).[82] A person could be a member of a local church, but not a member of the church "whose members are known to God alone." He based this belief on the parable of the wheat and the tares: "the Church in its visible character in this world must always be a mixture of the true and the false."[83] Loane concluded that the only true church is the spiritual house spoken of in 1 Peter 2:5. The believer's citizenship is in heaven; hence, the true church must be a heavenly one, not an earthly one. The destiny of the true church is to gather around Jesus in heaven. The local church is a foretaste of that fact.[84]

The emphasis of the evangelicals on the universal church was significantly greater than that of the fundamentalists, who placed their emphasis on the local church. This allowed for unregenerate members in

---

[80] Ibid.

[81] Marcus L. Loane, "Christ and His Church," in *Fundamentals of the Faith*, ed. Carl F. H. Henry (Grand Rapids: Zondervan, 1969), 177–78.

[82] Ibid., 178.

[83] Ibid.

[84] Ibid., 185.

a local church and less emphasis on the purity of the visible church than the emphasis placed on purity by the fundamentalists.

Unity and Purity in the Church

Henry was opposed to two extremes. In "The Perils of Ecumenicity" he rejected the ecumenical movement because in general it "elevates the doctrine of the unity of the body above every other doctrine."[85] In "The Perils of Independency" he decried the lack of union among the evangelicals.[86] Henry was representative of early evangelicalism and its attempt to strike a balance between these two positions. Addison Leitch called Henry the "rallying point in another kind of ecumenical movement."[87]

Henry, like most of the early evangelicals, was disillusioned with the establishment or institutional ecumenical movement represented by the National and World Councils of Churches. He rejected the ecumenical movement for six basic reasons.[88] First, the ecumenical movement ignored the traditional understanding of evangelism and missions. Henry believed evangelism to be the primary concern of the church. Ecumenism redefined evangelism in terms of socio-political action. Second, ecumenism made social and political goals the key to unity, not doctrine and mission. Henry argued for social and political involvement on the part of new evangelicalism but rejected the ecumenical intrusion into government affairs as a replacement for biblical ethics. Third, Henry accused the ecumenical leaders of undermining new evangelicalism and

---

[85] Carl F. H. Henry, "The Perils of Ecumenicity," *Christianity Today* 1 (26 November 1956): 20–22.

[86] Carl F. H. Henry, "The Perils of Independency," *Christianity Today* 1 (12 November 1956): 20–23. Beyond these two extremes, there is little in Henry's own writings to identify the nature of the church. In fairness, however, it must be noted that Henry centered much of his thinking and writing on theology proper, bibliology, and philosophy. However, to critique a movement for its poor ecclesiology and fail to correct that ecclesiology is problematic.

[87] Addison Leitch, "Modern Theologies: As Seen from the Gospel," review of *Christian Faith and Modern Theology*, ed. Carl F. H. Henry, *Christianity Today* 9 (31 July 1964): 32.

[88] Sharp, *Carl F. H. Henry*, 133–36.

its concerns.[89] He was especially troubled that the ecumenists had not given conservatives a forum in proportion to their numbers, while they seemed eager to listen to Roman Catholics and other non-evangelical groups. Fourth, Henry feared that ecumenical overtures to Roman Catholicism would result in a formal disavowal of some of the first principles of the Reformation, especially the final authority of the Bible and the rejection of any kind of homage to the papacy.[90] Henry's fifth fear was that the bureaucracy of the proposed national ecumenical body, recommended by the Consultation on Church Union, would be unfriendly toward conservatives. As a Baptist Henry was especially "distrustful of the emergence of a powerful monolithic structure whose ecclesiological and theological character is unsure."[91] Finally, Henry was suspicious of any organization that failed to commit itself to a minimum set of tenets. Henry was in full opposition to theological pluralism. Henry used terms like "vagueness," "sterility," and "unbiblical" to describe the theological stance of ecumenical leaders.

The official position of *Christianity Today* was a rejection of institutional ecumenism. "The effort to overcome the ailments of existing denominations by a process of merger into a giant church need not be viewed as the divine ideal. In fact, merger momentum may simply substitute 'ecclesiastical elephantiasis' for Protestant fragmentationalism, and the leprous-like condition would be no improvement."[92]

Ockenga likewise rejected "non-orthodox Protestantism" by declaring, "These cooperative interchurch movements are largely modernistic and liberal and in some cases even Unitarian. The importance of conviction and doctrine is pared down in the interests of unity and cooperation. Such unity can never be effective."[93] Ockenga also stated, "A truly converted evangelical church often has hesitancy and reluctance to

---

[89] For instance, Henry was critical of an American ecumenist's attempt to undermine the World Congress on Evangelism. Carl F. H. Henry, *Faith at the Frontiers* (Chicago: Moody, 1969), 99.

[90] Carl F. H. Henry, *Evangelicals at the Brink of Crisis* (Waco: Word, 1967), 100ff.

[91] Henry, *The God Who Shows Himself*, 131.

[92] "Vatican Rejects Protestant View of Church Unity," *Christianity Today* 6 (6 July 1962): 979.

[93] Ockenga, *Our Evangelical Faith*, 70.

join hands with other churches where the most precious truths, like the deity of Christ, the atonement for sin, and the second coming of our Lord are denied."[94]

Carnell rejected Catholic and liberal ecumenism. He rejected Catholic ecumenism because the Vatican eliminated the threat of disunity by eliminating religious liberty; this could not be accepted by anyone who believed that humanity is made in the image of God. He rejected Protestant ecumenism because Protestants, while seeing the evil in disunity, failed to see the evil in untruth. His conclusion was: "When a decision must be made between unity and truth, unity must yield to truth; for it is better to be divided by truth than to be united by error."[95]

Lines of division over ecclesiastical separation were drawn primarily in the local church and in the affiliations of those churches, not the universal church. Ockenga was critical of the fundamentalists' emphasis on the purity of the local church when he stated, "Whenever any individual church sets itself up as identical with the universal church, it is guilty of schism because it divides itself from the other brethren, and it separates itself from those which have also the right to be called the children of God."[96]

Packer repeated this theme.

> If a visible organization, as such, were or could be the one true church of God, then any organizational separation would be a breech [sic] of unity, and the only way to reunite a divided Christendom would be to work for a single international super-church. . . . The proper ecumenical task is not to create church unity by denominational coalescence, but to recognize the unity that already exists and to give it worthy expression on the local level.[97]

Based on Ephesians 4:1–6, Ockenga argued that a believer becomes a member of the one body by the Spirit when he is born again of the Spirit.

> This body must never be identified with any one organizational church. . . . To claim that any one organization is the only true church

---

[94] Ockenga, *The Church in God*, 150.

[95] Edward John Carnell, "Orthodoxy and Ecumenism," *Christianity Today* 2 (1 Sept 1958): 17.

[96] Ockenga, *The Church in God*, 330.

[97] Packer, *The Nature of the Church*, 246–47.

must be considered bigotry in the minds of enlightened, biblical Christians. . . . The one body already exists and it is the spiritual, mystical body of Christ.[98]

The ground of this unity is the Holy Spirit.

Ockenga viewed the fundamentalists' emphasis on purity as faulty. Fundamentalists identified the church with believers who were "orthodox in doctrine and separatist in ethics. Purity of the Church was emphasized above the peace of the Church." This emphasis on purity was problematic for fundamentalism, in Ockenga's opinion, for it diverted strength "from the great offensive work of missions, evangelism, and Christian education to the defense of the faith."[99]

Because the emphasis on purity was part of the basis for separation among the fundamentalists, Henry was concerned about the resultant fracturing of fundamentalism. He noted that Machen's independent American Presbyterian Church had divided into the Orthodox and Bible Presbyterian denominations. In 1956 the Bible Presbyterian Church experienced another split. Thus, in only twenty-one years, Machen's denomination split into an additional three groups. Henry's argument was that the militant fundamentalists tended toward extreme dogmatism on even minor issues and that a harsh, divisive spirit led to fragmentation.[100]

Ockenga was not afraid to separate when the occasion called for it. On June 25, 1957, the Congregational Christian Churches and the Evangelical and Reformed Church united to form the United Church of Christ. Ockenga was opposed and served notice that Park Street Church would become independent if the merger went through. Ockenga separated from the new denomination because there was no doctrinal unity therein. "I refuse to sell my integrity and liberty for a man-made unity."[101] He believed that when a church became apostate, Christians must withdraw from that church. He disagreed, however, with McIntire and the ACCC that all of the present major denominations were apostate. Lindsell said of Ockenga:

---

[98] Harold J. Ockenga, "The Reality of Church Unity," *United Evangelical Action* 2 (10 August 1943): 2.

[99] Ockenga, "Resurgent Evangelical Leadership," 12.

[100] Henry, "The Perils of Independency," 20–23.

[101] Ockenga, "The Body Christ Heads," 10.

Historically, no man identified with a Protestant group can state that separatism as understood by Calvin and Ockenga is wrong. To do so would conclude that Protestants must return to the Roman church, a movement which is hardly likely in the light of historical facts. . . . [U]p to this point he is not convinced that many of the so-called apostate churches are actually apostate. . . . [E]cumenically, Dr. Ockenga believes that all Bible-believing Christians ought to unite in a fellowship of a non-organizational type.[102]

He did not view himself as a separatist, however. "Ockenga himself would be loath to concede that it makes him a 'come-outer' in a negative sense. Rather, he sees himself and the church with the historic stream of such movements and not with a side eddy."[103] Ockenga's emphasis was on unity. He did not believe he needed to create a unity; he only needed to expose the unity that already existed.

From this idea of the body we can gain a true conception of the unity of the Church. It is utterly erroneous to conceive of local organizations as independent churches and to plan or talk about promoting organizational unity with other groups. Unity in Christianity is not something to be obtained. It is something which already exists.[104]

Ockenga argued that the unity of the church is based on the indwelling of the Holy Spirit.

The same Spirit who convicts, regenerates, sanctifies, illumines, empowers and preserves the individual believer is the Spirit who binds us together as one in the body of Christ. . . . It is for this reason that wherever saved men, men who are already members of the spiritual body of Christ gather together a church inevitably forms. The one Spirit causes the one body.[105]

Ockenga also believed that another basis for unity in the church was the "one baptism." He viewed this as water baptism, "the bond of the covenant proclaiming us to be members of His spiritual community." He acknowledged that there could be various ways of administrating

---

[102] Lindsell, *Park Street Pulpit*, 121–22.

[103] Ibid., 124.

[104] Ockenga, *Everyone That Believeth*, 188.

[105] Ockenga, "The Reality of Church Unity," 2.

baptism, but there is only one true baptism in Christ's name. As such the church becomes the habitation of God through the Spirit. "God abides in all the church pervading it and filling it with His presence." This unity is not an organizational unity, but a spiritual unity. He believed that the churches in the New Testament were all autonomous, but also that "spiritually all the churches were a unity. Their life was one. They had no organizational unity." He argued that spiritual unity is more difficult to maintain than organizational unity. Violations of this unity come when there is separation between brethren. "Schism is a sin against the brethren, against spiritual unity, but also it is a sin against the Holy Spirit and therefore is one of the greatest of all sins."[106]

Henry argued that the unity of the believers was an accomplished fact.

> [It is] already a fact of the historical order, not something which remains to be consummated. This is apparent from the Apostle Paul's exhortation to believers "to *preserve* the unity of the Spirit" in the very passage in which the theme of oneness is most conspicuous in his writings.[107]

The unity could be disturbed or promoted, but it could not be ultimately destroyed. Henry raised the question of how was an "emphasis on spiritual unity to be translated practically into the concrete historical setting of our generation?" He gave no answer, except to say that "a comprehensive answer . . . must be forged by the evangelical conscience at large."[108] This was the struggle between fundamentalism and evangelicalism; putting the theology of fellowship and separation into practice was the unsettled distinction between the two movements and to a lesser extent between factions within each movement. He did, however, give several basics. His goal was to avoid what he considered to be the extremes of inclusivism and exclusivism.

> Independency tends to be intolerant, Church Unionism to be tolerant. The former moves in the direction of exclusivism, the latter towards inclusivism. One holds a low view of the Church in its visible

---

[106] Ibid.

[107] Carl F. H. Henry, "The Unity That Christ Sustains," *United Evangelical Action* 14 (1 January 1956): 3.

[108] Ibid., 3.

and historical aspects, and the other a high view. The one glorifies separateness, while the other reaches out toward ecclesiasticism. Independency remains highly creedal in minute detail, while Church Unionism becomes vague and ill-defined in theological basis.[109]

Amalgamation of groups without similar doctrinal bases for union was an illegitimate exercise. Independency, merely on the basis of fear of inclusivism, was equally illegitimate. Outward amalgamations "neither create nor maintain the essential unity of the body."[110] Henry viewed unity as a result, not a goal. It was the result of obedience to the commission of Christ to make disciples among all men and races.

The problem was that while the church cannot be divided in its inner, spiritual life, "the painful disunity of the outward manifestation of that life is all too real."[111] There were three possible solutions to this problem. One was to conclude that the outward manifestation of that life was not significant and could be divided without disrupting the inner life, but to the apostles the inner and outer lives were inseparable. A second way was to conclude that since the inner life of the church was the essential life, divisions could be healed at the sacrifice of what was necessary to the true manifestation of the inner life. But this, too, was not the apostolic way; in the New Testament the outward manifestation was to be kept pure because it is the manifestation of the church's inner life. The third option was the only genuine one:

> We shall have to live with our terrible contradiction and never allow its painfulness to tempt us to take the easy way out. The tension is terrible; in seeking the purity of our Lord's church we seem involved in a denial of the Church's real and essential self.[112]

For Henry, the good news is that the last word will be said when the Lord brings the institutional life of the church into harmony with the inner essence of the church—the hope of glory and the fullness of unity.

This was the reason for the founding of the NAE. It was not nearly as separatistic as the ACCC or the fundamentalist denominational groups, but it did reject the modernistic ecumenism of the National and World

---

[109] Henry, "The Perils of Independency," 20.

[110] Henry, "The Unity That Christ Sustains," 4.

[111] Smedes, "The Essence of the Church," 51.

[112] Ibid., 51.

Council of Churches. The NAE had no intention to be divisive, but no denomination could join the association if it was already part of the National or World Councils. Additionally, an individual church could not belong to any other interdenominational organization if it belonged to the NAE. It was left to each particular church to determine whether to leave or stay in its denomination.

Henry saw the NAE as a middle ground between independence and church unionism:

> [The NAE's] position is not so easily defined since the lines are not so sharply drawn. It subscribes to some concepts of each of the extremist groups, but opposes others, finding its rationale in a mediating view, or perhaps better described as a perspective above the extremes. Extreme positions are easier to perceive and less difficult to defend to the popular mind.[113]

The differences between the NAE and ACCC were occasionally evaluated in the *United Evangelical Action*. A 1948 editorial by Stephen Paine called the separation of believers from apostates or unbelievers still in the visible church to be "the issue" between the NAE and ACCC. He indicated that the "principle of purity of the church, or the separation of belief from unbelief, certainly is not without standing in Protestantism historically."[114] In reaction to two accusations that the NAE was not a separatist organization, the Executive Committee of the Association approved a statement on separation and polled the sixty-seven men on the Board of Administration. The statement declared:

> With reference to separation, the NAE holds that the growing liberalism of denominations sometimes reaches that final apostasy when the only proper course for Evangelicals is to withdraw in loyalty to the Scriptures, but the NAE does not presume to decide when that point has been reached, recognizing at this point the responsibility of the individual conscience.[115]

The difficulty with this statement is that the NAE was made up mostly of churches and denominations, not individuals. Therefore, the argument

---

[113] Henry, "The Perils of Independency," 21.

[114] Stephen W. Paine, "NAE and Separation," *United Evangelical Action* 7 (15 September 1948): 11.

[115] Ibid., 22.

that separation was to be left to the conscience of the individual created confusion between personal separation and corporate or ecclesiastical separation.

Ockenga believed that some form of unbelief could be allowed to exist in the church.

> Some believers have earnestly tried to purify their congregations and denominations but have failed in the attempt. Therefore, they have separated themselves from the organization, believing that they were acting on Biblical authority. This has been the cause of many divisions within the church. Some go to the extreme of cutting off from fellowship all of those who are not sincerely convinced of the unbelief in the churches of which they are members. Thus, even Bible-believing Christians have been divided into two groups with the resulting confusion, misunderstanding and weakness. Effort which ought to go toward the advancement of missions, evangelism and Christian education is now used to condemn and criticize fellow Christians who sincerely work within their churches.[116]

He also argued that "there is no such thing as pure local church." The church at Corinth, for instance, consisted of the "sanctified" or "brethren," and it was complete with the sacraments and preaching of the Word, but "they were not pure." The same thing could be said of the churches in Galatia and Colosse. It is wrong to "try to erect an absolutely pure individual church and separate . . . from the brethren."[117]

This raised a question, however. "Does that mean that we shall remain constantly in fellowship with people who are not Christian people?"[118] Churches are to separate from the world. Based on 1 Corinthians 5, fornicators, adulterers, thieves, violent men, and others like them are to be kept out of the church. If they are already in the church, they must be reformed or removed.[119] Likewise, the church is to separate from idolatry (2 Cor 6:14–17). The typical evangelical argument was that this passage, however, has nothing to do with individual Corinthians leaving their church, but with the church coming out of the

---

[116] Harold John Ockenga, *he Epistles to the Thessalonians: Proclaiming the New Testament* (Grand Rapids: Baker, 1962), 138.

[117] Ockenga, *The Church in God*, 331–32.

[118] Ibid., 332.

[119] Ibid., 333.

world. The church should leave the world, but Christians do not need to leave a church with unregenerate members. This explanation, however, does not reflect the emphasis on the individual in 1 Corinthians 5.

J. Elwin Wright, one of the key leaders of the NAE, wrote an article for Rice's *Sword of the Lord* in 1950, emphasizing the need of unity among evangelicals. He argued that "it is a sin against God and His Church for any individual or group of individuals to believe or practice spiritual isolationism."[120] The article dealt primarily with the evangelical/ modernist battle. He indicated, however, that organic union was not the goal of the NAE. He believed that the NAE (and particularly its Commission on International Relations) represented a "movement for spiritual unity, rather than organic union."[121]

Carnell argued a rather simplistic approach. His contention was that a denomination was faithful to the gospel as long as the gospel remained in the denomination's creed or confession, no matter what theological positions were actually proclaimed or practiced in the churches or the denomination.[122] He believed that denominational distinctives "are an index to our blindness, not our vision, for if we knew Christ as we ought, we would succeed in mediating the gospel without dividing brother from brother."[123]

Graham viewed the doctrinal differences of the churches as superficial; these were the conflicts that came from the slightly different interpretations of the general's orders and in no way reflected upon the wisdom of "the general" or his absolute authority in issuing his orders.[124] While Graham's crusades were "church-centered," there was never one organized church under whose auspices the crusades were held. The theological differences between the sponsoring churches were kept in the background for the sake of bringing the gospel to the lost.[125]

Liberal ecumenism recognized that unity must center around two issues: faith and order. The issue of faith centered on the definition of

---

[120] J. Elwin Wright, "Evangelicals Must Unite Now," *Sword of the Lord* 12 (4 August 1950): 1.

[121] Ibid., 3.

[122] Carnell, *The Case for Orthodox Theology*, 157.

[123] Ibid., 131.

[124] Graham, *Peace with God*, 190–91.

[125] Ibid.

"members of Christ." The World Council of Churches concluded that it was sufficient to declare that Jesus Christ is God and Savior. The Reformers, however, had insisted on more than this. So, too, did both the NAE and the ACCC. Issues of order were equally important. The question was whether or not the Scriptures support a particular form of church government. Congregational, Presbyterian, and Episcopal governments all claim for themselves support from the Scriptures. One must conclude either that one form is biblical and the others therefore sinful or that no one form is biblical, but they are all "creative expressions of the sovereign working power of the Holy Spirit."[126] It was easy for the liberals and the evangelicals both to conclude that faith provided more unity than did order.

Carnell accused fundamentalism of making the "pompous theological error" of confining the true church to those in possession of true doctrine.[127] He also defined fundamentalism as cultic.

> [S]chism in the church is often interpreted as a sign of Christian virtue.... Perhaps the day will come when the fundamentalist will temper his separatism by the wisdom of the ages. Perhaps not. But in the meantime let us not be too disturbed by his vanity. The fundamentalist means well. He wants status in the church, but he errs in the way he goes about getting it. Having missed the way, he needs our pity, not our scorn.[128]

Carnell disagreed with Machen's position concerning separation of the orthodox from the modernists. Machen had stated:

> We are not dealing with delicate personal questions: we are not presuming to say whether such and such an individual man is a Christian or not. God only can decide such questions; no man can say with assurance whether the attitude of certain individual "liberals" toward Christ is saving faith or not. But one thing is perfectly plain—whether or not liberals are Christians, it is at any rate perfectly clear that liberalism is not Christianity. And that being the case, it is highly undesirable that

---

[126] "Unity: Quest and Questions," *Christianity Today* 6 (24 November 1961): 198.

[127] Edward John Carnell, "Post-Fundamentalist Faith," *Christian Century* 76 (26 August 1959): 971.

[128] Carnell, *Case for Orthodox Theology*, 121.

liberalism and Christianity should continue to be propagated within the bounds of the same organization.[129]

Instead, Carnell declared that anyone who denied the "fellowship of all who share in the blessings of the Abrahamic covenant" was separatistic in nature and thus "cultic."[130]

Conclusion

The evangelicals differed from the fundamentalists in some areas of ecclesiology. Both believed the church was for believers only, although the evangelicals were more willing to allow error into the churches and denominations and generally refused to identify error.

> The position taken by all but six delegates voting on April 8th at St. Louis, and officially the position of the National Association of Evangelicals for United Action is that we will not attack the Federal Council. . . .
>
> Let others organize to attack the Federal Council or to attack the National Association of Evangelicals for United Action, if they please; that is their right. But we renounce such strategy and tactics.[131]

Both movements agreed, for the most part, that there was a spiritual universal or invisible church which was composed only of believers, while the local church was composed of a mix of saved and lost. The evangelicals were willing to live with this mixture, while fundamentalism sought to purify both local churches and denominations or leave them because of their failure to obey Scripture. The evangelicals were more willing than the fundamentalists to tolerate unbelief in their churches and denominations.

The evangelicals placed their emphasis on unity, while the fundamentalists placed their emphasis on purity. The evangelicals believed that separation was incompatible with Christian love.

There was a shift away from dispensationalism and a move toward the covenant concept that the church was a continuation of Israel, the

---

[129] Machen, *Christianity and Liberalism*, 160.

[130] Nash, *The New Evangelicalism*, 88–91.

[131] Harold J. Ockenga, "Contentious Versus Evangelical Christianity," *United Evangelical Action* 1 (1 August 1943): 2.

"spiritual Israel of the New Testament." The evangelicals believed separation divided Christ's body and was a sin against unity. They rejected fundamentalism's belief that a pure church was a biblical commandment and that believers should separate from local churches and denominations that failed to maintain that purity.

Interestingly, while evangelicalism began with a strong organic connection between churches and even between denominations, that connection has been lost. Henry was gravely concerned that the separatism of fundamentalism would result in the fracturing of the fundamentalist movement. The emphasis on unity in evangelicalism would, in Henry's mind, prevent that in his own movement. That was not to be the case. Many evangelicals in the twenty-first century view themselves as far more independent than the evangelicals of the mid-twentieth century; evangelicals today tend to be part of loose organizations in which individuals just show up at the meetings or in regional associations that are frequently centered around a large ministry. It is beyond the scope of this study to determine the reasons for this loss. Perhaps the emphasis of the universal church over the local church for the purpose of evangelism drove this shift. Perhaps doctrinal precision was viewed, even unconsciously, as a detriment to evangelism and unity. Perhaps there was a pragmatic feeling that parachurch organizations could function more effectively than individual local churches. Nevertheless, Henry's belief that the evangelical emphasis on unity would keep the movement from fragmenting has been found invalid.

CONCLUSION

Public discussions of theology or religion are not restricted to theoretical concerns. They should and often do result in action. It is, in fact, a poor theology that has no relevance to life. The results of the application of theology on practice can be both positive and negative. Discussions of the application of biblical truth must be carefully crafted and be genuinely and legitimately theological. While broad theological discussions are profitable, it is when the attention becomes centered on specifics that the most profit is generated. The more detailed and narrow the selection of material and the more significance the discussion has for practical ramifications, the greater the necessity of a solid theological basis for the discussion.

There has been almost universal agreement that unity exists in a spiritual sense in the invisible church. Augustine, Luther, Calvin, and others ascribed to the invisible church a unity that is indivisible because of its center in the living Christ. The fundamentalists and evangelicals in the time frame discussed in this work came from similar backgrounds and, for the most part, agreed that there was (or at least would be in the eschaton) unity in the universal church. Therefore, the discussions of fellowship and separation had to center around the visible "church," whether that view of church was seen to be local churches, denominations, associations or Christendom as a whole. The National Council of Churches, the National Association of Evangelicals, the American Council of Christian Churches and the various denominational groups connected to these broader organizations were all expressions of unity in one form or another as those within these organizations saw it.

In any theological discussion, the participants must first ask what it is they are trying to determine. In this case the desire of the evangelicals was to perceive the reasons for and correct the malaise that they believed had set in on fundamentalism. The new evangelicals concluded that fundamentalism had lost its strength and ability to solve the problems it faced in the twentieth century because it had withdrawn from the religious scene and had no impact on society. To resolve this problem, evangelicalism sought to unite in a broad body. In this debate the ultimate question was one of fellowship. With whom may a Bible believer fellowship in a local church? And in the larger scene, with what churches or denominations may a church fellowship? This issue was phrased in various ways, but the final question was where the possibility of fellowship ended and separation had to begin.

Theological discussions never occur in a vacuum. The fundamentalists and evangelicals approached the issue of ecclesiastical separation with very similar presuppositions and backgrounds. Ockenga and McIntire had attended school together and both were students of Machen. Graham and Rice had ties to the Southern Baptists. Graham, Rice, and Jones were all evangelists who held large, inter-church campaigns. Both movements had associations with similar denominational and theological traditions. Both claimed the Bible as their source of authority. Both believed firmly that what they did and taught was in keeping with the Word of God.

Graham's city-wide evangelism intrigued and interested the fundamentalists. Rice and Jones held many similar city-wide, inter-denominational campaigns. The difference was that Rice and Jones would not think of holding meetings in cooperation with liberals who rejected the deity of the very Jesus to whom they sought to win lost souls. Their approach to the church was not based on indifference to evangelism. Instead, they were convinced that cooperation with the liberals would actually break down the true message of salvation.

The fundamentalists never denied that the evangelicals were their brothers and sisters in Christ. They prayed for them and had often fellowshipped and ministered together with them in earlier years, but they believed that there must be a church where people would be challenged to forsake their sins and come to the risen Christ for salvation. "No man will be really challenged the way he should be challenged to oppose the powers of darkness if the trumpet of the church, supposedly the pillar and ground of the truth, sends forth an uncertain sound."[1]

The biblical data garnered on each side of this issue was inconclusive. Had one movement had a clear and profound biblical basis for its beliefs, more than likely the other would have recognized it. As it was, the debates were unconvincing. Neither movement was willing to concede to the other. One problem is that there is a susceptibility to search the Scriptures to reinforce one's own position. Every interpreter carries certain personal, philosophical, and religious preunderstandings. "Whoever we are, our interpretation of the Bible will largely depend on

---

[1] Van Til, *New Evangelicalism*, 24.

how we come to it. The ideas we begin with will in many ways dictate our conclusions."[2]

One problem facing fundamentalists and evangelicals alike was the lack of a clear understanding of the term "church." Both movements used the term freely, but rarely explained whether they were discussing the visible church, the invisible church, the universal church, a local church, a denomination, or Christendom as a whole. The result was a measure of confusion. Most of the writers seemed to assume that a reader would understand of which church they were speaking. While that was often true, it was also the case that at times two individuals could be speaking the same words and not understanding each other. For instance, in 1946 John Macquarrie wrote:

> Probably more gets written on the Church nowadays than on any other single theological theme. Most of this writing has a practical orientation. We hear about the Church in relation to rapid social change, the Church in a secular society, the Church and reunion, the Church in missions. But, however valuable some of the insights gained in these various fields may be, they need to be guided and correlated by a theological understanding of the Church.[3]

This problem has not been solved. While much more has been written since then on the doctrine of the church, there is still a lack of clarity in the use of the term. A half-century after Macquarrie, Millard Erickson wrote:

> The church is at once a very familiar and a very misunderstood topic. . . . Church structures, even though sometimes very few persons gather within them, are proof of the reality of what we call the church. The church is mentioned in the media, but without much specification as to what is meant. Legislative documents refer to it. In the United States the church is to be kept separate from the state. People belong to a church; they go to church on Sunday. But for all of this familiarity,

---

[2] John F. Balchin, *Understanding Scripture* (Downers Grove, Ill.: InterVarsity, 1982), 17.

[3] John Macquarrie, *Principles of Christian Theology* (New York: Scribner, 1946), 346.

there are frequently considerable confusion and misunderstanding concerning the church.[4]

Another reason for the division between fundamentalists and evangelicals was the lack of agreement on the concepts of fellowship and separation. There was not a common understanding of what fellowship meant to individuals and organizations. Was it merely agreement on certain theological truths, or did it also involve working together as a result of that agreement? While separation was a commonly discussed concept and both movements practiced separation in one form or another, each took a significantly different view of and approach to the concept.

An additional reason for the inability of the fundamentalists and evangelicals to agree scripturally was their diverse hermeneutical approaches. The goal of theology is to establish a norm. Hermeneutics is the means by which individuals explain the biblical data. Fundamentalism was essentially dispensational; evangelicalism was moving away from dispensationalism and toward covenant theology. As such, their interpretation of the same biblical material was sometimes significantly different. Each movement's view of the inauguration and constituency of the church was different. The evangelicals were more willing to accept a reformation emphasis on the universality of the church, its spiritual character, and the unity that such a spiritual entity would have. The fundamentalists were more affect by the concept of the autonomous local church with a minimal emphasis on the universal or invisible church. Fundamentalism looked at the future of the church with the pessimism of dispensationalism; the visible church was heading toward apostasy. Evangelicalism looked at the future of the church with the optimism of covenant theology; the church would emerge victorious.

Orthodoxy has always sought to match its theology with the objective reality of scriptural revelation, but the fundamentalists were confronted with a cultural situation that had no precedence in the New Testament. They sought to establish a biblical basis for separation from an apostate church, when the New Testament had no example of such a church, much less of a Bible believer leaving such a church and starting a new one. While they faltered in their interpretation on occasion, they sought to be

---

[4] Erickson, *Christian Theology*, 1036–37.

faithful to the principles of Scripture in the new context of apostate churches.

Orthodox theology must be placed in the dynamic doctrinal tradition of the church. Church history and the history of doctrine establish "a broad perspective for the study of Christianity and do have the effect of bridging the gap between biblical study and the various contemporizing disciplines."[5] These disciplines reveal how Christians have developed dogmatic positions, ethics, and practical theology. This provides both positive and negative models for the present:

> [T]he recovery of useful concepts and tools from the past, the identification of the origins and reasons for ongoing problems, and the clarification not only of the ideas and teachings we presently hold but also of ways in which useful and valid ideas and teachings are constructed within the community of faith and brought to bear on its present. Finally, the historical and religious trajectory of Christianity has its own theological significance when it is understood as the fundamental reality of the life of the community of faith and as the key to our own grasp of the ongoing significance of the biblical and churchly materials that remain, today, the primary statements of the faith of Christians.[6]

History is an important guide. The goal in historical studies is to attempt to determine that which has been commonly accepted as biblically orthodox. One step toward a valid theology is to identify the historical position that best correlates with the biblical data. History can help prevent one from falling into heterodoxies over which the church has already struggled. It also provides the student of history with an understanding of what has been considered orthodox. It must be acknowledged, however, that "orthodoxy" is not the norm; Scripture is. "Orthodoxy" is not infallible; only Scripture is. Therefore, the goal is conformity to the rule of faith, not necessarily conformity to history.[7] While the fundamentalists and evangelicals agreed that the norm should

---

[5] Richard A. Muller, *The Study of Theology* (Grand Rapids: Zondervan, 1991), 39.

[6] Ibid.

[7] G. W. Bromiley, "Orthodoxy's Task in an Age of Theological Confusion," *Christianity Today* 11 (28 April 1967): 12–13.

be the apostolic witness, there was no consensus on how that witness should be understood.

Both evangelicalism and fundamentalism agreed that true unity could be grounded only in biblical doctrine. Both movements looked back to the early church for support of their positions. The evangelicals claimed to be the heirs of the Reformation. Fundamentalists tended to go back beyond the Reformation and look to the early Anabaptist movements for insight into the separatist position. Because Christendom has been divided historically in its theological understanding of the church, both fundamentalists and evangelicals could claim historic precedent for their positions.

After examining the biblical and historical data and with an understanding of one's own presuppositions, the theologian should then set forth an answer to the question or issue initially raised. The message of God's Word needs to be transmitted in a form that is as faithful as possible to the biblical text and yet as pertinent as possible to the time and situation in which one finds oneself.

There is a danger in overreacting to a situation. The swinging of the pendulum is a problem in theological discussions and actions.

> Reaction is a phenomenon in Christian thought that has played a large role in the history of the Church and its theology. Reaction from some unbiblically one-sided proposition has often landed theology in another unbiblically one-sided proposition. Theologians attacking a caricatured theology have often created their own caricature of Christian thought. Observing that a given aspect of faith was neglected, Christians have often proceeded to accentuate that aspect so much that it became the be-all of the faith, with a resulting neglect of other aspects.[8]

Fundamentalism had reacted to the modernism in the denominations by withdrawing from them and organizing their own associations, schools, and mission organizations. Evangelicalism reacted to the separatism of the fundamentalists and changed the strategy of separation into a strategy of infiltration.

The exposition of the truth involves linguistic restatement. There must be the translation of former statements between languages and

---

[8] G. C. Berkouwer, "Election and Doctrinal Reaction," *Christianity Today* 5 (10 April 1966): 586. Although Berkouwer applied this to soteriology, it is equally valid in all areas of theology, including ecclesiology.

within a language as well. Terms and concepts must be brought into a language understandable to the contemporary population. Historic forms and terms must not, however, be abandoned merely because they are no longer in vogue. There must be some education of biblical and theological terms among Christians, for "historic forms . . . will always have, under Scripture, a certain normative value."[9] There was a failure on both sides in this regard. The term "church" should not be abandoned. It has a historic validity that should not be discarded. Because "church" has a variety of meanings, however, some of which are extra-biblical, it is imperative that distinctions be made and the term explained or identified in specific contexts.

One task of theology is to bring good out of confusion; in this way orthodoxy will become stronger even in an age of apparent defeat and be better able to present the true Word of God to a world that otherwise has only the impotent word of man. There has been a significant increase of interest in ecclesiology and a further explication of the doctrine among evangelicals and fundamentalists in the last half-century.

The structure of biblical, historical, and systematic theology leads a person from theological formulation to practical application. Practical theology is the practice of the church. The apostles, led by the Spirit, established organized, visible churches. It certainly seems that it is the organized church that Paul called the pillar and ground of the truth. The importance of the visible church cannot be overestimated. It is the heart of practical Christianity. It is the center of ministry, the arena of Christian concern, and the storehouse of theological truth. The study of ecclesiology is an important undertaking.

One practical outgrowth of a careful study of the church should be the establishment of the definition of what the church is. Fellowship between "churches" must be maintained by true churches. A misinterpretation of the nature of the church will inevitably lead to the wrong concept of fellowship. The fundamentalists accused the evangelicals of being too broad in their associations; the evangelicals accused the fundamentalists of being too narrow.

Henry accused fundamentalism of concentrating on the fundamentals and displacing the doctrinal responsibilities of the church in the wider

---

[9] Bromiley, "Orthodoxy's Task," 752.

dimensions of historic creeds and confessions of faith.[10] He also indicated that most fundamentalists "seldom treat deeper theological issues with scholarly precision, yet they arrogate to themselves at times an unbecoming authority in fields beyond their mastery."[11] According to Henry, fundamentalism had neglected the doctrine of the church, except to define ecclesiastical separation as a special area of concern.[12]

On the other hand, Van Til accused the evangelicals of abandoning the church of the Reformers, because he argued that the evangelicals' church was no longer composed strictly of those who accept the Christ of the Scriptures. "If therefore Fundamentalism was weak in that it manifested a tendency toward sectarianism, the new evangelicalism appears to be weak in that it tries in vain to combine the historic Protestant view of the church with that of modern liberalism."[13] Carnell defined the church as a "fellowship of all who share in the blessings of the Abrahamic covenant,"[14] while allowing within the church those who reject the atonement provided by the One in whom the promises to Abraham were to terminate. Carnell argued, "Since love is higher than law, the organization [of the church] is a servant of the fellowship. If love were perfect, law would be transcended. Christ alone would rule the church. Laws are made for the unrighteous."[15] In response, Van Til argued that love in the church must be expressed by means of obedience to the Head of the Church. According to Van Til, this was the Reformed view of the church that Machen had accepted and Carnell rejected.

There is a need to further explore the theologies of the leading evangelicals and fundamentalists. Sociological and historical works have too often ignored the theological rationale and purposes of the actions of these individuals. Likewise, the biographies usually provide minimal theological content. Historians need to take into consideration the theological underpinnings of the fundamentalists and evangelicals to fully comprehend their actions.

---

[10] Carl F. H. Henry, *Evangelical Responsibility in Contemporary Theology* (Grand Rapids: Eerdmans, 1957), 32.

[11] Ibid., 34.

[12] Ibid., 35.

[13] Van Til, *The New Evangelicalism*, 12.

[14] Ibid.

[15] Ibid.

The ecclesiologies of the fundamentalists and evangelicals had similarities, and neither movement had within itself a consistent ecclesiology. There were variations in each movement concerning when the church began and concerning the nature or even the existence of an invisible church. Some fundamentalists and most evangelicals included Old Testament saints in the church. Others from both movements believed that the church was strictly a New Testament phenomenon.

There were also consistent differences between the two movements. Fundamentalists insisted on a regenerate church membership. They extended that requirement to the denominations. While they acknowledged that unregenerate individuals could be admitted into a church, it would only happen because the church was misled. Many evangelicals were willing to admit the unregenerate into the denominations; some even expected it.

The primary difference between the two movements centered in the relationship between purity and unity in the churches and denominations. Evangelicals stressed unity (in obedience to Scripture's emphasis on love). For the sake of the unity of the church (and denomination or association), they were often willing to overlook differences in doctrine. The early strategy of new evangelicalism was to infiltrate the modernist denominations in an attempt to return them to the truth, although by the end of the twentieth century that strategy had been abandoned. The fundamentalists stressed the purity of the church and the denomination or the association. As a result, they emphasized the doctrine of separation.

While there were differences between the new evangelical and the fundamentalist ecclesiologies, it must be acknowledged that theology sometimes gave way to emotion. The positions expounded by the evangelicals and fundamentalists were sometimes first practical in nature, then theological in defense. Where fundamentalism and the new evangelicalism were once united on the basic doctrinal issues against those who denied the essentials of the faith, the fundamentalists and evangelicals entered into an all-too-often acrimonious debate over what the evangelicals viewed as non-essentials and what the fundamentalists saw as absolutes of Scripture. In spite of the occasional acrimony of the discussion, the debate yielded positive results, for it resulted in more attention being paid to the doctrine of the church in the following decades.

Theology has often developed out of a crisis, when a given situation forces Bible believers to examine more carefully their positions. Such was the case here. No one can deny that part of the rationale for separation on one hand and union on the other was personality and politics. Pragmatic arguments were frequently raised on each side of the debate. There was, however, a theological basis for the division, a basis that cannot be overlooked and that must be studied further for a clearer understanding of the division between these two movements.

The intervening years have seen changes take place in both evangelicalism and fundamentalism. Both have become broader movements, with greater internal divisions. Both continue to struggle with the issues of separation and the rationale for or against it. The evangelicals have been unable to reclaim the mainline denominations. While some have remained in the mainline denominations, fellowship and involvement in those denominations have been replaced by association with smaller, more cohesive groups. Some of these are national and others regional; the majority are focused on particular concepts (such as Together for the Gospel), linked to a megachurch (such as the Willowbrook association of churches) or personalities (the current popularity of the evangelical gurus and multi-campus churches). Fundamentalist ecclesiology has remained fairly consistent. While the large fundamentalist organizations have decreased in numbers, local associations have been strengthened. The emphasis on the local church and its purity remains essentially unchanged. Fundamentalists continue to engage the culture from a dispensational perspective. The focus on ministry and service through the local church remains important and productive.

The edges of both movements have been coalescing, since neither side has been able to carefully craft a position on fellowship or separation that has captured the minds or hearts of its adherents. Much has been and still could be said about the current state of both movements. Theological critique is always appropriate.

INDEX

Bibliography

Monographs

Ammerman, Nancy. *Bible Believers: Fundamentalists in the Modern World*. New Brunswick: Rutgers University Press, 1987.

_____. "North American Protestant Fundamentalism." In *Fundamentalisms Observed*, ed. Martin E. Marty and R. Scott Appleby, 1-65. Chicago: University of Chicago, 1991.

Aquinas, Thomas. *The Summa Theologica of Saint Thomas Aquinas*.

Ashbrook, John. *Axioms of Separation*. Mentor, Ohio: Here I Stand Books, n.d.

_____. *New Neutralism II*. Mentor, Ohio: Here I Stand Books, 1992.

Ashbrook, William E. *Evangelicalism: The New Neutralism*. Columbus, Ohio: William E. Ashbrook, 1969.

Ashman, Chuck. *The Gospel According to Billy*. Secausuc, N.J.: Lyle Stuart, 1977.

Augustine. *De Baptismo, Contra Donatistas*.

_____. *Sermons on Selected Lessons of the New Testament*.

Averill, Lloyd. *American Theology in the Liberal Tradition*. Philadelphia: Westminster, 1967.

Balmer, Randall, and John D. Woodbridge. "The Princetonians' Viewpoint of Biblical Authority: An Evaluation of the Ernest Sandeen Proposal." In *Scripture and Truth,* ed. D. A. Carson and John D. Woodbridge, 251-286. Grand Rapids: Zondervan, 1983.

Baranowski, Shelley. "Carl McIntire." In *Twentieth-Century Shapers of American Popular Religion*, ed. Charles H. Lippy, 256-263. New York: Greenword, 1989.

Barnhart, Joe E. *The Billy Graham Religion*. Philadelphia: United Church, 1972.

Barth, Karl. "The Church--The Living Congregation of the Living Lord in Jesus Christ." In *Man's Disorder and God's Design*, 67-76. New York: Harper, 1949.

_____. *Dogmatik im Grundriss*. Zurich: Zollikon, 1947.

Bauder, Kevin and Robert Delnay. *One in Hope and Doctrine: Origins of Baptist Fundamentalism 1870-1950*. Schaumburg, IL: Regular Baptist Books, 2014.

Beale, David O. *In Pursuit of Purity: American Fundamentalism Since 1850*. Greenville, S.C.: Unusual Publications, 1986.

Berk, Stephen E. *Calvinism Versus Democracy: Timothy Dwight and the Origins of American Evangelical Orthodoxy*. Hamden, Conn.: Archon Books, 1974.

Berkhof, Louis. *History of Christian Doctrines*. Grand Rapids: Eerdmans, 1937. Reprint, Grand Rapids: Eerdmans, 1994.

Bettenson, Henry. *Documents of the Christian Church*. New York: Oxford, 1947.

Bierman, Bud. *The Local Church and the University*. Greenville, S.C.: Bob Jones University Press, 1973.

Bloesch, Donald. *The Evangelical Renaissance*. Grand Rapids: Eerdmans, 1973.

_____. *The Future of Evangelical Christianity.* Colorado Springs: Helmers and Howard, 1988.

Boles, John B. *The Great Revival, 1787-1805: The Origins of the Southern Evangelical Mind.* Lexington, Ky.: The University Press of Kentucky, 1972.

Bradburn, John W. "Co-operation Among Evangelicals." In *United . . . We Stand: A Report of the Constitutional Convention of the National Association of Evangelicals, LaSalle Hotel, Chicago, Illinois, May 3-6, 1943,* 16-20. Boston: National Association of Evangelicals, 1943.

Bumsted, J. M., ed. *The Great Awakening: The Beginnings of Evangelical Pietism in America,* Primary Sources in American History Series. Waltham, Mass.: Blaisdell Publishing, 1970.

Burnham, George. *Billy Graham: A Mission Accomplished.* Westwood, N.J.: Fleming H. Revell, 1955.

_____. *To the Far Corners: With Billy Graham in Asia.* Westwood, N.J.: Fleming H. Revell, 1956.

_____, and Lee Fisher. *Billy Graham and the New York Crusade.* Grand Rapids: Zondervan, 1957.

Burrage, Champlin. *Early English Dissenters in the Light of Recent Research.* New York: Putnam, 1912.

Buswell, James Oliver, Jr. *A Systematic Theology of the Christian Religion.* Grand Rapids: Zondervan, 1962.

Calvini, Ioannis. *Institutionis Christianae Religionis.* Brunsvigae: C. A. Schwetschke et Filium, 1864.

Campbell, Robert. *Spectrum of Protestant Beliefs.* Milwaukee: Bruce, 1968.

Carlson, Leland H., ed. *The Writings of Henry Barrowe, 1587-1590.* London: George Allen and Unwin, 1962.

Carnell, Edward John. *An Introduction to Christian Apologetics.* Grand Rapids: Eerdmans, 1948.

_____. *A Philosophy of the Christian Religion.* Grand Rapids: Eerdmans, 1952.

_____. *Christian Commitment: An Apologetic.* New York: MacMillan, 1957.

_____. "Fundamentalism." In *A Handbook of Christian Theology,* ed. Marvin Halverson and Arthur A. Cohen, 142-43. Cleveland: World, 1958.

_____. *The Case for Orthodox Theology.* Philadelphia: Westminster, 1959.

_____. "The Government of the Church." In *Basic Christian Doctrines,* ed. Carl F. H. Henry, 248-54. New York: Holt, Rinehart and Winston, 1962.

_____. *The Case for Biblical Christianity.* Grand Rapids: Eerdmans, 1969.

Carpenter, Joel. "The Fundamentalist Leaven and the Rise of an Evangelical United Front." In *The Evangelical Tradition in America,* ed. Leonard I. Sweet, 257-88. Macon: Mercer University, 1984.

_____. "From Fundamentalism to the New Evangelical Coalition." In *Evangelicalism and Modern America,* ed. George Marsden, 3-16. Grand Rapids: Eerdmans, 1984.

_____. *Revive Us Again: The Reawakening of American Fundamentalism.* New York: Oxford University Press, 1997.

Carter, Paul. "The Fundamentalist Defense of the Faith." In *Change and Continuity in Twentieth Century America: The 1920's,* ed. John Braeman, Robert Bremner, and David Brody, 179-214. Columbus, Ohio: Ohio State University Press, 1968.

Cauthen, Kenneth. *The Impact of American Religious Liberalism.* New York: Harper and Row, 1962.

Clabaugh, Gary. *Thunder on the Right: The Protestant Fundamentalists.* Chicago: Nelson-Hall, 1974.

Cleveland, Catharine C. *The Great Awakening in the West, 1797-1805.* Chicago: University of Chicago, 1916. Reprint, Gloucester, Mass.: Peter Smith, 1959.

Cohen, Gary. *Biblical Separation Defended: A Biblical Critique of Ten New Evangelical Arguments.* Philadelphia: Presbyterian and Reformed, 1966.

Cole, Stewart G. *The History of Fundamentalism.* New York: Richard R. Smith, 1931.

Colquhoun, Frank. *Harringay Story: The Official Record of the Billy Graham Greater London Crusade, 1954.* London: Hodder and Stoughton, 1955.

Cyprian. *De unitate Ecclesiae.*

_____. *Epistolae.*

Dalhouse, Mark Taylor. *An Island in the Lake of Fire: Bob Jones University, Fundamentalism, and The Separatist Movement.* Athens: University of Georgia Press, 1996.

Dana, H. E. *A Manual of Ecclesiology.* Kansas City: Central Seminary, 1945.

Dixon, A. C., Louis Meyer, and R. A. Torrey, eds. *The Fundamentals: A Testimony to the Truth.* Chicago: Testimony Publishing Company, [1910-1915].

Dollar, George. *A History of Fundamentalism in America.* Greenville, S.C.: Bob Jones University Press, 1973.

_____. *The Fight for Fundamentalism: American Fundamentalism, 1973-1983.* Sarasota, Fl.: George Dollar, 1983.

Epstein, Benjamin, and Arnold Forster. *Danger on the Right.* New York: Random House, 1964.

Erickson, Millard. *Christian Theology,* 2d ed. Grand Rapids: Baker, 1998.

_____. *New Evangelical Theology.* Westwood, N.J.: Revell, 1968.

Evangelical Action! A Report of the Organization of the National Association of Evangelicals for United Action. Boston: Fellowship, 1942.

Falwell, Jerry, ed. *The Fundamentalist Phenomenon: The Resurgence of Conservative Christianity.* Garden City: Doubleday, 1981.

Ferm, Robert O. *Cooperative Evangelism: Is Billy Graham Right or Wrong?* Grand Rapids: Zondervan, 1958.

_____. *The Psychology of Christian Conversion.* Westwood: Revell, 1959.

Findley, J. F., Jr. *Dwight L. Moody: American Evangelist, 1837-1899.* Chicago: University of Chicago, 1969.

Foster, Frank Hugh. *A Genetic History of the New England Theology.* New York: Russell and Russell, 1963.

Ford, Leighton. *The Christian Persuader.* Minneapolis: World Wide Publications, 1966.

Frady, Marshall. *Billy Graham: A Parable of American Righteousness.* Boston: Little, Brown, 1979.

Furniss, Norman. *The Fundamentalist Controversy 1918-1931.* New Haven: Yale University, 1954.

Gabler, Johann Phillip. "Von der richtigen Unterscheidung der biblischen und der dogmatischen Theologie und der rechten Bestimmung ihrer beider Zeile." In *Biblische Theologie des Neuen Testaments in ihrer Anfangszeit,* ed. Otto Merk, 178-89. Marburg: N. G. Elwert, 1972.

Garret, James Leo, E. Glenn Hinson, and James E. Tull, eds. *Are Southern Baptists "Evangelicals"?* Macon: Mercer, 1983.

Gasper, Louis. *The Fundamentalist Movement: 1930-1956.* Netherlands: Mouton and Co., 1963. Reprint, Grand Rapids: Baker, 1981.

Gaustad, Edwin Scott. *The Great Awakening in New England.* New York: Harper and Brothers, 1957.

George, Timothy, and David S. Dockery. *Baptist Theologians.* Nashville: Broadman, 1990.

Giobney, Ezra P., and Agnes M. Potter. *The Life of Mark A. Matthews, "Tall Pine of the Sierras."* Grand Rapids: Eerdmans, 1948.

Graham, Billy. *Peace with God.* Waco: Word, 1953.

_____. *The Challenging Church.* Minneapolis: Billy Graham Evangelistic Association, 1960.

_____. *My Answer.* Garden City: Doubleday, 1960.

_____. *Just As I Am.* San Francisco: HarperCollins, 1997.

Gundry, Stanley N. *Love Them In: The Proclamation Theology of D. L. Moody.* Chicago: Moody Press, 1976.

Haroutunian, Joseph. *Piety Versus Moralism: The Passing of the New England Theology.* New York: Henry Holt, 1932. Reprint, New York: Harper and Row, 1970.

Hatch, Nathan, and Mark Noll, eds. *The Bible in America.* New York: Oxford University, 1982.

Henry, Carl F. H. *Remaking the Modern Mind.* Grand Rapids: Eerdmans, 1946.

_____. *The Uneasy Conscience of Modern Fundamentalism.* Grand Rapids: Eerdmans, 1947.

_____. *The Protestant Dilemma: An Analysis of the Current Impasse in Theology.* Grand Rapids: Eerdmans, 1949.

_____. *Fifty Years of Protestant Theology.* Boston: A. W. Wilde, 1950.

_____. *The Drift of Western Thought.* Grand Rapids: Eerdmans, 1951.

_____. *Contemporary Evangelical Thought*. Great Neck, N.Y.: Channel, 1957.

_____. *Evangelical Responsibility in Contemporary Theology*. Grand Rapids: Eerdmans, 1957.

_____. *Frontiers in Modern Theology: A Critique of Current Theological Trends*. Chicago: Moody, 1966.

_____. *The God Who Shows Himself*. Waco: Word, 1966.

_____. *Evangelicals at the Brink of Crisis: Significance of the World Congress of Evangelism*. Waco: Word, 1967.

_____. *Faith at the Frontiers*. Chicago: Moody, 1969.

_____. *A Plea for Evangelical Demonstration*. Grand Rapids: Baker, 1971.

_____. *Evangelicals in Search of Identity*. Waco: Word, 1976.

_____. *God, Revelation and Authority*. Waco: Word, 1976-1979.

_____. *Confessions of a Theologian: An Autobiography*. Waco: Word, 1986.

Henry, Carl F. H., ed. *Basic Christian Doctrines: Contemporary Evangelical Thought*. New York: Holt, Rinehart and Winston, 1962.

Henry, Carl F. H., and Kenneth S. Kantzer, eds. *Evangelical Affirmations*. Grand Rapids: Zondervan, 1990.

High, Stanley. *Billy Graham: The Personal Story of the Man, His Message, and His Mission*. New York: McGraw-Hill, 1956.

Hodgson, Leonard. "The Doctrine of the Church as Held and Taught in the Church of England." In *The Nature of the Church*, ed. R. Newton Flew, 121-46. New York: Harper, 1952.

Hofstadter, Richard. *Anti-Intellectualism in American Life*. New York: Alfred A. Knopf, 1964.

Hordern, William. *A Layman's Guide to Protestant Liberalism*. New York: MacMillan, 1960.

Horton, Michael Scott. *Made in America: The Shaping of Modern American Evangelicalism*. Grand Rapids: Baker, 1991.

Hubbard, David. *What We Believe and Teach*. Pasadena: Fuller Theological Seminary, n.d.

Hudson, Winthrop S. *American Protestantism*. Chicago: University of Chicago Press, 1961.

Hull, Merle R. *What a Fellowship! The First Fifty Years of the GARBC*. Schaumburg, Ill.: Regular Baptist Press, 1981.

Hulse, Errol. *Billy Graham--The Pastor's Dilemma*. Hounslow, Middlesex, England: Maurice Allen, 1966.

Hunt, George L., ed. *Ten Makers of Modern Protestant Thought*. New York: Associated Press, 1958.

Hunter, James Davison. *Evangelicalism: The Coming Generation*. Chicago: University of Chicago Press, 1980.

_____. *American Evangelicalism: Conservative Religion and the Quandary of Modernity*. New Brunswick, N.J.: Rutgers University Press, 1983.

Hutchinson, Thomas. *The History of the Colony of Massachusetts Bay*. Boston: Prince Society, 1865.

Hutchison, William R. *The Modernist Impulse in American Protestantism*. Cambridge, Mass.: Harvard University Press, 1976.

Hutson, Curtis. *New Evangelicalism, An Enemy of Fundamentalism*. Murfreesboro, Tenn.: Sword of the Lord, 1984.

_____. *Unnecessary Divisions Among Fundamentalisms*. Murfreesboro, Tenn.: Sword of the Lord, 1990.

Ignatius. *Pro.j Filade,lfeij*.

_____. *Pro.j Smurnai,ouj*.

Irenaeus. *Adversus haereses*.

Jackson, Paul R. *The Position, Attitudes and Objectives of Biblical Separation*. Des Plaines, Ill.: General Association of Regular Baptist Churches, n.d.

Johnson, Edward. *The Wonder Working Providences of Zion's Saviour in New England*. Original Narratives of Early American History, ed. J. Franklin Jameson, vol. 15. New York: Barnes and Noble, 1959.

Johnson, R. K. *Builder of Bridges*. Murfreesboro, Tenn.: Sword of the Lord, 1969.

Johnston, Robert K. *Evangelicals at an Impasse*. Atlanta: John Knox, 1978.

Jones, Bob, Sr. *Things I Have Learned*. New York: L. B. Printing, 1944.

_____. "Evangelism Today--Where Is It Headed." In *Do Right!*, 209-228. Murfreesboro, Tenn.: Sword of the Lord, 1971.

Jones, Bob, Jr. *Scriptural Separation*. Greenville, S.C.: Bob Jones University Press, 1971.

_____. *Heritage of Faith*. Greenville, S.C.: Bob Jones University Press, 1973.

_____. *Cornbread and Caviar: Reminiscence and Reflections*. Greenville, S.C.: Bob Jones University Press, 1985.

Jones, Bob, III. *Facts John R. Rice Will Not Face*. Greenville, S.C.: Bob Jones University Press, 1977.

Jones, Rufus. *Mysticism and Democracy in the English Commonwealth*. Cambridge: Harvard, 1932.

Jorstad, Erling. *The Politics of Doomsday: Fundamentalists of the Far Right*. Nashville: Abingdon, 1970.

Kantzer, Kenneth, ed. *Evangelical Roots*. New York: Thomas Nelson, 1978.

Keller, Charles Roy. *The Second Great Awakening in Connecticut*. New Haven, Conn.: Yale University Press, 1942.

Ketcham, Robert. *The Answer*. Chicago: Regular Baptist, 1949.

_____. *Facts for Baptists to Face*. Waterloo, Iowa: Walnut Street Baptist Church, 1936.

Kidd, B. J. *The Thirty-Nine Articles: Their History and Explanation*. New York: Edwin S. Gorham, 1906.

Laman, Clarence. *God Calls a Man*. Collingswood, N.J.: Christian Beacon, 1959.

Leetscher, Lefferts. *The Broadening Church*. Philadelphia: University of Philadelphia, 1954.

Leibman, Robert C., and Robert Wuthrow. *The New Christian Right: Mobilization and Legitimation*. New York: Aldine, 1983.

Lewis, Gordon S. "Edward John Carnell." In *Handbook of Evangelical Theologians*, ed. Walter A. Elwell, 321-37. Grand Rapids: Baker, 1993.

Lewis, Leicester C. "The Anglican Church." In *The Nature of the Church*, ed. R. Newton Flew, 309-17. New York: Harper, 1952.

Lightner, Robert P. *New Evangelicalism*. Des Plaines, Ill.: Regular Baptist, 1954.

_____. *Neo-Liberalism*. Chicago: Regular Baptist, 1959.

_____. *Neo-evangelicalism*. Des Plaines, Ill.: Regular Baptist, 1969.

_____. *Neoevangelicalism Today*. Schaumburg, Ill.: Regular Baptist, 1978.

Lindsell, Harold. *The Battle for the Bible*. Grand Rapids: Zondervan, 1976.

_____. *The Battle in the Balance*. Grand Rapids: Zondervan, 1979.

_____. *Park Street Prophet: A Life of Harold John Ockenga*. Wheaton: Van Kampen, 1951.

Littell, Franklin Hamlin. *The Origins of Sectarian Protestantism: A Study of the Anabaptist View of the Church*. New York: Macmillan, 1964.

Loane, Marcus L. "Christ and His Church." In *Fundamentals of the Faith*, ed. Carl F. H. Henry, 169-86. Grand Rapids: Zondervan, 1969.

Lockard, W. David. *The Unheard Billy Graham*. Waco: Word, 1971.

Longfield, Bradley J. *The Presbyterian Controversy: Fundamentalists, Modernists, and Moderates*. New York: Oxford, 1991.

Luther, Martin. "Ad librum eximii Magistri Nostri Magistri Ambrosii Catharini, defensoris Silvestri Prieratis acerrimi, responsio." In *D. Martin Luthers Werke*, Weimar edition (1521).

_____. "Von den Conciliis und Kirchen." In *D. Martin Luthers Werke*, Weimar edition (1914).

_____. "Von dem Papsttum zu Rom wider den hochberühmten Romanisten zu Leipzig." In *D. Martin Luthers Werke*, Weimar edition (1888).

Machen, J. Gresham. *Christianity and Liberalism*. New York: Macmillan, 1923.

Marsden, George, ed. *Evangelicalism and Modern America*. Grand Rapids: Eerdmans, 1984.

Marsden, George M. *The Evangelical Mind and the New School Presbyterian Experience*. New Haven: Yale University, 1970.

_____. "From Fundamentalism to Evangelicalism: A Historical Analysis." In *The Evangelicals: What They Believe, Who They Are, and Where They Are Changing*, ed. David F. Wells and John D. Woodbridge, 122-42. Nashville: Abingdon, 1975.

_____. *Fundamentalism and American Culture*. New York: Oxford, 1980.

_____. *Reforming Fundamentalism: Fuller Seminary and the New Evangelicalism*. Grand Rapids: Eerdmans, 1987.

_____. *Understanding Fundamentalism and Evangelicalism*. Grand Rapids: Eerdmans, 1991.

Martin, William. *Prophet with Honor: The Billy Graham Story*. New York: William Morrow, 1991.

Marty, Martin E., and R. Scott Appleby, eds. *Fundamentalisms Observed*. Chicago: University of Chicago, 1991.

Marty, Martin. "Tensions Within Contemporary Evangelicalism." In *The Evangelicals: Who They Are, What They Believe, Where They Are Headed*, ed. David F. Wells and John D. Woodbridge, 170-88. Nashville: Abingdon Press, 1975.

Maxon, Charles H. *The Great Awakening in the Middle Colonies*. Chicago: University of Chicago, 1920.

McGrath, Alister. *Christian Theology, An Introduction*. Oxford: Blackwell, 1994.

MacGregor, Geddes. *Corpus Christi: The Nature of the Church According to the Reformed Tradition*. Philadelphia: Westminster, 1958.

McIntire, Carl. *Christ and Him Crucified*. New York: American Council of Christian Churches, 1944.

_____. *The Testimony of Separation*. Collingswood, N.J.: Christian Beacon, 1944.

_____. *Twentieth Century Reformation*. Collingswood, N.J.: Christian Beacon, 1944.

_____. *For Such a Time as This*. Collingswood, N.J.: Christian Beacon, 1946.

_____. *Modern Tower of Babel*. Collingswood, N.J.: Christian Beacon, 1949.

_____. *The Epistle of the Apostasy*. Collingswood, N.J.: Christian Beacon, 1958.

_____. *Author of Liberty*. Collingswood, N.J.: 20th Century Reformation Hour, 1963.

_____. *Servants of Apostasy*. Collingswood, N.J.: Christian Beacon, 1965.

_____. *The Death of a Church*. Collingswood, N.J.: Christian Beacon, 1967.

_____. *Outside the Gate*. Collingswood, N.J.: Christian Beacon, 1967.

McLachlan, Douglas R. *Reclaiming Authentic Fundamentalism*. Independence, Mo.: American Association of Christian Schools, 1993.

McLoughlin, William G. *Modern Revivalism: Charles Grandison Finney to Billy Graham*. New York: Ronald, 1959.

_____. *Billy Graham: Revivalist in a Secular Age*. New York: Ronald, 1960.

_____. *Revivals, Awakenings, and Reforms: An Essay on Religion and Social Change in America, 1607-1977*. Chicago: Chicago University Press, 1978.

Migne, J. P., ed. *Patrologiae*. Paris: Apud Garnier Fratres, various dates.

Miller, Perry. *Orthodoxy in Massachusetts, 1630-1650*. Cambridge: University Press, 1933.

"Minutes of the Committee for United Action Among Evangelicals" (27-28 October 1941, Chicago). Records of the African Inland Mission, Collection 81, Box 14, Folder 27, Billy Graham Center Archives, Wheaton, Ill.

Mitchell, Curtis. *God in the Garden: The Story of the Billy Graham New York Crusade*. Garden City: Doubleday, 1957.

Moore, R. Laurence. *Religious Outsiders and the Making of Americans*. New York: Oxford, 1986.

Morgan, Edmund S. *Roger Williams: The Church and the State*. New York: Harcourt, Brace, 1967.

Moritz, Fred. *"Be Ye Holy" The Call to Christian Separation*. Greenville, S.C.: Bob Jones University Press, 1994.

Morris, James. *The Preachers*. New York: St. Martin Press, 1973.

Mowry, George. *The Urban Nation*. New York: Hill and Wang, 1965.

Murch, James D. *Cooperation without Compromise: A History of the National Association of Evangelicals*. Grand Rapids: Eerdmans, 1956.

_____. *The Growing Super Church*. Cincinnati: The National Association of Evangelicals, 1952.

Murdoch, J. Murray. *Portrait of Obedience: The Biography of Robert T. Ketcham*. Schaumburg, Ill.: Regular Baptist, 1979.

Nash, Ronald. The *New Evangelicalism*. Grand Rapids: Zondervan, 1963.

Nelson, Rudolph. *The Making and Unmaking of an Evangelical Mind*. New York: Cambridge, 1977.

Niebuhr, H. Richard. "Fundamentalism." In *Encyclopedia of Social Sciences*, 526-27. New York: 1937.

Noll, Mark. *Between Faith and Criticism: Evangelicals, Scholarship, and the Bible in America*. San Francisco: Harper and Row, 1986.

Noll, Mark, and David Wells, eds. *Christian Faith and Practice in the Modern World*. Grand Rapids: Eerdmans, 1988.

Ockenga, Harold J. *These Religious Affections*. Grand Rapids: Zondervan, 1937.

_____. *Our Protestant Heritage*. Grand Rapids: Zondervan, 1938.

_____. *Everyone That Believeth: Expository Addresses on St. Paul's Epistle to the Romans*. New York: Revell, 1942.

_____. *Our Evangelical Faith*. New York: Revell, 1946.

_____. *The Spirit of the Living God*. New York: Revell, 1947.

_____. *Faithful in Christ Jesus*. New York: Revell, 1948.

_____. *The Church in God: Expository Values in Thessalonians*. Westwood: Revell, 1956.

_____. *The Church God Blesses*. Pasadena: Fuller Missions Fellowship, 1959.

_____. *The Epistles to the Thessalonians, Proclaiming the New Testament*. Grand Rapids: Baker, 1962.

_____. Foreward to *The Battle for the Bible*, by Harold Lindsell. Grand Rapids: Zondervan, 1976.

_____. "From Fundamentalism, Through New Evangelicalism, to Evangelicalism." In *Evangelical Roots*, Kenneth Kantzer, ed., 35-48. New York: Thomas Nelson, 1978.

Odell, Calvin. *The GARBC and Its Attendant Movement*. Salem, Ore.: Western Baptist Bible, 1975.

Ogden, Schubert M. *Doing Theology Today.* Valley Forge: Trinity Press International, 1996.

Otten, Bernard John. *Manual of the History of Dogmas.* St. Louis: Herder, 1918.

Packer, James I. *Fundamentalism and the Word of God.* Grand Rapids: Eerdmans, 1959.

_____. "The Nature of the Church." In *Basic Christian Doctrines: Contemporary Evangelical Thought,* ed. Carl F. H. Henry, 241-47. New York: Holt, Rinehart and Winston, 1962.

Paine, Stephen W. *"Separation" Is Separating Evangelicals.* Boston: Fellowship, 1951.

Patterson, Bob E. *Carl F. H. Henry.* Makers of the Modern Theological Mind Series. Waco: Word, 1983.

Pickering, Ernest D. *Biblical Separation: The Struggle for a Pure Church.* Schaumburg, Ill.: Regular Baptist Press, 1979.

_____. *The Tragedy of Compromise.* Greenville, S.C.: Bob Jones University Press, 1994.

Poling, David. *Why Billy Graham?* Grand Rapids: Zondervan, 1977.

Pollock, John. *Billy Graham: The Authorized Biography.* New York: McGraw-Hill, 1966.

_____. *Billy Graham, Evangelist to the World: An Authorized Biography of the Decisive Years.* New York: Harper and Row, 1979.

Price, Theron D. "The Anabaptist View of the Church." In *What is the Church?,* ed. Duke McCall, 97-117. Nashville: Broadman, 1958.

Quebedeaux, Richard. *The Young Evangelicals: Revolution in Orthodoxy.* New York: Harper and Row, 1974.

_____. *The Worldly Evangelicals.* San Francisco: Harper and Row, 1978.

_____. *By What Authority: The Rise of Personality Cults in American Christianity.* San Francisco: Harper and Row, 1982.

Radmacher, Earl D. *What the Church is All About.* Chicago: Moody, 1978.

Ramm, Bernard. *The Evangelical Heritage.* Waco: Word, 1973.

_____. *After Fundamentalism.* San Francisco: Harper and Row, 1983.

Rauschenbusch, Walter. *Christianity and the Social Crisis.* New York: Macmillan, 1910.

_____. *A Theology for the Social Gospel.* New York: Macmillan, 1922.

Reese, Ed. *The Life and Ministry of Carl McIntire.* Christian Hall of Fame Series. Glenwood, Ill.: Fundamental Publishers, n.d.

Reese, Ed. *The Life and Ministry of Bob Jones, Sr.* Christian Hall of Fame Series. Glenwood, Ill.: Fundamental Publishers, 1975.

Rian, Edwin H. *The Presbyterian Conflict.* Grand Rapids: Eerdmans, 1940.

Ribuffo, Leo. *The Old Christian Right: The Protestant Far Right from the Great Depression to the Cold War.* Philadelphia: Temple University Press, 1983.

Rice, John R. "'Churches' and 'The Church.'" In *Twelve Tremendous Themes,* 149-161. Wheaton: Sword of the Lord, 1943.

_____. *The Unequal Yoke*. Murfreesboro, Tenn.: Sword of the Lord, 1944.

_____. *Come Out or Stay In?* Nashville: Thomas Nelson, 1974.

_____. *I Am a Fundamentalist*. Murfreesboro, Tenn.: Sword of the Lord, 1975.

Roberts, Alexander, and James Donaldson, eds. *The Ante-Nicene Fathers*, American Reprint of the Edinburgh Edition. Grand Rapids: Eerdmans, 1971.

Robinson, John. *Works*. Edited by Robert Ashton. Boston: Doctrinal Tract and Book Society, 1851.

Rosas, Joseph L. "Edward John Carnell." In *Baptist Theologians*, ed. Timothy George and David Dockery, 606-26. Nashville: Broadman, 1990.

Roy, Ralph Lord. *Apostles of Discord: A Study of Organized Bigotry and Disruption on the Fringes of Protestantism*. Boston: Beacon, 1953.

Russell, C. Allyn. *Voices of American Fundamentalism*. Philadelphia: Westminster, 1976.

Rutman, Darrett B., ed. *The Great Awakening: Event and Exegesis*. New York: John Wiley and Sons, 1970.

Sandeen, Ernest. *The Roots of Fundamentalism: British and American Millenarianism, 1800-1930*. Chicago: University of Chicago Press, 1970.

Schaeffer, Francis. *The Great Evangelical Disaster*. Westchester, Ill.: Crossway Books, 1984.

Schaff, Philip. *The Creeds of Christendom*. Harper and Row, 1931. Reprint, Grand Rapids: Baker, 1985.

Schaff, Philip, and Henry Wace, eds. *A Select Library of Nicene and Post-Nicene Fathers of the Christian Church*, Second Series. Grand Rapids: Eerdmans, 1969.

Schleiermacher, Friedrich. *The Christian Faith*. Translated by H. R. Mackintosh and J. S. Stewart. Edinburgh: T. and T. Clark, 1928.

_____. *On Religion: Speeches Addressed to Its Cultured Despisers*. Translated by Terrence N. Tice. Richmond: John Knox, 1969.

Scofield, C. I. *Rightly Dividing the Word of Truth*. N.p.: n.p., n.d.

_____. *The Scofield Bible Correspondence Course*. Chicago: Moody Bible Institute, 1907.

_____. *The Scofield Reference Bible*. New York: Oxford, 1945.

Shelley, Bruce. *Conservative Baptists, A Story of Twentieth Century Dissent*. Denver: Conservative Baptist, 1960.

_____. *A History of Conservative Baptists*. Denver: Conservative Baptist, 1960.

_____. *Evangelicalism in America*. Grand Rapids: Eerdmans, 1967.

Sims, John A. *Edward John Carnell: Defender of the Faith*. Washington, D.C.: University Press of America, 1979.

Stonehouse, Ned B. *J. Gresham Machen: A Biographical Memoir*. Grand Rapids: Eerdmans, 1954.

Stott, J. R. W. *Fundamentalism and Evangelicalism*. Grand Rapids: Eerdmans, 1959.

Stowell, Joseph M. *Background and History of the General Association of Regular Baptist Churches*. Hayward, Calif.: J. F. May, 1949.

Strickland, Arthur B. *Roger Williams: Prophet and Pioneer of Soul-Liberty*. Chicago: Judson, 1919.

Sumner, Robert L. *A Man Sent from God*. Grand Rapids: Eerdmans, 1959.

Sweet, Leonard I., ed. *The Evangelical Tradition in America*. Macon: Mercer University Press, 1984.

Sweet, William Warren. *Revivalism in America: Its Origin, Growth and Influence*. New York: Charles Scribner's Sons, 1944.

Tice, Margaret Beall. *Bob Jones University*. Greenville, S.C.: Bob Jones University Press, 1976.

Tracy, Joseph. *The Great Awakening: A History of the Revival of Religion in the Time of Edwards and Whitefield*. Boston: Tappan and Dennet, 1842.

Triglot Concordia: The Symbolic Books of the Ev. Lutheran Church. St. Louis: Concordia, 1921.

Trollinger, William Vance, Jr. *God's Empire: William Bell Riley and Midwestern Fundamentalism*. Madison: University of Wisconsin, 1991.

Tulga, Chester. *The Case against Modernism*. Chicago: Conservative Baptist Fellowship, 1949.

_____. *The Case against Modernism in Evangelism*. Chicago: Conservative Baptist Fellowship, 1949.

_____. *The Case against Modernism in Foreign Missions*. Chicago: Conservative Baptist Fellowship, 1949.

_____. *The Case against the Federal Council of Churches*. Chicago: Conservative Baptist Fellowship, 1949.

_____. *The Case against the National Council of Churches*. Chicago: Conservative Baptist Fellowship, 1951.

_____. *The Independence of the Local Church*. Chicago: Conservative Baptist Fellowship, 1951.

_____. *The Doctrine of Holiness in These Times*. Arlington Heights, Ill.: Conservative Baptist Association of America, 1952.

_____. *The Doctrine of Separation in These Times*. Chicago: Conservative Baptist Fellowship, 1952.

_____. *The Doctrine of the Church in Times Like These*. Chicago: Conservative Baptist Fellowship, 1953.

_____. *The Fundamentalism of Yesterday, The Evangelicalism of Today, and the Fundamentalism of Tomorrow*. Chicago: Conservative Baptist Fellowship, n.d.

"United We Stand: A Report of the Constitutional Convention of the National Association of Evangelicals. Chicago, May 3-6, 1943." In *A New Evangelical*

Coalition: Early Documents of the National Association of Evangelicals, ed. Joel Carpenter, 1-63. New York: Garland, 1988.

Van Til, Cornelius. *The New Evangelicalism.* Philadelphia: Westminster Theological Seminary, n.d.

Van Impe, Jack. *Heart Disease in Christ's Body: Fundamentalism . . . Is It Sidetracked?* Royal Oaks, Mi.: Jack Van Impe Ministries, 1984.

Walden, Viola. *John R. Rice: "The Captain of our Team."* Murfreesboro, Tenn.: Sword of the Lord, 1990.

Walker, Williston. *Creeds and Platforms of Congregationalism.* Boston: Pilgrim, 1960.

_____. *A History of the Congregational Churches in the United States.* The American Church History Series, ed. Philip Schaff, vol. 3. New York: Christian Literature, 1894.

Ward, Charles G. *The Billy Graham Christian Worker's Handbook.* Minneapolis: World Wide, 1984.

Weber, Timothy. *Living in the Shadow of the Second Coming: American Premillennialism, 1875-1925.* New York: Oxford, 1979.

Webber, Robert and Donald Bloesch. *The Orthodox Evangelicals.* New York: Thomas Nelson, 1978.

Weisberger, Bernard A. *They Gathered at the River: The Story of the Great Revivalists and Their Impact upon Religion in America.* Boston: Little, Brown, 1958.

Wells, David. "No Offense: I Am an Evangelical: A Search for Self-Definition." In *A Time to Speak Out: The Evangelical-Jewish Encounter,* ed. A. James Rudin and Marvin R. Wilson, 20-40. Grand Rapids: Eerdmans, 1987.

Wells, David F., and John D. Woodbridge. *The Evangelicals: Who They Are, What They Believe, Where They Are Changing.* Nashville: Abingdon, 1975.

Westin, Gunnar. *The Free church Through the Ages.* Translated by Virgil A. Olson. Nashville: Broadman, 1958.

Wirt, Sherwood Eliot. *Crusade at the Golden Gate.* New York: Harper and Brothers, 1959.

Witmer, S. A. *The Bible College Story: Education with Dimension.* Manhasset, N.Y.: Channel, 1962.

Woodbridge, Charles J. *The New Evangelicalism.* Greenville, S.C.: Bob Jones University Press, 1969.

_____. *Biblical Separation.* Halifax, Nova Scotia, Canada: People's Gospel Hour, 1971.

_____. *Reaping the Whirlwind.* Collingswood, N.J.: Christian Beacon, 1977.

Woodbridge, John D., Mark A. Noll, and Nathan O. Hatch. *The Gospel in America.* Grand Rapids: Zondervan, 1979.

Wright, J. Elwin. "An Historical Statement of Events Leading Up to the National Conference at St. Louis." In *Evangelical Action! A Report of the Organization of the National Association of Evangelicals for United Action,* 3-16. Boston: United Action Press, 1942.

Wright, Melton. *Fortress of Faith.* Grand Rapids: Eerdmans, 1960.

Yoder, John H. "The Prophetic Dissent of the Anabaptists." In *The Recovery of the Anabaptist Vision,* ed. Guy Franklin Hershberger, 93-104. Scottdale, Penn.: Herald, 1957.

Young, Alexander, ed. *Chronicles of the First Planters of the Colony of Massachusetts Bay, 1623-1636.* New York: Da Capo, n.d.

Periodicals

"About Billy Graham's New York Crusade: Dr. Bob Jones Says." *Sword of the Lord* (3 May 1957): 12.

Bell, Nelson. "On Separation." *Christianity Today* 16 (8 October 1971): 26-27.

Bell, Robert D. "The True Unity of the Church." *Biblical Viewpoint* 9 (April 1977): 42-46.

Bradbury, John W. "The N. B. C. Fundamentalists." *Watchman-Examiner* 25 (12 August 1937): 916-918.

Bromiley, Geoffrey W. "Orthodoxy's Task in an Age of Theological Confusion." *Christianity Today* 11 (28 April 1967): 748-752.

Buswell, J. Oliver, Jr. "The American and International Councils of Christian Churches." *Christianity Today* 9 (29 January 1965): 429-431.

Carnell, Edward John. "Orthodoxy and Ecumenism." *Christianity Today* 2 (1 September 1958): 15-18, 24.

_____. "Post-Fundamentalist Faith." *The Christian Century* 76 (26 August 1959): 971.

_____. "Orthodoxy: Cultic vs. Classical." *The Christian Century* 77 (30 March 1960): 377-79.

_____. "The Government of the Church." *Christianity Today* 6 (22 June 1962): 930-931.

Carpenter, Joel. "A Shelter in the Time of Storm: Fundamentalist Institutions and the Rise of Evangelical Protestantism, 1929-1942." *Church History* 49 (March 1980): 62-75.

_____. "Understanding Fundamentalism." *Evangelical Studies Bulletin* 4 (March 1987): 4-6.

Custer, Stewart. "The Walk of the Church." *Biblical Viewpoint* 9 (April 1977): 47-63.

Davis, Ralph T. Open Letter, The Committee of United Action Among Evangelicals. 2 March 1942. Records of the African Inland Mission, Collection 81, Box 14, Folder 27, Billy Graham Center Archives, Wheaton, Illinois.

Dollar, George W. "An Inauguration by Independents." *Faith for the Family* 1 (May/June 1973): 9-10, 27.

Ervin, Howard M. "A Re-examination of 2 Corinthians 6:14-7:1." *Baptist Bulletin* 15 (April 1950): 4-5, 20-21.

Fea, John. "Carl McIntire: From Fundamentalist Presbyterian to Presbyterian Fundamentalist." *American Presbyterians* 72 (Winter 1994): 253-268.

_____. "Understanding the Changing Facade of Twentieth-Century American Protestant Fundamentalism: Toward a Historical Definition." *Trinity Journal* 15 (1994): 181-199.

Feinberg, Charles L., et al. "An Answer to Is Evangelical Theology Changing." *The King's Business* (January 1957): 23-28.

Ferm, Robert O. "Evanston, 1954: Unity Through Compromise." *United Evangelical Action* 13 (15 Jan 1955): 5-10.

_____. "Cooperative Evangelism: Why Not?" *Christianity Today* 2 (14 April 1958): 16-18.

George, Timothy. "Partly Fearing, Partly Hoping: Evangelicals, Southern Baptists, and the Quest for a New Consensus." *Perspectives in Religious Studies* 17 (Summer 1990): 167-172.

Graham, Billy. "Billy Graham on Separation." *Eternity* 9 (November 1958): 17-19, 47.

_____. "Taking the World's Temperature: An Interview with Billy Graham." *Christianity Today* 21 (23 Sept 1977): 16-19.

Grounds, Vernon. "The Nature of Evangelicalism." *Eternity* 7 (February 1956): 12-13, 42-43.

_____. "Separation--Yes, Schism--No." *Eternity* 14 (August 1963): 17-22.

Hamilton, H. G. "Secretary Lerrigo Struggles Hard to Explain." *Baptist Bulletin* 1 (August 1933): 2.

Handy, Robert T. "The American Religious Depression, 1925-1935." *Church History* 29 (March 1960): 1-29.

Henry, Carl F. H. "The Vigor of the New Evangelicalism." *Christian Life and Times* 9 (January 1948): 30-32; 9 (March 1948): 35-38, 85; 9 (April 1948): 32-34, 65-69.

_____. "The Theology of Billy Graham." *The Churchman* (January-March 1954): 46-54.

_____. "What is this Fundamentalism?" *United Evangelical Action* 14 (15 July 1955): 3-6.

_____. "The Unity That Christ Sustains." *United Evangelical Action* 15 (1 January 1956): 3-4, 15.

_____. "Why 'Christianity Today'?" *Christianity Today* 1 (18 October 1956): 20-21.

_____. "The Perils of Independency." *Christianity Today* 1 (12 November 1956): 20-23.

_____. "The Perils of Ecumenicity." *Christianity Today* 1 (26 November 1956): 20-23.

_____. "Dare We Renew the Controversy? Part 2. The Fundamentalist Reduction." *Christianity Today* 1 (24 June 1957): 23-26.

_____. "Dare We Renew the Controversy? Part 4. The Evangelical Responsibility." *Christianity Today* 1 (22 July 1957): 23-26, 38.

_____. "Twenty Years a Baptist." *Foundations* 1 (January 1958): 46-54.

_____. "Evangelicals and Fundamentals." *Christianity Today* 3 (30 March 1959): 4-5.

_____. "A Door Swings Open." *United Evangelical Action* 24 (July 1965): 9-11.

_____. "Firm on the Fundamentals." *Christianity Today* 32 (18 November 1988): 19.

Hodge, Charles. "The Unity of the Church." *Eternity* 9 (June 1958): 27.

"In a Tent." *Time* 31 (11 April 1938): 46-47.

"Is Evangelical Theology Changing?" *Christian Life* (March 1956): 16-19.

Jones, Bob, Jr. "Editorial." *Faith for the Family* 4 (Sept/Oct 1976): 1, 40.

Jones, Bob, Sr. "Dr. Bob Jones Says." *Sword of the Lord* 22 (14 September 1956): 1, 10.

_____. "About Billy Graham's New York Crusade: Dr. Bob Jones Says." *Sword of the Lord* (3 May 1957): 12.

_____. "Comments on here and hereafter." *Faith for the Family* 3 (May/June 1975): 39.

Ketcham, Robert T. "An Open Letter to Dr. W. B. Riley from Dr. R. T. Ketcham." *Baptist Bulletin* 2 (November 1936): 3-4.

_____. "Through Ecumenical Glasses." *Baptist Bulletin* 14 (November 1949): 4.

_____. "The Billy Graham Controversy." *Baptist Bulletin* 17 (December 1952): 6, 23-24.

_____. "The Doctrine of Separation." *Baptist Bulletin* 17 (December 1952): 10, 21-22.

_____. "A New Peril in our Last Days." *Christian Beacon* 21 (17 May 1956): 2, 6-7.

_____. "*Christianity Today*--An Analysis." *Baptist Bulletin* 22 (March 1957): 8-9, 21.

Ladd, George. "The Evangelical's Dilemma: Doctrinal Purity vs. Visible Unity." *Eternity* 13 (June 1962): 7-9.

_____. "First Impressions." *Bulletin of Fuller Theological Seminary* 1 (Jan-Mar 1951): 7.

Laws, Curtis L. "Convention Side Lights." *The Watchman-Examiner* (1 July 1920): 834.

Leitch, Addison. "Modern Theologies: As Seen from the Gospel." Review of *Christian Faith and Modern Theology*, ed. Carl F. H. Henry. *Christianity Today* 9 (31 July 1964): 32.

Marsden, George. "The New School Heritage and Presbyterian Fundamentalism." *Westminster Theological Journal* 32 (1970): 129-147.

_____. "Defining Fundamentalism." *Christian Scholar's Review* 1 (Winter 1971): 141-151.

Marty, Martin. "Fundamentalism Reborn." *Saturday Review* 7 (May 1980): 37-38.

_____. "Fundamentalism as a Social Phenomenon." *Review and Expositor* 79 (Winter 1982): 19-29.

_____. "Modern Fundamentalism." *America* 155 (27 Sept 1986): 134.

McIntire, Carl. "The Ship is Sunk." *Christian Beacon* 1 (2 July 1936): 4.

_____. "Premillennialism." *Christian Beacon* 1 (1 October 1936): 4.

_____. "Dr. Machen." *Christian Beacon* 2 (7 January 1937): 4.

_____. "Bible Presybterian Fellowship Formed." *Christian Beacon* 2 (10 June 1937): 1, 8.

_____. "Proposed Changes to Confession of Faith." *Christian Beacon* 3 (18 August 1938): 1, 2.

_____. "American Council of Christian Churches Organized in New York." *Christian Beacon* 6 (19 September 1941): 1.

_____. "Discussing the Issues of the Present Hour." *Christian Beacon* 8 (11 February 1943): 1, 2, 5.

_____. "American Council Resolutions From Sixth Annual Convention." *Christian Beacon* 12 (30 October 1947): 1.

_____. "The National Association of Evangelicals and Separation." *Christian Beacon* 13 (7 October 1948): 4.

_____. "NAE, Fuller Seminary, Championed by Ockenga." *Christian Beacon* 16 (10 May 1951): 4.

_____. "Christianity in Eclipse." *Christian Beacon* 21 (25 October 1956): 1, 8.

_____. "Twentieth Century Reformation." *Christian Beacon* 31 (23 June 1966): 3.

_____. "Behold! To Obey is Better than Sacrifice." *Christian Beacon* 36 (30 September 1971): 8.

_____. "World Congress of Fundamentalists." *Christian Beacon* 41 (4 March 1976): 7.

_____. "A Generation that Knew Not Machen." *Christian Beacon* 41 (29 July 1976): 3, 5, 7.

_____. "The International Council on Biblical Inerrancy --An Analysis." *Christian Beacon* 43 (1 March 1978): 8.

_____. "National Association of Evangelicals." *Christian Beacon* 47 (18 February 1982): 3-8.

_____. "Separation." *Christian Beacon* 47 (25 February 1982): 3-8.

Moore, Leroy. "Another Look at Fundamentalism: A Response to Ernest R. Sandeen." *Church History* 37 (June 1968): 195-202.

Murch, James DeForest. "We Must Work Together." *United Evangelical Action* 10 (1 July 1951): 5.

"New Officers and Commissions." *United Evangelical Action* 9 (1 May 1950): 6.

Ockenden, F. "Why I am a Fundamentalist." *Christian Beacon* 20 (4 August 1955): 4.

Ockenga, Harold J. "Editorial." *United Evangelical Action* 2 (January 1943): 1.

_____. "Contentious Versus Evangelical Christianity." *United Evangelical Action* 2 (1 August 1943): 2.

_____. "The Reality of Church Unity." *United Evangelical Action* 2 (10 August 1943): 2-3.

_____. "Can Christians Win America?" *Christian Life and Times* 2 (June 1947): 13-15.

_____. "What the N.A.E. is and What It is Doing." *United Evangelical Action* 7 (15 April 1948): 5-6.

_____. "The Reality of Church Union." *United Evangelical Action* 15 (1 March 1956): 3-4, 6.

_____. "The Body Christ Heads: A Symposium." *Christianity Today* 1 (19 Sept 1957): 3-13.

_____. "The New Evangelicalism." *The Park Street Spire* (February 1958): 2-7.

_____. "Resurgent Evangelical Leadership." *Christianity Today* 5 (10 October 1960): 11-15.

Paine, Stephen W. "NAE and Separation." *United Evangelical Action* 7 (15 September 1948): 11, 22-23.

Pyles, Volie E. "Bruised, Bloody and Broken: Fundamentalism's Internecine Controversy in the 1960s." *Fides et Historia* 18 (October 1986): 45-55.

"Resolutions of the Fundamentalists." *Sunday School Times* 75 (July 22, 1933): 472.

Rice, John R. "The New Paper and Its Policies." *Sword of the Lord* 1 (28 September 1934): 1.

_____. "Do Not Be Unequally Yoked with Unbelievers." *Sword of the Lord* 1 (26 October 1934): 2-3.

_____. "The Orthodox Baptist Tradition." *Sword of the Lord* 1 (29 March 1935): 1-3.

_____. "Questions and Answers on 'The Church.'" *Sword of the Lord* 2 (3 July 1936): 1-2.

_____. "Fellowship with Convention Brethren: How Far to Go? What We Want: Some Reservations." *Sword of the Lord* 3 (8 April 1937): 1-3.

_____. "Name Changed: Fundamentalist Baptist Church Becomes Galilean Baptist Church." *Sword of the Lord* 5 (December 1939): 1, 4.

_____. "'Churches' and 'The Church.'" *Sword of the Lord* 7 (30 May 1941): 1-4.

_____. "National Association of Evangelicals Convention: Columbus, Ohio, April 12-17." *Sword of the Lord* 6 (24 March 1944): 1, 3.

_____. "Editor Visits Bob Jones College." *Sword of the Lord* 7 (8 June 1945): 1.

_____. "Misunderstood Pentecost." *Sword of the Lord* 10 (9 April 1948): 1-6.

_____. "Dr. J. Oliver Buswell's Charges against Bob Jones University Answered." *Sword of the Lord* 10 (8 June 1948): 2.

_____. "Billy Graham and Revival Critics." *Sword of the Lord* 13 (2 March 1951): 6-8.

_____. "The Editor Answers: Bible Questions," *Sword of the Lord* 13 (12 October 1951): 1-2.

_____. "Billy Graham Seattle Campaign Reviewed." *Sword of the Lord* 14 (6 June 1952): 9.

_____. "Reformed and Covenant Doctrine." *Sword of the Lord* 20 (5 November 1954): 3.

_____. "Questions Answered About Billy Graham." *Sword of the Lord* 21 (17 June 1955): 1, 9-11.

_____. "Truth and Falsehood about the Bible Doctrine of the Church." *Sword of the Lord* 21 (4 November 1955): 1, 10-12.

_____. "Christ Builds His Church." *Sword of the Lord* 22 (13 January 1956): 3, 12.

_____. "The Christian and the Old Testament." *Sword of the Lord* 22 (20 January 1956): 4, 6.

_____. "Our Beloved Intellectuals Again." *Sword of the Lord* 22 (18 May 1956): 1, 12.

_____. "Can Theology Change?" *Christian Life* 8 (May 1956): 3.

_____. "New Magazine: 'Not Anti-Anything.'" *Sword of the Lord* 22 (13 July 1956): 2.

_____. "Bible Problems Concerning the Church." *Sword of the Lord* 22 (26 October 1956): 2, 6-8.

_____. "Fuller Seminary's Carnell Sneers Fundamentalism." *Sword of the Lord* 22 (30 October 1956): 7, 11.

_____. "Which Way, Billy Graham?" *Sword of the Lord* 22 (23 November 1956): 2.

_____. "Billy Graham Openly Repudiates Fundamentalism." *Sword of the Lord* 23 (17 May 1957): 2, 10.

_____. "Our Life Long Fight Against Modernism." *Sword of the Lord* 24 (2 May 1958): 11.

_____. "If We Compromise What Happens?" *Sword of the Lord* 24 (9 May 1958): 12.

_____. "Cooperative Evangelism." *Sword of the Lord* 24 (20 June 1958): 1-12.

_____. "Christian Leaders Dec. 26 in Chicago Restate the Historic Position of Bible-Believers." *Sword of the Lord* 25 (16 January 1959): 1, 5.

_____. "The Road to Sodom." *Sword of the Lord* 25 (1 May 1959): 1, 9.

_____. "Ceremonial Law Forbids N. T. Christians the Unequal Yoke." *Sword of the Lord* 25 (7 August 1959): 1, 9-12.

_____. "Co-operation Among Christians--Is it Baptistic? Scriptural?" *Sword of the Lord* 25 (21 August 1959): 1, 5-6.

_____. "Separation from Infidels, Not from Good Christians: How Our Bible Position Differs from a Denominational Position." *Sword of the Lord* 26 (2 September 1960): 1, 9-10.

_____. "Pentecost Does Not Mean New Dispensation." *Sword of the Lord* 29 (21 August 1963): 3.

_____. "Goodbye Dr. Bob." *Sword of the Lord* 34 (9 February 1968): 1.

_____. "They Did not Hold to Secondary Separation." *Sword of the Lord* 42 (17 Dec 1976): 1.

_____. "Here is Historic Fundamentalism." *Sword of the Lord* 44 (22 Sept 1978): 1, 7.

_____. "Bible Separation--From Saints or Sinners?" *Sword of the Lord* 45 (13 April 1979): 9.

Riley, W. B. "The Denominational Division Among Baptists." *The Pilot* 20 (January 1940): 104-105.

Rosas, L. Joseph, III. "The Theology of Edward John Carnell." *Criswell Theological Review* 4 (1990): 351-371.

Runia, Klaas. "When Is Separation a Christian Duty?" *Christianity Today* (23 June 1967): 939-941 and (7 July 1967): 982-984.

Sandeen, Ernest. "Toward a Historical Interpretation of the Origins of Fundamentalism." *Church History* 36 (March 1967): 66-83.

_____. "Defining Fundamentalism: A Reply to Professor Marsden." *Christian Scholar's Review* 1 (Spring 1971): 227-232.

_____. "Fundamentalism and American Identity." *Annals of the American Academy of Social and Political Sciences* 387 (January 1970): 64-66.

Smedes, Lewis B. "The Essence of the Church." *Christianity Today* 4 (26 Oct 1959): 49-51.

Sweeney, Douglas A. "The Essential Evangelicalism Dialectic: The Historiography of the Early New-Evangelical Movement and the Observer-Participant Dilemma." *Church History* 60 (March 1991): 70-84.

Talley, John D. "The Basis for Ecclesiastical Separation." *The Fundamentalist Journal* 2 (April 1983): 22-25+.

Tulga, Chester. "More than Evangelicals." *Sword of the Lord* 22 (27 July 1956): 1-5.

_____. "Fundamentalism: Past and Future." *Sword of the Lord* 23 (4 October 1957): 2, 11-12.

_____. "The Christian and the Problem of Religious Unity." *Sword of the Lord* 25 (2 January 1959): 1, 11-12.

"Unity: Quest and Questions." *Christianity Today* 6 (24 November 1961): 196-98.

"Vanishing Fundamentalism." *Christian Century* 43 (June 24, 1926): 799.

VanOsdel, O. W. "How About It?" *Baptist Bulletin* 1 (November 1933): 2.

"Vatican Rejects Protestant View of Church Unity." *Christianity Today* 6 (6 July 1962): 979.

Walvoord, John F. "What's Right About Fundamentalism?" *Eternity* 8 (June 1957): 6-35.

Weniger, Archer. "Separation Systematized." *Faith for the Family* (Nov/Dec 1976): 8-9.

"What Does It Mean to Be Evangelical?" *Christianity Today* 33 (16 June 1989): 60, 63.

Woodbridge, Charles. "The Book of Acts." *Biblical Viewpoint* 4 (April 1970): 16-22.

Woodbridge, John. "Stunted Growth or Stunning Growth?" *Eternity* 27 (October 1976): 64-66.

Wright, J. Elwin. "A Few Observations." *New England Fellowship Monthly* (April 1937): 8.

_____. "A False Doctrine." *United Evangelical Action* 7 (15 April 1948): 16-17.

_____. "Evangelicals Must Unite Now." *Sword of the Lord* 12 (4 August 1950): 1, 3.

Dissertations

Bevier, William A. "A History of the I.F.C.A." Th.D. diss., Dallas Theological Seminary, 1958.

Blakemore, Peter J. "Toward an Honest Portrait of Fundamentalism, 1930-1980: A Historical Study of Progressive Development in the Working Definition of Fundamentalism." Ph.D. diss., Bob Jones University, 1982.

Butler, Farley Porter. "Billy Graham and the End of Evangelical Unity." Ph.D. diss., University of Florida, 1976.

Carpenter, Joel A. "The Renewal of American Fundamentalism, 1930-1945." Ph.D. diss., John Hopkins University, 1984.

Delnay, Robert. "A History of the Baptist Bible Union." Th.D. diss., Dallas Theological Seminary, 1963.

Fea, John. "Come Out From Among Them: Separatist Fundamentalism in America, 1941-1991." M.A. thesis, Trinity Evangelical Divinity School, 1992.

Holland, John Steward. "A Biblical Theology of Separation." Ph.D. diss., Bob Jones University, 1976.

James, Edgar C. "The Theological Distinctives of New Evangelicalism." Th.M. diss., Dallas Theological Seminary, 1959.

Jones, Bob, Jr. "American Evangelicalism." M.A. diss., University of Pittsburgh, 1933.

Mulholland, Robert Joseph. "Carl McIntire: The Early Radio Years (1932-1955)." Ph.D. diss., Bowling Green State University, 1984.

Perry, Everett L. "The Role of Socio-Economic Factors in the Rise and Development of American Fundamentalism." Ph.D. diss., University of Chicago, 1959.

Porter, Butler F., Jr. "Billy Graham and the End of Evangelical Unity." Ph.D. diss., University of Florida, 1976.

Sharp, Larry Dean. "Carl Henry: Neo-Evangelical Theologian." D.Min. diss., Vanderbilt University Divinity School, 1972.

Stroman, John Albert. "American Council of Christian Churches: A Study of Its Origin, Leaders and Characteristic Positions." Th.D. diss., Boston University, 1966.

Tinder, Donald. "Fundamentalist Baptists in the Northern and Western United States." Ph.D. diss., Yale University, 1972.

Walzer, William Charles. "Charles Grandison Finney and the Presbyterian Revivals of Central and Western New York." Ph.D. diss., University of Chicago: 1944.

Weaver, Donald A. "The Theological Deviations of the New Evangelicalism." Th.M. diss., Dallas Theological Seminary, 1962.

Whiteman, Curtis Wayne. "The General Association of Regular Baptist Churches, 1932-1955." Ph.D. diss., St. Louis University, 1984.

Correspondence

Davis, Ralph T. to Harry Ironside, 28 April 1944. Records of the African Inland Mission, Collection 81, Box 8, Folder 61. Billy Graham Center Archives, Wheaton, Ill.

Graham, Billy to Bob Jones Sr., 19 February 1949; 29 December 1949; and 23 October 1950. Bob Jones University Archives. Greenville, S.C.

Graham, Billy-Robert T. Ketcham correspondence. Palmer Muntz Papers, Collection 108, Box 1, Folder 1. Billy Graham Center Archives. Wheaton, Ill.

Bibliographies, Lists of Holdings

Blumhofer, Edith and Joel A. Carpenter. *Evangelicalism in the Twentieth Century: A Guide to the Sources*. New York: Garland, 1990.

Branson, Mark Lau. *The Reader's Guide to the Best Evangelical Books*. New York: Harpers Row, 1982.

Fea, John. "American Fundamentalism and Neo-Evangelicalism: A Bibliographical Survey." *Evangelical Journal* 11 (Spring 1993): 21-30.

Hedstrom, James. "A Bibliography for Evangelical Reform." *Journal of the Evangelical Theological Society* 19 (Summer 1976): 225-238.

Lippy, Charles H. *A Bibliography of Religion in the South*. Macon, Ga.: Mercer University Press, 1985.

Magnuson, Norris and William G. Travis, ed. *American Evangelicalism: An Annotated Bibliography*. West Cornwall, Conn.: Locust Hill Press, 1990.

Pierard, Richard V. "The Quest for the Historical Evangelicalism: Bibliographical Excursus." *Fides et Historia* 11 (Spring 1979): 60-71.

Shuster, Robert D., et al. *Researching Modern Evangelicalism: A Guide to the Holdings of the Billy Graham Center Archives with Information on Other Collections*. Westport, Conn.: Greenwood Press, 1990.

Wacker, Grant. "Twentieth Century Evangelicalism: A Guide to the Sources." *Evangelical Studies Bulletin* 7 (Fall 1990): 6-7.

Made in the USA
San Bernardino, CA
25 January 2018